Heartbreaker

Heartbreaker

A Memoir of Judy Garland

John Meyer

CITADEL PRESS
Kensington Publishing Corp.
www.kensingtonbooks.com

*I would like to thank Anne Bryant, Larry Lowenstein, and Priscilla Meyer
for sharing their recollections with me; Leila Martin, for her imaginative
support . . . and Sharon Messitte for providing me with an essential ingredient.*

CITADEL PRESS BOOKS are published by

Kensington Publishing Corp.
850 Third Avenue
New York, NY 10022

All Kensington titles, imprints, and distributed lines are available at special quantity discounts for bulk purchases for sales promotions, premiums, fund-raising, educational, or institutional use. Special book excerpts or customized printings can also be created to fit specific needs. For details, write or phone the office of the Kensington special sales manager: Kensington Publishing Corp., 850 Third Avenue, New York, NY 10022, attn: Special Sales Department; phone 1-800-221-2647.

CITADEL PRESS and the Citadel logo are Reg. U.S. Pat. & TM Off.

First printing: May 2006

10 9 8 7 6 5 4 3 2 1

Printed in the United States of America

Library of Congress Control Number: 82-456000 (text only)

ISBN 0-8065-2754-4

This book is for Harold Arlen, Richard Rodgers, Frank Loesser, and all the other writers of America's film and theater music. Their work informed Judy's life and still informs mine.

One must try to distinguish history from
the wistful preservation of a legend . . .

ARLENE CROCE

Part One

❀ ❀ ❀

New York

This is the story of two months I spent with Judy Garland, two months in which I was given the chance to help her. It seemed, at the beginning, as if a capricious and wanton Providence had dropped this fascinating hot potato in my lap; I had been chosen by some divine prankster because of my unique abilities—you needed humor, stamina, and finally compassion . . . and it helped if you were musical. But, as I was to learn, what started as a divine prank ended in an all too realistic tragedy, because these were the only resources I had . . . and they were not sufficient.

But then nobody's would have been.

FRIDAY, OCTOBER 18, 1968

I guess this story properly begins on East Seventy-second Street, in a bar called Three. That's where I met Richard Stryker, and he was the one who introduced me to Judy.

I was the entertainer at Three. I sat behind the piano singing show tunes. I'm an expert on shows and movie musicals. I can tell you what songs were cut from *South Pacific*, for instance, or in what picture Dick Haymes sang "The More I See You." I can do a Fred Astaire medley, or a Cole Porter medley, or all the songs from the Hope/Crosby *Road* pictures. And, of course, from Judy's pictures, because the songs Judy introduced are central to the literature: "Over the Rainbow," "The Trolley Song," "The Man That Got Away."

Not an evening went by that I wasn't conscious of Judy, her songs, and her mystique. Her Legend, they called it at Three. Poor Judy, the Legend went, what a shame. Such a pity that a woman with such talent has let herself become a bum, penniless, dependent on pills and booze. Did you hear about the St. Moritz Hotel? They kicked her out for not paying her bills, and they're holding her luggage until she pays up.

This fellow Richard Stryker was often the bearer of fresh tidings about Judy. He was not a particularly important or prepossessing man, but somehow, through the network of homosexuals that was rumored to surround Judy, he knew her.

Being the Messenger gave Richard a certain celebrity at

Three. He was a truly bizarre person. There was a terribly unhealthy aspect to him (indeed he was to die in his early forties of a heart attack). His skin seemed to ooze a diseased kind of perspiration. He wore his hair in little points which stuck jaggedly from his scalp, giving him the appearance of a gay Mark Antony. He always asked me to play Judy tunes, and he'd sit by me on the piano bench and offer me sniffs from his poppers.

One night in October he said to me in an offhand manner, "Listen, do you have any material that might suit Judy?" He knew I wrote songs.

"Are you kidding?" I answered him. "Of course I do."

"Why don't you come over tomorrow?" he smiled in his sickly way. "We're listening to new material."

"Great," I said.

"It's the Carnegie Hall apartments," said Richard. "How's five?"

SATURDAY, OCTOBER 19

Well, five was all right, I supposed. It seemed a little cocktail-ey and too close to work, which was at ten, but if this was a chance to show one of my songs to Judy Garland, I could put up with the inconvenience.

Richard's apartment was unhealthy in the same way he was. Chaotic and filthy, with no room for anything. But it was spacious, with a high ceiling and a sleeping platform at the top of a flight of stairs.

Along the walls, piled haphazardly into shelves, were hundreds of boxes of reel-to-reel recording tape (this was before cassettes) and an enormous collection of records, both LPs and 78s.

Richard ran a company called the Institute of Sound, a recording service. He made his living by selling the material in his archives, which were extensive. He had records of Caruso and Jussi Bjoerling; he had Gallagher and Shean and Nora Bayes, he had Eva Tanguay. He had the opening night performance of *Gypsy*.

As I walked in, the unique Garland voice was blaring "Rock-a-bye Your Baby with a Dixie Melody" from two giant speakers. Richard greeted me with glass in hand. "Have a drink," he said. He lowered the volume of "Rock-a-bye" as I looked round the room, sipping my drink. It was vodka and tonic, and Judy was nowhere to be seen. "Is she upstairs?" I asked, indicating the balcony.

"Oh no, she's in Boston, didn't you know? She's coming down later this week."

"Boston? What's she doing in Boston?" Richard waved a hand airily. "She's absolutely queer for Boston, don't ask me why. Now my dear"—he gestured toward his piano, a spinet—"you must play me your song because we're putting together a lot of new material for her. A friend of mine, Sydney Shaw, is writing her a whole new act. It's something she's never done before, a totally new concept. Can I tell you?" He took a step back, put two fingers to his mouth. The word "coy" took on new meaning. He looked demurely at his carpet, which was matted with dust and hair. "Promise me you won't tell anyone," he said.

"Richard, come *on*."

"Well, it's this." He glanced slyly from side to side and lowered his voice conspiratorially. "*Three acts*," he whispered. "Judy will do a concert composed of three acts." He twinkled at me, waiting for my response. I truly didn't know what to say. "That's great, Richard," I managed. "Really unique."

"Well, you can see how it changes her whole"—he gestured wildly, searching for the word, couldn't find it—"and my dear, she gets to wear *three different gowns*."

"One for each act."

"Well ex*actly*."

I nodded. I knew now that I was on a wild-goose chase here. It was hard to believe that Judy would grant someone like Richard Stryker any part in her life.

"So you see," Richard was saying, "we're open to new material. Now you mentioned you had a song . . ."

I did have a song. It's called "I'd Like to Hate Myself in the Morning" and, as it turned out, it was perfect for Judy. I played it once through and stood up. It was time to get out of there. Judy wasn't coming, and I didn't need to spend any more time with Richard and his fantasies.

"Wait, wait a minute, I like it. It's cute. Have you eaten?"

"Yes, I have."

"Well then, how about an orgy?" He stepped back again, grinning. "Oh, I forgot. You're straight." He twinkled at me again, challenging me to deny it. He came forward suddenly and thrust his hand into my face. I caught the ammoniac smell of amyl nitrate. "Have you tried these?" he breathed at me. "It's a popper."

I stepped past him. "Momma don't need no poppers tonight," I said, and left.

THURSDAY, OCTOBER 24

That was on a Saturday. Five days later, on Thursday, I was on my way out when the phone rang, about seven-fifteen. It was Richard.

"She's here," he breathed dramatically. "And she's asked for someone who plays the piano. Do you want to come down?"

"She's there?" I countered, suspicion in my voice. I didn't want to go traipsing down there again for nothing.

"Yes, she's here, we're together." This with great impatience. "Now, do you want to come down? It could be an excellent opportunity."

I considered it briefly; bizarre as he was, Richard wouldn't dare bullshit me again. "All right," I said.

"In about twenty minutes? Can you get here?"

"Make it half an hour. I have to shave."

I nearly sliced my face to ribbons. I drove down to Carnegie Hall in the battered Dodge van my father uses in his frozen food business. As I parked, I realized I was too hungry to survive the next hour without food, so I stopped in the market on Fifty-eighth and Seventh and bought two Bonbel cheeses, the round kind. Excited beyond measure, I rang Richard's bell.

He opened the door, smiling, and handed me another vodka and tonic. As I walked briskly past him into the room, I wondered if he greeted all his guests this way. Judy was nowhere to be seen. "Richard . . ." I began, in a menacing tone. He pointed upward significantly. He took my arm and led me to the center of the room, calling up to the sleeping platform. "Judy, this is John Meyers."

"No 'S,'" I hissed at him. He nudged my arm. "Say hello."

"Hi, Judy," I blurted. A voice came from the balcony.

"Well hello-*hoh* . . ." There was no mistaking the voice. It had cracked a little, broken on the second syllable, but that was because she'd put too much energy into it.

"How aah ya?" she continued, adopting a comic Bronx-ey intonation.

"I'm good," I replied. "How are you?"

"Well, I'm nn, *crip*pled, but . . . I'll be all right. I'm one of the Crips. My leg is about to fall right over this nn, *bal*cony . . . I'll be down in a minute . . . just let me put on my nn, *le*per bell . . ."

A pair of black panty hose sailed over the balcony railing and fluttered gracefully to the floor, settling into a filmy dark mound like the Wicked Witch of the West. It was the most astounding thing. I looked at Richard, amazed. Before either of us could react, a bra followed the panty hose over the rail, joining it on the floor like a homing pigeon. I glanced up to the balcony.

"Hey," I yelled, "wouldja like me to toss up my Jockey shorts?" And suddenly this exchange, with its sexual implications, connected a circuit within me, and my excitement, already total, became almost too much to bear. It was the wildest feeling. I wanted to pull Judy's bra over my scalp like two big ears and sing M-I-C-K-E-Y M-O-U-S-E. I felt like pulling her panty hose over my head and shouting "This is a stickup!" But Richard was talking, quite calmly.

"You haven't met Jenny, John," he was saying. "This is Jenny Wheeler, Judy's secretary." There was a woman with brown hair sitting on Richard's couch, between two stacks of magazines. It's indicative of how manic I was that I hadn't even noticed her. I mumbled a greeting and she smiled as we shook hands. I was cogent enough to notice that, even sitting, she was taller than I. She was the only person in the room with a sense of repose.

Richard was pulling me to the piano. "Play something," he whispered.

I felt my stomach clutch. God, what should I play? This was a woman who'd had composers like Cole Porter and Harold Arlen audition their scores for her. Not that I was going to play *my* song yet, before she was in the room. But this would be Judy's first impression of my ability and talent. I had to pick something distinctive, witty, something sophisticated in an offbeat way, a song that said to her Hey, this is a special guy, someone exceptional, for who else would know *that* song (and what it secretly signifies). My fingers were poised above the keys.

I played "Blue Moon." The dumbest, least significant song I could have chosen. My fingers seemed to move of their own accord. As soon as I realized what I was playing, I stopped. I skittered through the Rolodex of songs in my mind, found "Here's That Rainy Day" which might be a little shopworn, but at least wasn't dopey, like "Blue Moon." I wouldn't be humiliating myself—

Judy's voice was coming from the balcony. "Do you know any of those, nn, Tony *New*ley songs from the . . . *Roar of the . . . Hoo-ha . . .* thing . . . ?"

Well yes, I did. I began to play "Look at That Face," and Judy started singing, from upstairs. My God, I thought, here I am at the piano accompanying the disembodied voice of Judy Garland, which was soaring out over the balcony like . . . like a pair of panty hose.

She went for a high F and cracked, of course, because it was out of her range. I cursed myself for picking the wrong key, but I heard Judy giggle, and it was all right because a minute later she was downstairs and clasping my hand in a very warm grip. Warm and firm and intense. She was in a high-necked black silk dress with cuffs that flopped out over her wrists and she was wearing black fishnet stockings, but no shoes. I could see she looked bright-eyed and alert, and that her weight was okay, and her hair was short and zippy and she was *not letting go of my hand.*

"Hello again," she said to me, and now, without the strain of shouting, her voice was rich and vibrant, with something so compelling in its timbre I wanted to melt. And she was talking about what? The IRS?

"Yes, I've had the most, nn, *wrack*ing day because the nn, *tax*

people have been here . . . a Chinese gentleman, his name was
Mr. nn, *Wong* . . . and I was finding it very difficult to nn, *con-
centrate*, I just kept singing you know kind of under my breath
. . . 'It's the Wong Time/and the Wong Place! . . .'"

I struck a chord. "And what about 'Let's Take the Wong Way
Home . . .'" I sang. Judy opened her mouth in delight. "Yes,"
she continued, "or 'Everybody Has the Right to Be Wong/at
Least Once.' Oh my, they were batting me around like a nn,
*vol*leyball . . . I was getting trainsick . . . like the Metro Bond
Train . . ."

"What's the Metro Bond Train?" I asked her, from the piano
bench. Jenny was on the couch behind her, Richard was leaning
against a table, and Judy was on her feet, performing for us. I
noticed that, in her stocking feet, Judy might come up to my
chin.

"Well, in 1942," Judy began, "when the Japs were kind of nn,
*win*ning, all the studios put their stars on a nn, *train* that toured
the country selling war bonds. We all had to go, Mickey and
Gene and Betty Hutton and nn, *every*body . . ."

Her manner of speaking fascinated me. She hesitated before
each essential word or phrase, making a small sound in her
throat—an N or an M—before enunciating it. It made you hang
on each word, anticipating everything she said.

". . . and at each stop we were all nn, *trot*ted out to sing, or
dance, or do magic tricks or whatever . . . and afterwards, the
people would nn, buy *bonds*. Well, Paul Henreid was on the
train, he was the nn, *ni*cest man, very dapper and nn, conti-
*nent*al, very quiet . . . he never joined in all our hijinks . . . and
his act was kind of nn, French *pa*triot, *Casablanca*-style. And
after Mickey and Betty and I had nn, sung our little *hearts* out,
Paul would go out to the back of the train and . . . kind of,
mmm . . ."

Judy put her right hand across her chest and clutched her left
lower rib, imitating Paul Henreid's stance of long ago. She
gazed into the distance and spoke in a thick French accent.

"'Mah fellow cahntree-main . . . we are fighting a war of
resistahnce . . . a war we weel nevair geev up . . . until the
boot of the Nazee oppressor ees leefted from our soil . . .'" Judy
giggled. "And they played the nn, 'Marseill*aise*' and Paul would

go back in the train." Judy smiled sympathetically. "It was kinda bad. It was just a nn, *dud.* I mean after all us nn, *vod*vil types doing—'Poor Johnny one note' and 'Got no diamonds/got no pearls . . .'" Judy belted out the phrases, enjoying herself. She was positively sparkling.

"And it made Paul very unhappy. He didn't like being a nn, *dud* when the rest of us were a nn, *hit.* So I thought, Well, he's just done *Now Voyager,* and he was a big hit in that so I said nn, *Paul,* why don't you do your nn, *cigarette* bit? And he said Judy, that's a wahnderfool ahdea . . . and the next town we came to he lit two cigarettes and gave one to, you know, some nn, *girl* in the crowd. Well, from then on he was a nn, *hit.* So he kept it in and did it nn, *everywhere* . . . and you know, we used to stop at, mmm, twenty-five or thirty towns a *day.* After about a week we noticed Paul had turned kind of, nn, *green* . . . and, a few days after that—" Judy could not contain her amusement. "He had to be sent back to his studio with, nn, nicotine *poisoning.*"

She's perfection I was thinking. Her eye for detail, her ear for dialect, her sweet sense of self-deprecation. And look how she's taking the trouble to entertain us.

"That's a *marv*elous story," I said. Judy beamed at me. "But Richard tells me you're a marvelous, nn, *songwriter* . . . do you think . . . would you mind very much . . . ?" She nodded toward the piano. Baby, you don't have to coax me, I was thinking. I was eager to prove myself to her. "Why don't you pull up that hassock?" I suggested, and I made Judy sit by the piano as I played my song with manic gusto:

"I'd like to hate myself in the morning" I sang,

"And raise a little hell tonight
   I've got the urge to carouse
   And maybe raise a few brows
      Cut loose and pull all the stops out
      Who cares if they call the cops out?

I'd like to wake at noon feeling guilty
And know somehow that something isn't quite right . . .

I'd like to hate myself in the morning
And raise a little hell . . . tonight

I'd like to wake at noon feeling guilty" I repeated,
"And leave the wrong hotel by dawn's early light

I'd like to lift my lids in the morning
And wonder who I kissed
And wonder—"

Judy broke in: "who I missed—" she sang. I was astounded.
Judy had anticipated exactly what I'd written.

"I just might hate myself in the morning" I finished,
"But what a dandy time I'll have . . . tonight!"

Judy began clapping her hands. "Oh, yes!" she said, enthusiastically.

"My God," I told her, "you know the song better than I do."
As I turned to Richard I heard the doorbell ring. "Did you hear
what Judy did? She anticipated the goddam lyric. She actually—"

Judy was giggling with delight. "It just seemed so nn, *natural*." As Richard moved to answer the door, he beamed at Judy.
"Didn't I tell you?" he asked her. "It could be very cute, kind of
a throwaway number." He disappeared into the little foyer. I
heard him murmur something, and then he came back into the
room. "Sydney's here," he said.

From behind him, Sydney Shaw floated languorously into the
room. He was about fifty, I judged, with gray, wet-looking hair.
You wouldn't want to lend him your comb. He looked as if he
bit his nails. There was the same clammy, hothouse quality to
him that Richard had . . . as if he never got any fresh air.

He crossed to Judy and, making a little moue of his mouth,
put his face on either side of hers, giving her two kisses, in the
French style. Was it my imagination, or did Judy seem to find
this distasteful?

"How aah ya?" she asked him, doing her Bronx voice.

"Oh, don't ask," Sydney sighed. "Cleopatra gave birth today."
He pronounced it Clay-oh-pahtra. He turned to me. "Clayoh's
my cat," he explained. "And I must tell you, it was frightening."
He swung round to face Richard, who had resumed his position
by the table. "You know, I've never been a mother before. Now I
know what you ladies go through. My heavens, I had no *idea*. It

seemed to take for*e*ver. But I must say she gave us a marvelous litter. Anybody want a kitten?" He smiled at Judy.

"Oh, sure," Richard smirked, patronizingly. "I can just see Judy taking care of an animal, can't you? *Uh*." He made a sound that meant "Forget it." It was a rude, unpleasant moment. Sydney leaped in hurriedly to cover it.

"I'm Sydney Shaw, by the way," he said to me. "And you're John, Richard's told me. Has Judy told you about the new act we're doing for her? We're going to change her whole image."

Yes, let's, I agreed inwardly. Let's throw out "The Trolley Song," "The Man That Got Away," "Over the Rainbow," all that trash. What do we need *them* for? They're only part of a great show-business Legend. I was suddenly very disturbed. As the talk continued, I rose from the piano bench and crossed irritably to the shelves of records, absenting myself from Sydney's intolerable conversation. *Damn.* I was all set to show Judy more of my songs when this fey and trivial *jerk* burst in. He spoiled everything, goddamit. Hold on now, wait a minute, I asked myself, is this really worth reacting to so strongly? Could I maybe be a little high? I'd had one stiff vodka and tonic on an empty stomach, was I maybe a little bombed? I *couldn't* be. Then all at once it hit me: I was jealous. Viciously, bitchily jealous of Sydney for having taken the attention away from me.

Across the room they were talking about the format of the act, whether Judy should talk more, perhaps tell a few stories. Well, of course, she should, asshole, I commented mentally. She's a brilliant raconteur, as any schmuck can see after spending two minutes with her. Jesus, it occurred to me, if anyone should put Judy's act together, it's me. Me, me, ME!

The hollow grinding of my stomach reminded me I was close to collapsing from hunger. I wondered where I'd put those little cheeses. I looked at my watch. It was nine forty-five.

As it happened, the talk had turned to dinner. Sydney clasped his hands together. "I've got it all arranged—we're going to Elaine's, soon as I get back from downtown. I have to feed my babies." Oh, shit, I thought.

"How long will this take you, darling?" Judy inquired. Sydney pondered it. "Well, let's say twenty minutes down, twenty minutes to change and feed the cats, twenty minutes back. Say an hour."

"All right, Sydney," Judy said to him, "you go down to your, nn, *cat*house . . ."

I glanced at Sydney. He hadn't really heard that. He started toward the hall, oblivious. Richard, seeing his guest out, turned to me from the doorway.

"You'll come with us, John . . . ?"

I assessed it rapidly: by the time Sydney returned, it'd be quarter to eleven. And Judy Garland or no Judy Garland, I simply could not wait that long for dinner. "Thanks, Richard, I can't," I said.

"Well, all right for *you*," Richard responded, in mock petulance. He followed Sydney into the hall, talking. As his voice swam in from the foyer, Judy rose from the hassock by the piano and met me in the center of the room. Standing before me, she pointed to herself, then to me, shaping a silent phrase with her lips: "I'm with you."

At first I didn't get it. Then, a fraction of a second later, there was sudden blood in my mouth, the rusty red taste of excitement, up from my throat and into my mouth. I was breathing so fast I could hardly speak.

I must have said something, because she answered me, "Let's get the fuck *out* of here."

"What about Richard and Sydney?" I asked inanely.

"Fuck *them*." She turned to Jenny for the first time. "The coat's upstairs," she whispered, "and the nn . . . *shoes*."

All at once we were galvanized into activity. Jenny scrambled upstairs, I slipped on my jacket, and Richard came back into the room.

"Richard . . ." Judy was Little Miss Innocent. "Weren't you going to take a shower?" Richard frowned.

"Well, I was, but if I take one now my hair won't be dry in time for dinner." He thought about it a moment. "Oh, screw it," he decided, "maybe I'll take one. I am a bit sticky."

I'll say, I thought. The bathroom was to the left of the front door. Richard vanished inside it as Jenny poked her head out from the stairs. She was carrying a mink coat and a pair of black pumps.

"Let's go," Judy mouthed, and we crept quietly to the door, a furtive trio, as we heard the water begin running in the shower not ten feet away from us. I turned the catch the wrong way, cursed silently. Then the door gave and we slipped out, sucking in our collective breath.

Once outside, my impulse was to flatten my back against the wall. Any minute the searchlight would be coming round again. The girls headed for the elevator.

"No!" I hissed. "Down a flight. In case he looks out."

It was an Escape picture. We tiptoed down an ominous black flight of stairs to the level below. I pressed the bell, urgently. Judy was hit by a fit of sudden giggles.

"Judy, shut up, he'll hear us."

It wasn't till we were safely outside the building that we allowed ourselves to let go. "A bit nn, *sticky!*" Judy squealed. "He thinks he's a bit sticky!" As we crossed Seventh Avenue toward Broadway, I remembered the ancient truck and tried quickly to convert it to a new limousine by sheer concentration. Well, okay, so Judy would ride in a truck. In the film *Summer Stock* she'd driven a tractor. A truck was not so far from a tractor.

Jenny's long legs and my New Yorker's gait had outdistanced Judy. Without realizing it, we were half a block ahead of her. I turned around. "Hurry *up.*"

"I nn, *can't,*" Judy complained. "It's my . . . foot."

Judy had a painful ulcer on the inside of her heel, an infection. Even to limp was difficult. Impulsively, I ran back and picked her up in my arms. The cool sensuality of her mink brushed my face. I began carrying her down Fifty-sixth Street, terribly conscious of the intimacy of what I was doing, terribly moved by the scent of her neck, terribly aware that my heartbeat was tripling.

I set Judy down by the door of the van, opened it, and motioned Jenny inside. Judy took it with surprising aplomb, matter-of-factly climbing up the high step to the cab, where she settled herself in the seat. Jenny sat above the motor, in the space between the two seats.

I climbed in on the driver's side, started the ignition, and pulled out onto Broadway. Judy smiled impishly at Jenny.

"He doesn't nn, *know* it," she said, "but we're his now."

I headed down Broadway, my wind whirring. I had to reconcile two bizarre and disparate facts: a) I had Judy Garland beside me in my father's van, and b) I was so hungry I could barely *see*. Plus which, I had about thirteen dollars in my pocket. Now where could I buy dinner for three for thirteen dollars?

I decided on the Buena Mesa, a Spanish place on Twenty-eighth and Lexington. Stucco walls and guitar music. It wasn't Lutèce, but it wasn't Bickford's either. It was a place I could buy three dinners for thirteen dollars.

Judy ordered vodka, I ordered wine, and I felt the mania surge through my veins again. I grabbed the salt and pepper shakers, one in each hand. "Did you hear?" I said to Judy. "Sammy Davis, Jr., and May Britt are"—I flung my arms apart—"splitsville!" I picked up a small china holder which contained individually wrapped packets of sugar and began picking through the packets. "Garland, Garland," I muttered, "I can't seem to find your file . . ."

The mania had me. I couldn't stop grabbing silverware, glasses, condiment bottles, doing every table *shtick* I knew. I was a pinwheel, rattling on, singing snatches of Betty Hutton songs, doing impressions. "Lishen, shweetheart (this was my Bogart imitation) what'sh a nishe girl like you doing in a joint like thish?"

Judy began to chortle. "That's *good*," she said.

"No, it's not," I contradicted her. "It's lousy. But why should I let that stop me? Okay, who's this?" I deepened my voice and adopted an English accent. "Every morning I take the mirror from the shelf and I say 'Mirror, mirror on the wall . . . who's the greatest star of all?'" I was doing a James Mason speech from one of Judy's biggest hits, *A Star Is Born*. I knew all the dialogue.

Judy fell right in with it. "Mmm . . . N . . . Norman Maine . . ." she said.

"Ex*act*ly," I said, still in character, and the two of us broke into laughter.

There was no time now, it seemed, to talk about anything real. We had been suddenly blasted, propelled into this shared frame of reference, and, to me, it was as if an exhilarating breath of the ionosphere had pervaded this tacky restaurant with its wooden beams and its cheap orange jars with candles in them. I thought of Richard Stryker and how dumbfounded he'd be when he came out of the shower and found us gone.

"You know what you are?" I said to Judy, laughing. "You're a *run*away. Wow. What a story!" I grabbed Judy's arm urgently. "I'm onto something hot, Chief—but you've gotta give me some cash!"

Again Judy fell in with it immediately. "I can't give you another penny, Lucky. I'm running a newspaper here . . . not a charity ward." She jerked her thumb over her shoulder, nearly stabbing the forgotten Jenny in the eye. "I've got a board of directors in there," she barked at me.

"Chief, this could be the biggest story of the *year*—" I insisted, doing Lee Tracy. "It's a runaway movie star. It's Judy *Gar*land. Nobody knows where she is but me, and I can get an exclusive on this, we can scoop every paper in *town*, if I can just stay *with* her. But I've got to have some cash!"

Judy glared at me, and I thought for an instant I'd said something wrong, but she was only taking a dramatic pause. "I know I'm gonna regret this," she said to me, in a deep, Eugene Pallette voice.

"Trust me, Chief," I hissed back at her. "It'll be the story of the year!"

"All right, Lucky—" Judy said, brightening. "Go to it!"

"Wire me a thou!" I yelled and ran from the table out the arched doorway. Judy's head was on her arms in giggles as I returned and brushed by four young men in black cassocks who had begun to serenade our table with a Castilian folk song. One of them handed me a card. The card said these boys were students at the University of Seville and were financing their trip to America by singing in cafes. Oh shit, I thought. I'm gonna have to give these guys one of my thirteen dollars.

After dinner, the maître d' offered us a drink in the bar. "We are very fortunate tonight at the Buena Mesa," he informed us. "We have with us Miguel from Madrid. He is one of the greatest dancers of the flamenco. When he dance, Miguel insist always on a floor of the finest wood and, as you can see, here we have only rugs, and so maybe he will not dance for us tonight—but I bring him to meet you, anyway."

So Miguel came over, and—after some greasy hand-kissing—allowed as how he might be persuaded to give us a demonstration of the flamenco after all. Seeing as how it was Mees Garlan' and because the arteest has the obleegation to the fellow arteest.

So we watched as this guy stomped the dust outta the carpet. Judy made several comments—ostensibly to me, but loudly enough for the room at large to hear. "Oh, he's *marv*elous . . ." she said. "Isn't he *won*derful?" Now the guy was okay, you know, he wasn't worth Marvelous or Wonderful. I figured this must be Judy's gracious lady act; the star acknowledging the performance of a peer.

Miguel, however, mistook Judy's enthusiasm as a come-on (maybe it was) and drew a chair to our table. "Miguel," Judy murmured with a dazzling smile, "you were fantastic." Miguel leaned forward in his chair. He was straddling it, of course. Flamenco dancers never sit in chairs the way you and I do, they straddle them. Judy leaned toward him.

Infuriated, I set down my Fundador, got up and left the table. Go ahead, I thought angrily. Go get laid by a pair of sideburns, what do I care? I was so upset I banged the wall above the urinal with the heel of my hand. What the hell was going *on* inside me?

On my way back to the table, I could see that Miguel had now appropriated my chair, and was locked in what looked like a deep and intimate tête-à-tête with Judy. As I approached, the maître d' glanced at me with a false smile that contained both disdain and fear. I caught the message immediately: I mus' not let the greengo take her away before Miguel can make hees move—

I turned on my heel, left the Buena Mesa, and dashed the three blocks to where I'd parked the truck. I drove back to the door of the restaurant and left the motor running. On the way to the bar I stopped by the checkroom and collected Judy's mink. When I reached the table, Miguel was not glad to see me.

I held Judy's coat out for her, gazing steadily at Miguel all the while. The dancer had no choice. He rose and pulled the table to allow Judy out.

"Perhaps we weel see each other soon again," he said to her.

Not if I have anything to say about it, I thought.

FRIDAY, OCTOBER 25

I pointed the truck west on Forty-second Street. "Th . . . there's a . . . poolroom around here somewhere," Judy said. "Let's see if we can find it."

We drove east and west, back and forth along Forty-second Street for half an hour, but Judy couldn't locate her poolroom. "Mmm, this *city* . . ." she said. "They keep nn, *chang*ing things around without . . . *tell*ing me."

"I know," I said. "Let's go to the pound." Judy looked at me curiously. "The . . . dog pound?"

"The car pound, where they tow the cars. It's out on a pier, we can see the river." I was thinking of the quarter and two dimes in my pocket. There wasn't much you could do in New York for forty-five cents. The pound might not have the greatest floor show in town, but it had one big attraction—it was free.

I steered the truck to the Hudson River and Fifty-sixth Street. The pier extends perhaps five hundred feet into the water and is lined on each side with a row of incarcerated automobiles. If you walk to the end of this pier you are out by the water, which was cold and shimmery in this October night.

I helped Judy down from the truck and took her arm. She began limping with me to the entrance. You idiot, I suddenly thought, are you going to make this woman hobble five hundred feet on a bad foot to freeze her ass on a *dock?*

Fortunately, the pound guard stopped us. "You got a car here?"

"No, officer, we just wanted a look at the river," I said.

"Sorry, nobody's allowed out there," said the guard, " 'f somep'n wazza happen to you'd be my 'sponsibility."

"What could happen?" I persisted. All at once Judy took up the struggle. "We *do* have a car out there," she told the man.

She's a game kid, I thought. Game in her left foot. The guard was giving us a suspicious once-over. "Yeah? What make?"

"Officer," I broke in, before we got too deeply into this, "this is Miss Judy Garland, and we just wanted to sing and dance a little, down by the river."

The guy peered at Judy. If he recognized her he was very cool about it. "I'm sorry," was all he said.

DISSOLVE TO: the Improvisation, a club on West Forty-fourth Street, where I know I can sign the check because I work there occasionally. By four in the morning we had been there two hours, and I found myself pooping out, which surprised me. Normally, I'm nocturnal, never in bed till three or four anyway. Why should I be this fatigued? I didn't realize how much adrenaline this evening was costing me.

To begin with, I'd just finished playing for Judy, who sang four tunes, and I'd had an anxiety attack about getting her keys right. Secondly, I was playing host at our table, introducing the gang of resident comics who hung out at the Improv—"Hiya, Rodney, whaddya say, saw the item in Lyons, beautiful, baby, just beautiful. Judy, this is Rodney Dangerfield, one of our better, cheaper comics—"

And Rodney practically genuflected and said "Miss Garland, I dowanna sound like a schmuck, but really, sincerely, there is no one, and I mean no one—"

And Budd Friedman, our genial bearded host, was bringing over everyone he could get his hands on; this was a big evening for his club. I mean Alan King, okay, Milton Berle, terrific, but Judy Garland . . . singing here? That was an event.

Around four-thirty, I saw Budd approaching with Murray, his baker, who was making a predawn delivery. Murray had always wanted to meet Judy Garland. He was so overwhelmed he gave her a bagel. Judy stared at it in some surprise.

"Ga 'head, take it," said Murray. "It's free."

Judy gave him a smile. "Well, mmm, thank you."

Budd turned his palms out in an explanatory gesture. "He's always wanted to meet you."

"Listen," said Murray the baker, "you want a lift home? I got the truck outside."

"Thanks," I countered, "we have our own truck." Budd laughed. He thought I was kidding.

"It's no trouble, believe me," said Murray. Like we were worried.

But Judy wasn't ready to go home. "I wish I could think where that pool hall disappeared to . . ." she murmured. Budd, sensing an opportunity (maybe he could still contact a photographer somewhere and get some publicity outta this), said, "I know an all-night parlor."

Judy perked up. "Where?" But I wanted to get home. "Listen, what time is it?" I asked. "Oh, come on," Budd argued, "it's only quarter to five, the shank of the evening."

I was moving our party outside. There, parked on West Forty-fourth Street, was the bakery truck, looking for all the world like Jimmy Gleason's milk wagon in *The Clock,* the cab lit up all warm and yellow.

But it was time to go home. I took Judy by the arm and guided her across the street to the other truck—mine. Budd followed us, walking behind Jenny. We stood by the truck door, the mood one of indecision.

"Come *on,*" Budd pushed, "the lady wants to play pool. You're not gonna let the Hustler down, are you?" I looked at Judy. She was rarin' to go, ready for action. "Where is this place?" I asked Budd, reluctantly.

And then, curiously, help arrived from an unexpected quarter. "I think we'd better get going," said Jenny. The three of us stared at her. There was an odd finality to her tone. It was the only thing she'd said all evening, and it therefore carried weight. What *is* her story? I wondered, but whatever it was, I was grateful to Jenny now.

I opened the door to the cab and Jenny climbed in taking her place above the motor. I pushed Judy up by her elbow, bouncing her gently into her seat, and hopped in on the other side. I started the engine.

But Budd's arms were on the window on Judy's side, and he hung there, making small talk, for another six or seven minutes.

He sure didn't want to let her go.

Judy gave me a quizzical look when I stopped the truck before the Park Avenue building I lived in with my folks. After the patched and soldered condition of the delivery truck she was expecting a warehouse on the waterfront.

I roused the sleepy doorman, and he let the three of us into the long, elegantly furnished lobby. We moved past marble tables, over plush carpet, beneath chandeliers. Judy turned to Jenny, "Too bad they had to leave the nn, Winter *Palace*."

Once upstairs, I led the two women quietly down the hall, careful not to wake anyone. At the end of this hall, separated by a bathroom, were two rooms, one with twin beds, the other a single. I put my guests in the double.

"Howsabout a drink?" Judy said, still perky, still rarin' to go at five-thirty in the morning. ". . . And one for, nn, *Jenny*," she added. Jenny made a small sound of demurral. Judy wouldn't allow it. "No, Jenny, you stick to your guns . . ." She turned to me, pulling up her top lip, baring her teeth. She tried on an oriental accent. "Get . . . hopping," she said.

But she wasn't kidding. She was trying to disguise her imperiousness with her Charlie Chan impression, but it didn't work. The harsh subtext of command, of disregard for my feelings, rang through. It was the first unpleasant thing she'd done all evening, and it shocked me.

But I got the drinks. And then I brought my tape recorder into the bedroom. "I've got something that'll surprise you," I said.

From my tape collection I dug out three radio broadcasts: the "Shell Chateau," hosted by Wallace Beery in 1935, and featuring a young vocalist named Judy Garland, only twelve years old. Her first radio appearance. On these rare tapes Judy sings "Broadway Rhythm" and "Zing! Went the Strings of My Heart." At the sound of her own voice, Judy's eyes brightened with pleasure and wonder. "Where did you get . . . those?"

She listened intently, smiling, in the alien sensation of hearing what she had been, nodding at times in agreement with herself but never commenting verbally. She didn't want to miss a note.

And she was right. Even at age twelve, it was there. Not all of it, naturally, not the visceral impact, the emotional gut pull, that would arrive with maturity; but already, at *twelve*, the voice was developed and robust, the style was polished and professional, and, if the vocal mannerisms sounded a shade gimmicky, a little precocious here on a kid, you could hear her beginning to evolve into the natural, direct artist who finally performed so simply and without artifice.

The tape ended, and Judy began talking about this early period. "Well, I could always be nn, *heard.* We had to practically, nn, *scream* the place down because half the time there were no . . . mikes . . ." She was talking about herself in the vaudeville days, talking unselfconsciously, amusingly, while I prompted her with questions. How did you feel about performing then? What was your mother like? Your father? I wanted to get closer to Judy now, wanted her to . . . what was the word? *Trust* me. Wanted her not to have to resort to Charlie Chan impressions . . .

"Oh, my neck . . ." she was saying. "It feels so nn, *tense* . . ."

I kneeled on the bed in back of her and took her shoulders beneath my fingers, kneading the flesh beneath her dress. This was our third physical encounter, I realized. First, the intense handclasp at Richard's, next lifting and carrying her to the truck . . . and now this. I pressed my palms into her shoulders strongly, applied a firm pressure with my fingers, easing the tension, soothing her, soothing her. Judy looked over her shoulder.

"Hey, take it easy . . . gently, gently . . ."

"Sorry," I muttered, feeling stupid. I stared blankly across the top of Judy's head and noticed Jenny sitting on the adjoining bed, silent as a shadow. Jenny had a disquieting tendency: she tended to disappear for minutes at a time.

I winced as I registered the clock on the night table. Seventen. I gritted my teeth as they clicked together with fatigue. Hold Back the Yawn. I gave Judy's shoulders a final pat and stepped from the bed to the floor.

"Well, ladies," I announced, "I think I've had it. I'm going to bed."

"Okay, buster." Judy's voice was harsh again. "You do that." She waved her hand in dismissal. "You can go now."

"Now is there anything you need? Can I get you anything?" Judy gave me what seemed like a genuine smile. And now her voice was soft as sachet.

"No . . . everything is, nn, *fine* . . ." The voice was nearly a whisper. "And . . . thank you."

I bent to her and kissed her on the cheek. Judy put a hand under my elbow and squeezed with a gentle pressure, and in that moment I knew she wanted me. Oh my God, I thought, She wants me. Jesus Christ, what do I do now? Of course I want her too. I've spent the entire evening trying to seduce her with my songs, my gags, my *shtick*, my impressions, my tapes—with everything I have. But it's seven-thirty in the morning, Jenny is right here in the room with us, I'm ready to drop from exhaustion, and it's just fucking impossible, that's all.

I squeezed Judy's shoulder with an answering pressure and crossed into the bath that separated the two bedrooms. As I brushed my teeth my mind was pondering the possibilities that lay in store tomorrow. Would Judy be here tomorrow? I might very well wake up and find her gone.

I never thought bed could be so good. I turned to the wall, allowing myself to relax for the first time in hours. Ooh, I didn't know how tired I was till I lay down. My lids began to close . . . well, howsabout that, fans, Judy Garland . . . the baker gave her a bagel, incredible . . . the whole thing's incredible . . . I wonder how my folks—

There was a knock. I raised myself on an elbow. "Come in?" Jenny was standing on the threshold. Her voice carried a certain urgency.

"John, I have to go back to Richard's to get some Seconal. Judy can't sleep without them."

"Okay."

"Can we . . . is there a TV set or a radio around? Judy doesn't like to be alone without something."

There was a TV set in here, a big Zenith console on a rolling cart. I dragged myself out of bed, slipped on my slacks, and knotted a shirt about my waist, Busby Berkeley rehearsal style. Together, Jenny and I pushed the set through the bathroom into Judy's room. I turned it on. It was Channel Thirteen, the educational channel. "Buenos días, señoras y señores. Hoy vamos a estudiar el pasado." Great. Judy could audit Spanish 101. Jenny had her coat on.

"Will you show me how to get out?"

"Yeah, come on." In the hall we passed my father, who was just getting up. He stared after us, blankly. As we reached the end of the hall he did a double take. Tell you later, I thought.

I pressed the bell and waited, wearily, with Jenny for the elevator to arrive. As the door opened she turned to me with a grave expression and gave me a warning filled with dark portent. "Don't leave her alone," she said.

I went back to Judy. She was lying on the bed, her head on her arm, her eyes fixed obliquely on the Spanish lesson. Was she in a trance? Trepidation and desire neutralized each other in my head as I approached the bed and sat with my left leg folded under me, by the pillow, above her. With my right hand I lifted her head gently and placed it on my left leg, just above the knee. I chanced a look down. Judy was smiling, very slightly, it's true, but enough to make me begin moving the back of my hand against her cheek, gently, caressingly, remembering the too-violent massage.

We stayed like that for a long time, it seemed, an eon compressed into minutes, as the Spanish teacher gesticulated silently five feet away from us, and my fingers toyed with Judy's cheek, her chin, her nostrils, her lips.

I bent my mouth to hers and kissed her from above, upside down. It was a mistake, it was not good, it was dry, dry and awkward. Holding the kiss, I tried to slide my leg out and lie face-to-face beside her, and this necessitated cupping the back of her head in my hand, trying to keep our mouths in some kind of alignment . . . it was awful, I was conscious only of the mechanics of everything, my eyes were closed but I could feel the sunlight, red through my lids, and in the midst of this cramped, fidgety, awkward moment, I was kissing Judy Garland.

I WAS KISSING JUDY GARLAND!

It was all I could think of. I'm kissing . . . I'm kissing . . . GOD. It was like kissing God in the back of a '53 Nash. A multiplicity of impressions, high school and Hollywood . . . and even as our bodies shifted on the bed, shifted so we could really join our mouths, finally . . . I couldn't help remembering that marvelous kiss Judy gives James Mason in A Star Is Born when they go tumbling over the couch and you can catch Judy just beginning to open her mouth to him . . . it is the sexiest thing, *Christ* . . . I wondered what kind of a kisser James Mason was . . . or Robert Walker or Gene Kelly or David Rose or Vincente Minnelli—Now *stop* it! I told myself, stop it and *con*centrate. I ran my hand along Judy's torso, from her shoulder to her flank. My immediate impression was of bone—collarbone, ribs, hip-bone, pelvic bone . . . Lord, she'd lost a lotta weight.

The chesslike progression of lovemaking had locked us into the next level, inexorably, with a sharp click, like the closing of a latch. The time for kissing and fondling had run down through the hourglass, and let's climb the stairs to the next plateau, which was . . . taking off our clothes.

"Too bad Jenny's coming back," I said. Judy smiled at me.

"Jenny's a big girl now," she said. "Why don't you leave her a note?" Judy plucked at my shirt sleeve, tentatively. "You know what I'd like?"

"What? Anything. Ask me."

"Could I nn, use the *john?*"

I sat up. "Of *course.*"

Judy disappeared into the bathroom, and a moment later I heard the tub begin to fill. Wow, I thought. We're really gonna *do* it. And then I remembered the towels in the bathroom—they were filthy. I dashed down the hall to the linen closet, grabbed a fresh towel and washcloth, ran back and handed them in through the door. Judy was singing in the bathtub, but I couldn't recognize the song. Now what had she asked me for? Oh, a note for Jenny.

I seized pen and paper and hurriedly scribbled the following:

> Dear Jenny,
> Judy says you're a big girl now
> and you will understand if I ask you
> to stay in my room for a while.
> Thanks, Johnny.

I Scotch-taped this to the hall door. Then I pulled down the shades against the sun. It didn't help. I turned down the bed-spread, rumpling the sheets for a casual effect. This didn't help either. I heard the water stop running in the bathroom. In a cou-ple of minutes she'll be out here, I thought. I was in a near seizure of agonized nerves. I tried to sit still on the foot of the bed and couldn't. I got up and checked my hair in the mirror. Oh, God, maybe I should take a Valium. But what if I fell asleep in the middle of screwing? That'd be great, wouldn't it?

Face it, I told myself, you're probably not gonna get it up anyway. You're about to go to bed with Judy Garland, and there's no way to make it anything other than total madness.

Judy emerged from the bathroom, wrapped in a towel from bust to thigh. "You know . . . I was thinking, in the nn, *tub* . . ."

"What?"

"I'm really a . . . a pickup."

"Aah, Judy, come on now." A droplet of moisture fell from the nape of her neck to the floor. She seemed oddly small now, standing on the carpet with her toes pointed in.

"No, I mean we just . . . nn, *met* a few hours ago . . . and it suddenly seems kind of . . . mmm, *cheap*."

I smiled to myself. She almost got me. This was a game, of course. Okay, I could play too. I dropped my voice to a murmur and said with such sincerity: "I respect you like crazy."

And Judy giggled and came into my arms and, as well as I could, I took her to bed.

I woke up first. It was five-thirty, and the afternoon was cross fading into evening. There was no moment of wondering for me, none of that was-it-all-a-dream uncertainty. Everything was crystal and remembered. Even as I turned my head to look I knew I was in bed with Judy after an incredible madcap night, a night climaxed by our tentative, unfulfilled, yet strangely satisfying coming together, all mouths . . . all lips and tongues and palates and the glowing red insides of cheeks.

I slid an arm gently under Judy's neck. She stirred, and I suddenly clutched with a terrible fear: will *she* remember *me?* Judy's catholic taste in bedmates was part of the Legend—she embraced everyone. All those lines about guys waking up in motel rooms after a one-night stand—Hi, GI, we're *married*—all those gags went through my mind in reverse from Judy's viewpoint.

But she smiled at me, and I saw recognition in her eyes. "I'm huuungry," she squeaked, in a Disney chipmunk voice.

"I'll see what's going on in the kitchen," I said. My father is the chef in our family, and I knew there'd be something on the stove. I slipped into my pants and headed down the hall. The first person I ran into was my grandfather Leo, who had moved in with my mother and father after his wife died. At eighty-six, he rarely left the apartment; typically, he was unshaven and in his bathrobe.

"We have a houseguest, Leo," I said to the device in his ear. "Judy Garland."

"Who?"

"Jew-dee *Gar*land."

"Oh." Leo turned slowly, bulkily, and retreated to his room, emerging minutes later into the kitchen minus the beard and in a blue serge suit with a red bow tie. He gave a short, courtly nod to the table where Judy was sitting.

"Hello, young lady," he said, which was perfect.

My mother, Marjorie, entered, in her velvet hostess gown with the gold thread in it. I'd told her who had come to visit, and she'd paid special attention to her hair and makeup.

My father, Herbert, on the other hand, was not about to be impressed. He just kept stirring the lentil soup. My mother sat down at the big oval table. "Hel*lo*," she said.

"Hi-iiiii . . ." Judy replied, drawing out the word. I began to see that Judy conveyed her intentions vocally, almost singing in her speech the primitive, animal noises of pleasure, irritation, whatever she was feeling. Now she embarked on a detailed account of how we'd sneaked out of Richard's like a pair of thieves, how we'd been ignominiously booted out of the nn, *car* pound, for heaven's sake . . . I mean you'd think we were going to steal one of their nn, *cars*, and the whole adventure. Once again she was onstage, entertaining an audience of four, the Meyer family.

My father put a bowl of soup before her, but Judy, though admittedly hungry, wouldn't touch it. She'd begin toying with it, raise the spoon to her lips, and be deflected by a fresh thought. It was more than mere distraction, however. Judy was embarrassed to consume food in front of people. "I don't like people to see me nn, *eat*," she told me later. "I don't think I look, nn, *pretty* when I eat."

Judy told my family about Mr. Wong (ong-ong), the tax man, and what a pickle she was in with the IRS. "I owe . . . at least as much money as there is, nn, in the *world* . . ."

Leo, my practical grandfather, was shocked. Judy Garland, the Legend, the internationally renowned star . . . broke?

"Not a nickel," Judy mourned, pathetically. "If it weren't for your nn, grandson's *kindness* . . ."

"But . . . can't you sing in nightclubs?" Leo wanted to know.

"Mmm, the IRS says I can't even . . . *burp* without giving them everything." It was true. Judy was not only broke, she was heavily in debt. She owed the government three hundred and sixty thousand dollars. Her cash on hand was, literally, a five-dollar bill.

I saw my mother and father, who are Park Avenue Jewish and very chic, politely masking their curiosity. Leo, less tactful, was able to pursue it.

"Don't you have any friends who could help you out?" he asked her. Judy looked down at the linoleum-covered floor. "Oh, I couldn't nn, *ask* them," she said.

No, Judy would not ask for money. There were many people who would have helped her, but Judy enjoyed playing the waif, destitute, homeless, battered and tossed by the cruel, unfeeling world. It was a role she could milk.

But I didn't know this then, in my father's kitchen. I left the room with an idea. I would get Judy some walking-around money. It was Friday, and I was due at the club tonight. What if Three were to hire Judy and slip her cash under the table? That way she could keep it and not have to declare it. I got on the phone to Mary McCarty, who ran the club. Mary, I knew, was a big fan of Judy's.

"Listen, Mary, Judy Garland's in town, and I think I can get her to work for you this weekend."

"To *work* for me?!"

"Yeah, incredible, right? She just feels like it. But listen, she wants a hundred bucks. Per night." I knew that was all the club budget could afford.

Mary was quite taken aback. "Well, my God, John . . . I don't know. I'll have to clear it with Brett . . . let me call you back."

Right. I popped into the kitchen, buzzing with energy. Judy

had returned to the bedroom, but Leo was still at the table. I told him what I was contemplating. My grandfather, however, was not enthusiastic.

"I think that's a stinko idea," he said. "Why should you let word get around that Judy Garland is working for a hundred bucks a night in some joint?"

"Leo," I said patiently, "No one's gonna know, and look, let's face it, she can use the money. You just heard her tell you about her tax situation." Leo gave me one of his I-think-yer-a-damn-fool looks.

"It's not being advertised or anything, ya know," I continued, irritated by his lack of enthusiasm. "She'll sing a few nights and make a few bucks, that's all." But Leo was adamant in his opinion. "I think it's a stinko punk idea," he reiterated. I was about to get angry with him when the phone rang.

"All right," said Mary. "It's okay."

"Great," I fairly shouted. "She'll be there at midnight."

"I mean anything we can do to help her out," Mary went on. "But I think it's shameful that none of her friends—" But I cut this short. I was too elated, too ridiculously proud of myself. I'd just made Judy a hundred bucks.

She was in the bathroom, making up. I dashed in, excited, chanting a new version of the "Madame Crematon" number Judy once sang:

"Guess what
Guess what
We're workin' tonight
(Workin' tonight?)
Yes, workin' tonight
 To ge-het food
 And ge-het shelter
And (vop) get money for to pay the rent—"

We began stomping round the bathroom, clapping our hands, making up our own lyrics. Judy was delighted, she was all for it. "Great!" she cried. "Let's go. I haven't worked since my last nn, col*lapse*."

We ran into the living room, and I sat down at the piano. If

Judy was "working" tonight we'd better rehearse a few numbers. I turned on the tape recorder.

We started with "Just in Time." The arrangement Judy was used to went through six keys, with an elaborate tag. I tried fumbling through it, without the music, but had to give up on it. Judy was contrite.

"I *wish* I had my orchestrations . . . that damn Sid has them all . . ."

"Let's try 'For Once in My Life.' "

"Oh, yes, I love that song . . ." said Judy, staring at the bar. "May I have a drink?"

We ran through "For Once in My Life." "It goes into . . . kind of a . . . determined tempo . . ." Judy told me. "Like nn . . . boots, slogging up and down, through the mud . . ." She remembered something. "Mmm . . . I used to sing, my mother had me sing . . . the most outrageous song when I was only about mmm . . . three . . . uh, 'Buddy, Can You Spare a Dime?'

> "Once in khaki suits
> Gee we looked swell
> Full of that Yankee-Doodleydum
>
> Half a mill—(yes) . . ."

I had begun to accompany her, but she shushed me, didn't want the interruption.

> "Half a million boots
> Went slugging through hell
> I was the kid with the drum
>
> Say, don't you remember,
> They called me Al???"

Judy burst into giggles. "No wonder people went (shrug) 'what the hell?' We emptied a lotta theaters."

"You know what we oughta learn . . . just for camps. 'Jippy Jippy Jap.' " Judy nearly choked on her drink. "Mmm!" she exclaimed, over the rim of her glass. "It's a *dreamy* song." During her last Palace engagement, I had heard Judy tell the story of Peter A. Follo, an amateur songwriter who, during World War Two, had sent Judy leather-bound copies of the most uninten-

tionally hilarious songs. This "Jap" song described the hideous
fate awaiting our yellow enemies.

"Teach it to me," I said.

"Well, I don't remember . . . *all* the lyric . . . but I know it's
a . . . *happy* song . . ."

Judy set the tempo: "Boom chicka boom chicka boom."

"You lousy jippy jippy Jap
  I hate you so much
  I'll make you go 'n buy a crutch
  Just wait and see

You lousy jippy jippy Jap
  You rotten big rats
  I'll make you some muh impetigo
  Rah dah rah dah something here . . .

You rousy jippy jippy Jap
  Go bomb your own selves
  And make us strollah rah dah rah
  Red white and blue

We're going to round up all the boys and girls
  And then we'll show the world . . . (*no*) . . . yours . . .

Jippy jippy Jap . . . Jippy Jap
  Just look out for us!"

There was another, by the same author. This one was a march.
"It has a kind of . . . in*duc*tion feeling," Judy told me.

"Uncle Sam is going to build an army
  Uncle Sam is going to build a navy
  And if you dare to come upon our shores
  If you do we'll punch you on your jores

We are cert'n'y gonn' surprise you
  And we'll knock you out
  For the U and S and A
  Is going to knock
                    You
                  Flat!"

I was convulsed. "Mmm . . . he wrote one ballad . . ." Judy recalled. "It went: 'I never laid eyes on you before, until we chanced to meet on the floor.' But it never talked about *dancing*."

We ran through two Cole Porter songs and some Tony Newley and "Here's to Us" by Cy Coleman. Judy worked, as I did, by ear and by instinct. It was marvelous to find that our instincts meshed; that, without any discussion, I put the piano fills just where Judy expected them, that I modulated up half a key just where she would do so herself. We seemed to respond to each other, we seemed to fit.

"W . . . would you teach me . . . your song?"

"I thought you'd never ask. Of course I will."

I gave her the lyric sheet to "Hate Myself." There was a misprint: Instead of "Raise a little hell tonight" I'd typed "raise a little heel tonight."

"Which is rather appropriate," Judy said, lifting her injured foot. "It goes with my gout." And she launched into a stream of extemporaneous rhyme:

> "That's how I feel
> With this heel
> Ceil,
> Real
> How about a meal, Lucille
> I'll see you in my heel
> 'Cause I really feel I need a meal with this heel."

I swiveled round from the piano and caught her by the middle. "You're so fucking cute," I said.

"That's because I have this . . . childlike, *wist*ful quality." Judy laughed. "Mary McCarthy and I met when we were five years old," she said, adding an H to Mary's name. "We were the Meiglin Kiddies."

"Who were the Meiglin Kiddies?"

"Well, they were a bunch of . . . they were thousands of kids in vaudeville . . . and she and I used to work for the Meiglin Kiddies, and we were both . . . disgusting . . . and she had a party . . . where I met her for the first time in years . . . and, I

must say it was rather dodgey . . . because . . . it just . . ."
Judy moved her butt like a matador dodging the horns of a
bull."

"Grabbing?" I said. "Mucho grabbing?"

"Women!" Judy widened her eyes in mock terror. "Terribly
. . . they really frighten me. Mmm . . . I can put up with nn
. . . *gentle*men who have mmm . . . problems—"

"Guys who are pawing you—"

"Mmm, y—no, I mean—"

"Oh, you mean fags," I said.

"Yeh-heh-ess . . ." Judy said, smiling at my bluntness. "But
. . . *fe*males . . . get with that . . . 'All right, Judes—'" Judy
dropped her voice a fifth, became harsh and loud and butch.
"'All right, Judes, baby' and I mean now hold—*wait* a minute—"
She was dodging the bull again, it was Manolete in my living
room. "You know, as you try to go to the ladies' room—" Judy
twitched her hips again, comically, evading unseen grabbing
hands. "It's really . . . *in*stant . . . *Key*stone—WRAAAAH!" She
gave one final jump of escape across the carpet.

"Mmm . . . I got trapped in one little tiny old john . . . in a
hotel in Provincetown . . . it was only *that* big and there were
four . . . 'bout sixty-year-old women . . . dykes . . . and I took
one look and I thought . . . mmm . . . maybe I should get in
my booth—there was only one, you know—"

Judy squatted like a catcher at home plate and began rum-
maging through an imaginary purse at her feet. "I'd brought my
handbag . . . you know, with everything . . . down there so I
could nn . . . *split* . . . and they were just waiting . . ."

"Oh boy," I said. God, I marveled, the way she tells a story is
as good as the way she sings.

"And, as I went by"—Judy continued—"they went (YANK)
. . . pulled me back, and I said, now, ladies, wait a min—you're,
we're *all* too old for this . . . and I said, really, now HOLD
THE PHONE here madam"—Judy bounced jerkily off the floor,
like a marionette pulled by opposing strings—"I don't like to be
—you're not a man and neither am—now, can't we try a li'l
femini—oh, FAAAAAHK! and I went rushing, *scream*ing outta
the place, and then—" Now Judy adopted the attitude of the

rejected dykes; she put on a dark scowl and mimicked the deep tone of their ill-natured comments: "Aaanh, yeah, y' think you're something, huh, who needs ya?" Judy made the dykes sound like Wallace Beery, contorting her mouth in a stream of garbled, obscene-sounding indistinct syllables: "Whay do rrrrowr olecun shiddowwwr nerr need her anyway, the old has-been." Judy put a hand on my shoulder. "So watch out for me tonight, will you?" she said.

Yes, I thought. And tomorrow night, too.

Judy's "booking" at Three was SRO. They were standing in the corners, hanging from the rafters. Mary had packed one hundred and thirty-five people into a room that held ninety. In the six hours between dinner and midnight, word had spread like brushfire, and they were waiting, buzzing with the electric expectancy that always preceded any appearance by Judy.

But Judy at Three? Amazing. Of course, no one knew she was getting paid. To the fans it was just one of those off-the-cuff, spur-of-the-moment caprices to read about in Leonard Lyons' column tomorrow.

I came to work at ten, played two sets, and left at eleven-thirty to cab back and fetch Judy. She had to be fetched, of course, had to be attended to, watched, nursed, looked after. It was obvious you couldn't ask The Lady to get anywhere under her own steam. Someone had to shepherd The Lady from Eighty-fourth and Park to Seventy-second and Second. They had been calling her that at the club, "The Lady." Is The Lady in shape? How does The Lady feel?

Well, The Lady was still fixing herself in the bathroom at twelve-thirty A.M., and I was learning a disturbing fact about Judy: it took her hours—literally *hours*—to get herself together. I fidgeted around the bedroom, looking at my watch.

"I just nn, *had* my eyeliner . . ."

"I think I saw it in the kitchen."

Yes, the eyeliner was in the kitchen. Judy trailed slippers and orange sticks, lipsticks and lashes all over the house. People thought Judy drank a lot because she was always asking for a drink. Well, every time she changed rooms she needed a fresh drink. The old glass was still full, but it was in the hall. Or the kitchen. Or the bathroom. It was like keeping track of the pieces of an apartment-sized puzzle to keep Judy together.

SATURDAY, OCTOBER 26

Mary called at twelve-thirty, frantic with worry. Where are you? We're on our way, I told her, guiltily. I felt responsible for the success of the evening. After all, I'd engineered it.

We arrived a little after one. Judy and Mary embraced, and Mary seated Judy with great ceremony at the table by the piano. From the corner of their eyes, everyone in the room watched, trying to keep up their conversations, as Judy ordered a vodka and tonic. Judy had become the focus of attention simply by entering the room.

Mary sat with Judy, and the two women smiled at each other as I played a couple of tunes. Then Mary caught my eye and we reached a tacit agreement: it was time. Mary rose, took the microphone, and delivered herself of a speech. How she'd known this little girl when they were Meiglin Kiddies together. How she'd followed her ups and downs through the years without ever losing the love she'd had for her. How honored she was to welcome her into the room tonight. Then she sang a chorus of "You Are My Lucky Star," and at the end of this she announced Judy, and everyone in the room stood and applauded. It was applause of genuine regard, it was a hip group, and you could see Judy register this.

I played the four-bar introduction to "Zing! Went the Strings of My Heart" five times before they quieted enough for Judy to sing, but when she did she belted that song right through Mary's exposed brick wall, singing with strength, power, and command. She was like a thoroughbred that's been in the paddock too long without a race. She bit into the song, embracing it, loving it.

And after that she sang "For Once in My Life," and "The Man That Got Away," and "Here's to Us," and "Melancholy Baby," and, just before the obligatory "Over the Rainbow," Judy picked my typed sheet of lyrics from the top of the piano and addressed the audience.

"And now, I think . . . we ought to sing a song that nn, *John*ny's written . . ." she murmured, and she began to sing "Hate Myself," with her glasses on, reading the words from the page.

I didn't know it would hit me the way it did. I remember Mary's face, in particular, sitting to my left, awed and impressed. I remember thinking, Yeah, I'm somebody else now, right Mary? Not just your weekend piano player. And I remember the frustration of having to concentrate on my hands at the keyboard instead of being able to watch Judy and the audience reaction . . . and I remember feeling something almost sexual, as if I'd suddenly been enveloped in a blinding ray of unearthly light that was changing my molecular structure . . .

Judy was to sing "Hate Myself" every other time we performed together, and later she sang it on television and in London, but this was its baptism, and, for me, its finest hour.

The ovation, of course, was unceasing and vociferous. Judy had done all her I-lost-my-place *shtick*, had entertained fabulously, and now, as she sat down again, her table was besieged, encircled by people who just wanted to . . . touch her. That's what it *was* about Judy, a warmth, a vulnerability that made you want to touch her . . . hug her, make sure she's all right. She won't mind. I love her, and I just want to . . . touch her.

Judy allowed herself to be touched, and praised, and adored for an hour and a half, while I finished playing. We left just before four, Mary and Judy exchanging the traditional show-biz kiss, lips to cheek. I saw Mary slip a single bill surreptitiously into Judy's hand. As I held the door, it occurred to me that Judy must be hungry. She hadn't eaten anything since she turned down the lentil soup nearly twelve hours ago.

"Do you want to eat something?" I asked her. Judy gave me an outrageous and provocative leer. "I'll see *you* later," she said.

Later. We had both bedrooms to ourselves, Jenny having been sent off to stay with a girl friend on the West Side. Judy did that with people; when she no longer needed them she dismissed them. But she would never make herself the heavy: "The Meyers really can't put up nn, *two* houseguests, Jenny . . . Mrs. Meyer told me this afternoon . . ."

Jenny had been useful when there was no one else around besides Richard and his friends, but now, you see, Judy was trading up. I could take over the duties Jenny had been performing. Being an audience for Judy, for instance. Or commiserating with her or diverting her. Oh, there was lots to do. And I could do all that now, maybe not as proficiently as Jenny, for I was new to the job and not versed in Judy's needs. But I had one essential feature Jenny lacked: I was a man.

We made real love for the first time. It was just fine. It wasn't that important. Does that make any sense? For me and Judy, lovemaking was not the ultimate pinnacle of the relationship, as it might be with many couples, it was simply another building block in the glittering, prismed, golden tower-for-two we were busily constructing around us. Lovemaking had to be prorated among the other jeweled girders, among the more unique gifts we could bring each other, like the music. I could make love to another woman, sure, but who except Judy could bring me to the point of simultaneous heartbreak and admiration when she sang for me? Who except Judy could stir me so immediately to laughter or pity, to sorrow or pleasure?

I didn't know it, but I was falling in love.

This afternoon I learned about the pills. The pills were as much a part of the Legend as "Over the Rainbow." In addition to Seconal, which she often needed to sleep, Judy took Ritalin—a cerebral stimulant that produces a sense of well-being without revving up your motor, the way Dexedrine does. Ritalin is a prescription drug, and doctors will only issue limited amounts. Judy was allowed twenty ten-milligram pills per order, but she was dependent on the drug, swallowing an average of four at a time. She'd popped eight the night we met. She was so adept at sneaking them I hadn't even noticed.

You can see twenty pills wouldn't last more than a day and a half, and that's a mild day. Judy needed four pills when she woke up, just to get her heart started. This afternoon she finished her supply, and brought me her makeup kit. In this kit Judy kept the empty vials that had been prescribed for her by physicians all over the country. There were five from New York, four from Boston, six from Los Angeles, dating back to 1965.

Wherever she lighted, Judy's ploy was to take the vial to the corresponding apothecary and get him to refill it. I shook my head.

"They're not gonna refill this, Judy. It's a year out of date."

"Oh, Johnny, yes they will . . . ask for, nn, *Ral*phie." The pharmacy was in midtown, but Ralphie wasn't around. I spoke to a Mr. Edmonds. As I'd predicted, he was not what you'd call tractable. He frowned at me.

"Look, I'd like to help her out," he said, "but I must have a prescription."

"Suppose we call the doctor," I said, taking a chance. The doctor was merely a name on a label, and Judy probably still owed him money. He could very easily turn me down. As Edmonds dialed, I tried to will myself inside this doctor's head, thirty blocks across town. Suddenly I wanted these twenty pills more than I had ever wanted anything. Getting Judy's Ritalin meant more, somehow, than getting my show on or my songs recorded.

Edmonds hung up the receiver. "The doctor's gone home," he said. "Oh, *Christ*," I fumed. "Listen, Mr. Edmonds, I am *really* not trying to get you in trouble. All I want is this minuscule amount of Ritalin. Please, wait a half hour and call the doctor at home, I guaran*tee* you he'll okay this."

And Edmonds gave me the Ritalin.

That night, Judy and I did a reprise of our act at Three, and she made another hundred dollars. I was beginning to feel like Mickey Rooney putting on the show in the barn.

Once again Judy granted an audience at her table to a throng of admirers, and by the time we left the club, it was close to four o'clock in the morning.

SUNDAY, OCTOBER 27

"I feel like some nn, *chili*," Judy said on the street, so we hopped in a cab and told the driver to take us to P. J. Clarke's. By the time we arrived it was past four and they were closed. But, of course, they opened the door for Judy.

The place was emptying out. The last few diehard drinkers were taking their final swallow of the evening. As we pushed past the bar to the back, one of these men turned around, recognizing Judy. He was a beefy man with a pug's face, and his eyes were dulled by a night of consistent boozing. It was Jake LaMotta, the former middleweight champ. "Eh," he wheezed heavily, "'sa li'l songbird. Eh, gi' the chanh a hunh . . ."

Judy smiled at him noncommittally. "Oh, hi, Jake . . ."

"Gi' the chanh a hunh . . ." Jake repeated. He was trying to say "Give the champ a hug," but he was so thick with liquor he was incomprehensible. As he lurched toward her, Judy took an involuntary step backward, instinctively avoiding the juggernaut bulk and the bourbon breath. Jake stopped, sensing Judy's distaste. Why had she done that? And then I saw him figure out the reason.

"'S'matta," he growled, turning to me. "'Iss guy gi'n ya tru'll?" And he drew back a fist so large, so meaty, I saw him draw it back so slowly, so ominously I could almost hear the spring tighten and lock into place. I was frozen, rooted to the floor, watching his hand; I was hypnotized. I couldn't run, shout, or strike out. Joe Walcott's whole life passed before my eyes. Say good-bye to your face, I told myself, 'cause it's going right through the wall.

All at once Judy threw herself on Jake and began covering his face with kisses, mwah, mwah, mwah, oh Jake, no, no trouble, there's nn, no trouble . . . And the fist came down, slowly, reluctantly. He turned back to Judy. "Well," he concluded, sullenly, "'f he gi's ya any tru'll . . ."

I led the way back weakly, on legs made of tripe, and we sat down at a table by the back wall. "I'm sorry you had to kiss Jake LaMotta," I told Judy, "I wouldn't wish that on anyone."

But our troubles were just beginning. First, a man from Chicago came over and, quite politely, asked Judy to sign the back of his plane ticket. His wife would get such a kick out of it. Judy complied, sweetly. Then the drunken blond woman at the table on our right insisted on accosting Judy, over the remonstrations of her escort.

"I jist wanna ask her how she's *feeling* . . ." this woman repeated, over and over, in her inebriation. Finally, after several agonizing minutes of this, she rose and tried to stand by our table. She had to put a hand down to steady herself.

"Judy . . . Judy . . . how do you f . . . how you feeling?"

"I feel fine, darling," said Judy. The woman was trying to form another sentence, but she was having difficulty coordinating her mind with her tongue, palate, and teeth. "Judy . . ." she said, finally, ". . . you're the best . . ."

"Look," I said to her, trying not to be unkind, "we've just worked all night, we're tired, and we'd like to relax awhile, so please . . . we'd just like to enjoy ourselves alone here."

The woman blinked. "Course y' kenjoy 'reselfs . . . I'm jist, I jist wanna find out how Judy's feelin', thassall. My name is Ann Miller," she added, which came as a surprise. She was not Ann Miller, the actress. What she was, was intolerable.

"Terrific, Ann," I said. "We've certainly enjoyed you in all your musicals, but right now—"

"That's what I like," said a voice on our other side. "A guy who knows something." It was the man from Chicago, the man whose plane ticket Judy had just autographed. He was back, in-explicably hostile. Boy, I thought, you never know with boozers.

"That's what I really like," he reiterated. "A guy who knows what it's all about. How'd you like to tell us some more?" I shook my head. This wouldn't happen if I were sitting here with Ethel Merman. People took a violently proprietary interest in Judy.

"C'mon," said Chicago. "Tell us some more." Howabout this, I was thinking. I get by Jake LaMotta—Jake La*Motta*, for chris-sake—and now I have to climb in the ring with this schmuck. I took a deep breath and was halfway out of my seat when Judy spoke.

"I think you people are just about the nn, *rud*est people I've ever seen. How *dare* you? How dare you impose on us this way? Who do you think you are? What gives you the right to inter-rupt us when we're eating? We're not bothering anybody." Judy paused. "Now let's everyone sit down at his own table and just quietly nn, mind his *bus*iness."

I looked pointedly at the blonde's escort. He put out his arm and pulled her back into her chair. Chicago slunk away, chas-tened. I looked at Judy, a scant five feet tall. Her speech of fire and dignity seemed to add inches to her. I felt as if I were look-ing up at her.

She was one surprise after another.

When my mother heard about Jake LaMotta nearly sending my face through the wall, she had to grab the back of a chair for support. All right, it was all very fun and games, but frankly, it had passed the point of being amusing. Yes, there was a certain pizzazz having Judy Garland as a houseguest, but, after the initial excitement, you had to look at the practical side of it. The household was totally disrupted, that bedroom looks like a cyclone hit it, and then, more seriously, there were the disturbing signs of my increasing infatuation. Lord, Marjorie's thinking went, the woman's fifteen years older than John, she looks like a wreck until she's spent God knows how long in front of a makeup mirror, she drinks like a fish, and she's always sending him out for those pills.

My father, too, was smarting. His domain, the kitchen, was invaded each morning by the goddam Legend, who might do nothing more than boil some milk and have a piece of toast. But the saucepan would be left in the sink, rimmed with white, and the butter would be out, limp and rancid, to greet him. Can't she even put the butter back in the fridge?

And Leo, my grandfather, couldn't understand why I wasn't dating some cute young chicks instead of wasting my time with an old Floradora girl.

And how did *I* feel? I felt defensive, sensing my family's disapproving attitude. Okay, maybe my view of Judy was idolatrous, but only two things gave me pause: one, the lady was never ready, and two, the lady did seem to require an excessive amount of Ritalin. But what the hell, she's *Judy Garland,* isn't she entitled to a couple of idiosyncrasies? We all know what Louis B. Mayer and M-G-M did to her when she was twelve, for chrissake, keeping her on the set fourteen hours a day, putting her to bed in the studio infirmary, giving her pills because she was too excited to sleep, getting her up the next morning with Dexedrine; was that Judy's fault? And even if it is, all right, let's say it *is;* doesn't she more than make up for it by being so, such a terrific—okay, wait a minute, I'll get the tape recorder and we'll put on *The Pirate,* for instance, not just the musical numbers, but the complete sound track. I've got them all, taped off TV, I've got *A Star Is Born* and *Meet Me in St. Louis* (and the lesser ones too, like *The Harvey Girls* and *Sum-*

mer Stock), but let's put on *The Pirate* and just see about this
hopped-up, has-been drunken old tramp, shall we? Let's just see
about the comic flair, the impeccable restraint, the truth of her
characterization. Let's just see if anyone with this sensitivity
could ever let herself be anything less than perfect. Let's just
see.

"You know, Anita nn, *Loos* was supposed to write *The Pirate*
originally . . . she'd done some work, and one Sunday morning
we all nn, *trooped* over to Cole's house to hear Anita read her
nn, *screen*play. I had never met . . . Anita Loos, all I knew was
she had written, mmm, *Gentlemen Prefer Blondes* and I guess
she was pretty nn, hot *stuff.*
"Well, we all sat down in Cole's lovely living room, there was
Arthur (Freed) and Vincente (Minnelli) and Gene (Kelly) and
in came Anita, one hundred and eight years old . . . she's only
about nn, *two* feet nn, *tall,* you know, with a little mmm, pillbox
hat and bangs that kind of nn, *dripped* into her eyes . . . and
she sat in an enormous chair and sort of . . . tucked her feet
under her and put on her glasses . . . oh, she had huge, tor-
toiseshell nn, *horn*-rims, and these . . . big, wide, baby eyes . . .
and she started to read in a little teeny, squeaky voice . . .
"Well in Anita's version, Gene was José, or Gomez, or someone
. . . and—he wasn't even a pirate! He was a nn, *fisherman!*
And teeny, squeaky Anita was reading along . . . and she came
to the part where mmm, Gomez and Manuela *meet* . . . and she
said 'When Gomez sees Manuela, he drops his nuts—uh NETS!'
Well, I thought I would nn, *die,* I was in hys*ter*ics, but I looked
around, and everybody else was nn, *terribly* serious . . . they
hadn't heard a thing. Well, you know *Vincente.*"

A disappointment hit us at sundown. Mary McCarty called to
say she hoped Judy wasn't expecting to come in tonight because,
well, Sunday was kind of slow, and Brett wasn't feeling well,
and when she got to the third excuse I knew it was because they
didn't want to spring for another hundred. However, I was to
come in and work my regular shift, ten till two.
I could sense the letdown when I told Judy. Not strong, noth-

ing tragic, but it was rejection, and Judy feared rejection more than death. Judy needed to feel people wanted her.

But onward. Okay, I told Judy, I'll get off early and we'll go out and do the town, kiddo, whaddaya shay, shweethaht (doing my Bogart impression), you know how to whishle, doncha, y' jush pucker up and raise your right hand and atsh what I call ballin' the jack and I'll shee ya later. If you could get Judy laughing, everything was all right.

MONDAY, OCTOBER 28

We were standing outside Jilly's, waiting for the doorman to get us a cab. I'd begged off work early, picked Judy up at home, and gone to visit this notorious hangout that had once featured Bobby Cole, a pianist we both knew. Bobby wasn't playing there anymore, but there were two other guys, and we listened to them perfectly happily as we demolished a plate of spareribs. We even did a turn ourselves, to make up for Mary's defection.

We climbed into the cab, and I gave the driver the Park Avenue address. Judy took immediate exception to this. "Hey, I thought you said we were going to nn, do the *town* . . ."

I'd forgotten. Judy had been hanging around the house all night and was ready to get into trouble. How about a little action? Well, it was close to four in the morning (why did it always seem to be close to four in the morning?), and the only place I knew to be open now was an after-hours club on top of an East Side hotel, the Shelton Towers, a real freak joint catering to gay midgets, asexual hunchbacks, and hermaphroditic cross-dressers.

"Just our kind of place," I said. Judy uttered her unique squeal of delight, and I curled my fingers into hers. "God," I murmured in the close intimacy of the backseat, "I know you so well . . . and it's been a fast five days."

"Four days," Judy corrected me.

"No, Judes, we met on Thursday . . ." I put out my first finger. ". . . and this is, let's see, Friday . . ." I put out my second finger. "Saturday . . ." Third finger. ". . . and here it is . . ."

Fourth finger. "Sunday." I stopped. Judy was watching me with half a smile. "You're right." I blinked, then blinked again. My four fingers were outstretched, substantiating her, starting something in me, something terribly intense.

"Do you really remember that?" I pressed her, almost angrily. "Do you really know how long we've been together?"

Judy nodded. "Yeh-heh-ess . . ." she laughed, breaking the syllable into a waterfall, dissolving me, liquefying me.

"Will you marry me?" I said, as steadily as I could. "I never asked anybody before, Judy, but . . . will you marry me?"

Judy took a moment, a beat to look serious, and then she raised her brows ever so slightly, as if there was never any question. "Why . . . yes . . . if . . . if you want me . . ."

I caught her by the throat of her mink and drew her to me and kissed her as romantically and as deeply as I knew how. I was thinking only a woman in love counts the days you've been together, and I was thinking how very human and feminine and lovely she is, and I was thinking—but the cab pulled up to the curb. I leaned through the plastic partition. "Guess who's just agreed to marry me?" I yelled at the driver. "Judy Garland!"

The driver was beautiful. "I think she's a very lucky girl," he said. So we took his name and address because, of course, he was going to be our best man, and, on a surge of elation, we zoomed upstairs to the freak club on the top floor.

They kept the jukebox really blaring at the Towers, and that was fine with us. We were riding an instant wave of New Year's Eve, a wave of balloons and champagne and such unbearable excitement it seemed we could light up the night forever. Our energy level was up to a zillion, and we didn't even bother with drinks, we jumped right on the dance floor and burst all the seams in an almost frenzied marathon, the beat way up a-one-two-three-four, one-two-three-four, one-two-three-four, bom-bom-bom-bom. I was in it and outside of it at the same time, dancing through the fizz of this unreal, magical moment, still able to marvel at Judy's performing instincts as she danced. It was very loud and very agitated, it was disco dancing, it was rock, a style Judy wasn't used to, but she was blending her show sensibility with the sound that was happening in a dazzling synthesis of timing, style, and imagination.

She kicked off her shoes (oh Lord, that heel) and I had to fall back to being a simple foil, giving her just an occasional spin, watching Judy build a whole show, all by herself, precise, vigorous, mannered (but not mired) in a Hollywood/hoofer dance tradition that she wedded somehow to the screaming, insistent beat of the Doors. Her face was glittering, a mask of intense, concentrated, joyful abandon, almost harsh, it was so driving and intense, but no, there was nothing harsh about Judy tonight . . . tonight she was totally warm, supple, and giving.

After twenty-five minutes of this almost religious exaltation, Dionne Warwick had the sense to come on with a Bacharach ballad, and we melted into each other's arms, falling into a floating sense of timelessness as we danced, a sense of cloudy suspension. Nothing mattered but the Two of Us. This was Romance with a capital R.

"I love you," I spoke softly into her wet hair.

"I . . . love you," she answered me, breathing heavily.

"Quite a workout you gave yourself."

"Let's . . . unh . . . let's have a drink." We took our glasses into the piano bar and sat down at a small, black formica-topped table. Curiously, no one seemed to recognize Judy here, and I was glad. This was our night. I didn't want to share it.

"Are we . . . going to have a wonderful life, Johnny?"

"Marvelous. It's going to be just marvelous, you know why?" I ran my hand up the flesh of her forearm. "Because we both know what's really and truly important . . . we know what the real values are."

"And Johnny, you'll have your work."

"And you'll have yours."

"But yours comes nn, *first*," Judy insisted. "Yours is the important work."

"All right, darling."

"And we're not going to have any of that, nn, *Mister* Judy Garland business . . . I won't permit it." I smiled.

"Honey, don't worry about that. There'll be a terrific balance, because, see, your work and my work, they complement each other. You'll sing what I write. It's like this beautiful, symbiotic thing . . . they both . . ."

I had to stop. I wasn't saying it right, I wasn't getting it, it was coming out mundane, pedestrian, the words were blurred and imprecise, they didn't begin to suggest the scope, the magnitude, the *grandeur* I knew was there for us, and why couldn't I express this, why was it coming out a tract, so academic, *why* for chrissake when I'm supposed to be a writer, why this clumsiness, this fumbling, why can't I *get* this, I could *write* it . . . I *had* written it, by God, and with music. I stood up.

"Come here," I said, bringing Judy to the piano. "I've got something for you." I placed her on a bar stool, facing the piano, and sat opposite her, behind the keys. And then I sang Judy the song that said what I needed to say.

"It's all for you
I live just for your sake
  With ev'ry move I make
  Breath I take
  Rule I break

  Each day I live
  Each thing I do
It's all for you
All for you

It's all for you
Let not a day go by
  When I don't reach up high
  Try to fly
  And touch the sky

  Some day I will
  And when I do
It's all for you
All for you

  There's no one else
   My heart adores
  And no one else's heart for me
   But yours

When life is through
When all my days are done
  The moon, the sun will know
  There's none but you . . .
  The only one

  And let them say
  This much is true
It was all for you
All for you."

I finished playing. The last, grand chord died away. I gazed with laser intensity into Judy's eyes. "And that's for you," I said.

Judy broke into a slight giggle.

"What's funny?" I inquired. It wasn't the reaction I'd expected. "I was just thinking," Judy said, hopping off the bar stool. "Now they're in love, and he's the mmm, bright young composer, and he wants her to know . . . he wants to nn, *dem*-onstrate his, you know, grand *passion,* so he takes her by the hand, and he sits her down . . . and plays her the *worst—*" Judy saw my face contort. "No, not you, darling, but he . . . he plays her the most nn, god-*awful* song in the world . . . and . . ."—here Judy squealed her squeal—". . . she has to pretend it's nn, mag*nif*icent, the most beautiful song ever written . . ." She went into a paroxysm of simulated rapture, clasping her hands to her throat, staring at the ceiling.

I confess it took me a moment to see the humor in this, but I finally had to agree. "Yes," I concurred, leaping back to the keyboard, "he's a songwriter, and he's written her this rotten ballad, and while he's singing it to her, she has to pretend—" I began to improvise the worst ballad ever written:

    "You are the one I'm *glad* that I met
    You are the one I'll *never* forget
      Under the stars and the sun
      You are the one."

And Judy gave me this pained smile, as if she were sucking on a lemon, and murmured, in a tone of false encouragement, "Go on, darling . . ."

"You are the one I've *been* dreaming of
You are the one I always will love
Under the stars and the sun
You are the one."

A waiter came and told us it was six A.M., and they were closing, but then he saw who was sitting there, and we told him we were getting married, so the club had to buy us a drink, and listen to a story or two, and let us stay a little longer, just long enough for us to watch dawn break over Manhattan through the grimy window of the Shelton Towers.

Marjorie was in the kitchen when we came home. She was up early, making herself breakfast before she went to work in Bloomingdale's furniture department. Her morning face, slack and sagging, and her morning movements, slow and heavy, were in dull contrast to our bubbly spirit. We were riding high on energy and emotion, plopping down breathlessly at the kitchen table. My mother was making toast in the pantry, ten feet away. Judy gave my arm a squeeze. "Shall we tell her?" she whispered.

"Mom . . ." I announced offhandedly, "guess what?" My mother raised her eyes. "We're gonna get married."

Well, thank God Judy's back was turned. My mother's face went ashen, went paler than the paleness of leftover sleep; the corners of her mouth began to work uncontrollably, in a Jell-O-ey way, and a look of blankness, of absence came into her eyes. It was not the usual reaction of a potential mother-in-law.

"Whe . . . when did this . . ." Marjorie managed to moan.

"Your son just asked me," Judy chirped brightly, "and I said, nn, *yes!*"

"You shoulda heard the cabdriver, Mom, he was beautiful. He—" But I stopped. Something in my mother's face stopped me. She came slowly to the table, passing behind us, and circled each of our shoulders with an arm. She put her face between our heads and pressed us, squeezed us together in a gesture of emotion. It was a beautiful and nearly impossible thing for her to do.

"Blessings, my children," she said. Judy put her arms up and

Marjorie bent down and the two women embraced in a warm hug. I'll always love and admire my mother for being strong enough to keep her own counsel, for never interfering, and for having faith enough in me to let me pursue things to the end without reproach. May all mothers be as perceptive and as wise. Especially with the condition of silence I placed upon her. She was not to mention it to anyone, not even Herbert, I told her later. I'd break the news, in my own way, when the time came. Strange? Maybe. But by the time I imposed this condition, the afternoon had passed, and I'd talked to my friend Larry.

Larry had driven his battered Mustang from his home in Long Branch, New Jersey, to the airport, where he met Jenny, who was returning from Boston. Wouldn't it be mmm, *nice,* Judy had remarked, if someone could meet Jenny's flight? Larry Lowenstein was the logical choice. A great fan of Judy's, Larry had been thrilled to be present for Judy's shows at Three, and nearly overwhelmed when she sang four of his favorite songs, directly to him.

This past Saturday, after Three, Larry and Judy had sat together in the Mustang while I bought sandwiches in Smiler's. Judy told him how she felt about our blossoming romance: it was thrilling, wonderful. She'd been up, she'd been down, and she'd be up again, but Johnny was all that mattered now, and she'd never been so happy. But not all Judy's hyperbole had prepared Larry for today's revelation. He nearly leaped down my throat.

"Are you out of your *mind?*" From the normally mild and easygoing Larry this vehemence was astounding. His whoop of dismay echoed off the kitchen walls. He looked around guiltily. "Come in here," he said, and we moved my breakfast coffee (at eight o'clock in the evening) into the dining room, where Larry carefully closed the doors.

"How can you even con*sid*er it? You'll ruin yourself in the business. You've got a career ahead of you as a writer, John, and it's not gonna do you any good to be known as Judy Garland's gigolo. You'll be a laughingstock, nobody will take you seriously."

"Oh, horseshit."

"John . . ." he was pacing back and forth. "If it were Streisand I'd say 'okay, go ahead, take a year off, do yourself some good.' But *Judy.*" His voice carried an implication of doom. "Well, you've heard the stories," he went on, his voice lowered, "she must run through a hundred men a year. Look at Mark Herron, he still hasn't recovered, she made him a wreck. She'd make a wreck out of Joe Namath. Sing with her, sleep with her if you want to, but marry her?"

"Larry, I've never met a woman like this. We laugh at the same things, we have the music, the *shtick,* we have the same interests—"

"John, you know I love her as a talent, there's nobody better. But she's old, she's faded, she's been through the mill. And you're just beginning. And she'll drag you down with her. She can't come back again, not like she was. It's *Star Is Born* in reverse."

"That's not true," I flared. "She can be greater than she's ever been, and I can help her do it, I can help her get back up there." Larry put out a hand to quiet me, but I slapped it aside.

"Larry, I *can't* give up this chance, even if I'm wrong, don't you see? Not for her. For anybody else, but not for her. Streisand, I wouldn't *do* it for Streisand, not that she's asked me, but she'll never have what Judy has . . . the warmth, the vulnerability." I was suddenly angry at Larry, cautious Larry, rational Larry.

"And how can you, the guy who stays up till all hours to watch *Presenting Lily Mars*—how can you try to louse this up for her?"

"John, you're seeing her as she was, not as she is. You have to separate the myth from what's really there. Okay—" he said, hurriedly, as he saw me start for the door, "just promise me one thing: think it over, wait a few days. Don't do anything hasty, that's all I ask you."

As I opened the doors Larry had another thought. "And what about children? Have you thought about children?" The idea sent me into a near ecstasy. "Larry, can you imagine our children?! Can you imagine the kids we'd have? Musical, and funny—"

"—and drunk and neurotic and myopic."

"Oh, fuck off. You're just jealous it's not happening to you."

Jealous or not, Larry drove us to Long Branch. But not before we'd had a sandwich at Reubens with Jenny—a very disconcerting sandwich.

We were just three at Reubens, Judy having elected to stay home and make up for the trip to Long Branch. We'd promised to bring her back her own sandwich, the one they'd named after her.

"No, don't bring me that one, it's got mmm, *tongue* in it. Bring me the Arlene Francis . . . no, bring me egg salad."

As we settled into our booth and ordered, Jenny's expression grew serious. "I'm having a terrible battle with myself," she said. "I've got to tell you something, but I don't want you to think that I'm . . . oh . . ."

"What?"

"Oh Lord . . . that I'm being disloyal. Or talking behind her back." She paused, and I could hear the hum of the restaurant's background conversation. "But if you're going to be with her any length of time," Jenny continued, "it's something you ought to know."

"Jenny, what is it, for God's sake?" Jenny toyed with the ashtray, absently. "I know my days with her are numbered," she said slowly. "People don't last long with Judy; she goes through them very quickly and uses them up. I hope it's different with you, John, she seems to like you, and I think you're good for her." She leaned forward urgently. "It's because I want so much to see Judy get what she wants at last that I'm afraid to tell you about this."

I gave Larry a look of impatience. Jenny finally plunged in. "All right, I suppose it's not such a secret. Lord knows it's been in the papers often enough. It's about Judy's suicide attempts. If you're going to be around Judy, you'd better know how to cope."

Larry, sitting beside Jenny in the booth, turned the color of stale oatmeal. Jenny caught this. "I'm not telling you this to scare you, or for any other reason except it might save her life someday."

"What do you have to do?" I asked.

"Well, she used to do the razor blade bit. You can see the scars, if you look, on the inside of her wrists. But that's out. Now she likes the pills, the Seconals. She'll swallow as many as she has on hand, unless she has more than say, forty. If you ask me, Judy really doesn't want to kill herself, but sometimes she thinks she does. Do you know what I mean?"

"Mmm," I said.

"I think it's basically a bid for sympathy and attention, but all right, she could misjudge her dosage and kill herself by accident."

I was struck by what good English Jenny spoke. She was eyeing us both, trying to determine our reactions. Larry, I could see, was remaining calm only with an effort. Curiously, I wasn't disturbed. If something like this came up, I'd deal with it.

"Don't call the police, whatever you do," Jenny was saying. "That only means more bad publicity, and it doesn't do any good anyhow. Call a doctor, and give her something to make her vomit. And keep her walking around, don't let her lie down, keep her up on her feet. When it happened this last time, Richard and I took turns walking her up and down the room, and she came out of it, finally. She was murder, but she came out of it. And boy, was she mad. She didn't like it at all. There she was in the same old room with the same old people she thought she was escaping forever. Oh, she was livid."

The sandwiches came, and Jenny paused discreetly till the waiter had gone. "Then, when she wakes up, she'll be full of hatred. She'll spew out the most unmentionable bile, she'll cuss you out, she'll call you every filthy name under the sun, she'll throw things, she'll break furniture. She broke all the mirrors in the house on Sixty-third Street. She's terribly strong. That sound doesn't come from nothing, you know, she's powerful, there's a lot of strength in that big chest cavity. And she'll start hitting and biting and spitting—"

And fighting, I thought, watching Larry sink lower and lower in his seat.

"—because she's angry at herself for not succeeding, for not being dead now. That's how she got the sore on her heel. She was so annoyed when she woke up the last time that she started to stamp her foot on the floor and wouldn't stop. Just kept at it, stamping, till I thought the floor would cave in." Jenny grimaced in distaste at the memory.

"And Richard's floors were filthy. I'm sure that's how it got infected." She bit into her sandwich. "Just filthy," she repeated. "Do you know," she said, looking at me across the tablecloth, "when we met you the two of us hadn't had a bath in a week?"

I remembered Judy, singing in the tub, bathing that first time to be clean for me. And then I saw Larry, three feet away, looking at me pointedly. All right, Cassandra, I thought, I hear you.

TUESDAY, OCTOBER 29

Larry and I had a backers' audition of my show, *The Draft Dodger,* scheduled on Thursday. The audition was to be in Long Branch, and I'd told Judy what fun we could have by the Jersey Shore. But when we got back from Reubens, Judy had changed her mind. She didn't want to go. She'd put down her roots, she was comfy where she was. Moving meant facing a set of unknown factors, it meant exchanging the security of here for the uncertainty of there.

But we needed a change of locale. By tomorrow this bedroom would become unbearable; we were spending hours here, closeted together, cooped up in a miasma of chairbacks hung with dresses and strung with gauze stripping (from the foot); trying to maneuver in a bathroom cluttered by cosmetics and strangling in panty hose, the whole place in chaos and disorder. In another day the atmosphere would close in and smother us.

But Judy stalled so long at the mirror that I finally picked up the message. I asked Larry and Jenny to wait in the living room.

"You know, we don't have to go the shore tonight," I told Judy when we were alone. "I just thought it might be fun. But we don't have to. Would you rather stay here?" Judy nodded.

"I think . . . I think so."

"Okay, fine," I agreed, but inwardly I began to feel uneasy. When would we get out of here? And what about Thursday's audition?

"Of cawss," I minced, slipping into an exaggerated, effeminate pose, "Bruce and Mary will be dsreadfully tisappointed."

Judy fell in with it immediately. "Oh, Bwuce and Mawy, Bwuce and Mawy," she responded, widening her eyes. "That's awl I evah heah fwum yew. If yaw so cwazy about Bwuce and Mawy, why donchew go live with them?" Judy made a fierce little beesting of her mouth. "I know awl aboutchew and Bwuce. Mawy told me the whole stowy while I was tsoo-ing her hair."

"Tsouch up those wroots, deah. She's going oh nat-yourel again." Then simultaneously, we both said:

"Now lissen, Gawgette—"

It was uncanny. Without premeditation, and with a thousand names to choose from, we'd each selected Georgette. It was enough to make you believe in thought transference. The awe this inspired was strong enough to change Judy's mood.

"Come on," I nudged her. "Let's go to Jersey and tear the place apart. It'll be fun." And I was able to kiss and hold her till she felt secure enough to relinquish the stricken, unhealthy bedroom for the unknown adventures waiting by the waves of the Jersey Shore.

We ensconced Judy carefully in the front seat of Larry's Mustang, a glass in her hand, a pillow to cushion her throbbing foot. Once on the move, Judy's anxiety evaporated, and, speeding down the Jersey Turnpike, she gathered momentum, telling stories, doing *shtick,* and firing instructions to Larry.

"Don't get too close to that truck. You don't know where it's been. Besides, he's bigger than you are. No, don't look at me! Watch the road!"

Larry was both enthralled and awed by finding himself suddenly beside the Queen of the Silver Screen, now magically transformed into a diminutive dynamo yakking at him from two feet away. He was cowed by Judy, and, somewhere along the way to Long Branch, Judy began to dislike him. Perhaps she sensed his disapproval of her as my prospective bride.

When we arrived, Larry took Jenny to a nearby motel, while Judy and I went upstairs to Larry's studio apartment, on the sixth floor of a high rise called the Sea Verge, because it overlooked the ocean.

Judy sat down on Larry's couch. "He's not coming back, is he?"

"I'm not sure, Judes. I know he was trying to make some other arrangement."

"He probably wants to watch," she said, swinging abruptly from hilarity to truculence. What a sensitive device the seismograph of her emotions was; how capriciously she switched gears, needing only the slightest provocation, the flick of an eyebrow, the hint of a vocal timbre to flip you off the delicate tightrope you were always treading with her. You had to be constantly on guard and anticipatory, like a chess player thinking five moves ahead.

Larry unwittingly brought Judy back into a good humor by reading her a critique of *A Star Is Born* in which her performance was highly praised. Judy sat on the couch, totally engrossed, as she was our first night, when I played her the tapes.

Then Larry brought out George Eells's biography of Cole Porter, who had written the songs for *The Pirate*. There was a story in the book that Larry wanted to verify. "He (Porter) appeared at M-G-M to hear Gene Kelly and Judy Garland record the number ('Be a Clown')," Larry read. "Miss Garland made no secret of how she felt about it. She did not want to sing it. 'She pointed out that there were hardly any laughs, where I had attempted to provide an infinite number. It was very embarrassing to have it pointed out,' he said."

Judy took violent exception to this. "Why, I *loved* "Be a Clown." Gene and I fell all over ourselves with it . . . it was nn, *mar*velous. Who *is* that man?" she demanded, referring to Eells, the author. When told, she cussed him out roundly. "What other nn, *lies* has he printed about me?" she wanted to know.

Around six in the morning Judy disappeared into the bathroom, and I had to confront Larry. Larry had tried to make other sleeping arrangements, but failed.

"Oh. Hmm. Gee, Larr, listen, uh . . . this is really stupid, but, um, you can't stay here." Larry's eyes were dim with fatigue.

"What do you *mean?*"

"Well, she just wants to be alone, Larr, and . . . well, it'd be very difficult."

"Are you staying?"

"Yeah, well, um, I have to, Larr." There was a painful pause.

"But John, I have nowhere to go."

"What about your folks?" Larry's folks lived upstairs. "Or Danny's?" Larry's brother wasn't far.

"There isn't room," he groaned dolefully, as I shut the door quietly on his defeated back.

Larry had to drive aimlessly around in the cold till eight in the morning, when he was finally able to borrow a bed in his brother's house after the kids went to school.

This afternoon Larry dropped us at Monmouth Clinic. Judy's foot had begun to suppurate and needed medical attention, finally. Dr. Lester Barnett wanted to place Judy in a ward, where she could stay off her feet, since walking aggravated the injury.

"Hospitalization would be best," he said, choosing a word that was anathema to Judy.

"Look, I didn't come down here to be mmm, incarcerated," Judy bridled. "I've been through enough nn, *pain* in New Jersey."

"Well, then, Miss Garland, the only thing I can suggest is to keep your foot dressed and bandaged, and soak it regularly in a bath of warm Epsom salts. Keep off it, and keep it elevated."

I hurried out to buy the salts, bandages, and ointment. When I returned to the clinic, Judy was happily rolling about in a wheelchair.

"I'm keeping off it," she informed me.

"You look like something out of *Night Must Fall.*"

Dr. Barnett's nurse was to drive us back to the apartment, and, as Judy and I exchanged a hidden, conspiratorial look, we casually bundled the clinic wheelchair into the trunk of her car. The nurse assumed the chair was ours. To this day there's a Monmouth Clinic wheelchair in the storeroom on Park Avenue.

Jenny and Larry were in the apartment when we returned. We made an adventure out of preparing a bucketful of warm Epsom salts, and then we dunked Judy's foot. Judy was pleased with her new toy, the wheelchair, and went careening about the L-shaped room feeling prime. In fact, she declared, "Why don't we stay down here all week?"

I saw Larry bend forward, slightly, as if he'd just caught a medicine ball in the abdomen. Judy picked up on it instantly.

"What's the matter, Larry, don't you want us here? I thought you invited us down for a visit!" She burst into song:

> "Be a host
> Be a host
>   Just for once
> Be a host."

I jumped in quickly. "Come on, Larr," I said, pulling him to the door, "let's go buy some food." I turned to Judy and Jenny. "You girls knit us a sampler or something, and we'll be back in an hour with food for dinner and six hundred thousand dollars in cash. Make it six-fifty. Come on, Larr, before the bank closes."

Coming from a gourmet family, I've learned to cook two or three impressive (but easy-to-prepare) dishes. Tonight I was going to make chicken breasts, boned and skinned, in a white wine sauce with butter and shallots (we went to three groceries to find shallots). With new potatoes and spinach, for Dr. Barnett had prescribed iron and protein to make the skin grow back on Judy's heel. A prescription dinner.

As I stood by Larry's stove, coordinating the boiling potatoes, the frying breasts, and the simmering spinach, Jenny set the table for four, and Larry kept his turntable supplied with Garland records. He had them all. We'd just been through the four sides of *Carnegie Hall,* and now Larry put on *That's Entertainment.*

Judy was cruising the room in her chair. She'd become attached to it and could maneuver quite adroitly now, even clutching her drink, which was a light one since I was now rationing her liquor. Alcohol retarded the healing process, Barnett had told us, so I was seeing to it that Judy cut down. She didn't mind, though, she was having such a good time; telling stories, bumping (on purpose) into Larry's Regency chairs (the only fine pieces of furniture he had), and singing along with her album, including the stings and fills in the orchestration:

> "The clown (wop!)
> With his pants falling down
> Or the lights (wop! wop!)
> On the lady in tights—"

Larry couldn't help loving it, though still concerned about being a refugee, bedless for the rest of the week. His fear was groundless. We had to be back by Friday to meet Harold Arlen, the composer who wrote "Over the Rainbow" for Judy. Lincoln Center was planning a benefit honoring Arlen, an evening of his music, and Judy had been asked to participate. A meeting was set three days from now, at the apartment on Park Avenue, so Larry could relax—we had to be back in Manhattan.

In her wheelchair, Judy began to giggle. A new Garland rendition was coming through the speakers, and it reminded her of the recording session:

"Mmm . . . we had to do this number a few times, because, I kept . . . breaking *up* . . . Kay Thompson had brought her nn, *dog* to the session, and . . . right at the bridge . . . the damn thing mmm, *fart*ed, and everybody went—Mmmwwwrrr-AAAAAH!! let's get *out*ta here!"

Judy watched me in the kitchen. There were a few times during the months I knew her when she allowed herself to be content; when the constant condition of instability and flux suspended itself for a brief instant. This was one of them. Maybe the music had something to do with it. The song was Kurt Weill's "It Never Was You." Judy was humming along with the lyric:

> "An occasional sunset reminded me
> Or a flow'r hanging high on a tulip tree
> Or one red star hung low in the west—"

"Hung Lo," I said to her. "On Pell Street. Great spareribs." This moved Judy. I saw her smile a deep down, whimsical smile at me, and rise from the wheelchair. "Meetcha round the corner," she said, meaning the post that separated the living room from the kitchen. I crossed three quick steps to meet her, hidden by the post from both Larry and Jenny. We were enveloped by a clandestine intimacy. We could be heard, but not seen.

Judy came into my arms, still singing:

> "But . . . it never was you
> It never was anywhere you . . ."

She sang in a voice so soft, so sweetly lyrical, and so obviously just for me that I thought I might faint. The tears rose to my eyes, preventing me from giving her the kiss we'd both mutely agreed upon a moment ago, and I had to content myself with burying my face in her shoulder. It was the first time she moved me in that precise way, touching me with the ineffable sweet joy so uniquely hers. It was also the last, for the next time she moved me, it was adulterated with the helpless pity of not being able to help her.

Dinner was ready. I'd set the chicken, potatoes, and spinach down and was returning to the table with a pan of wine sauce, when I noticed the plates were gone. But that couldn't be. I'd just set the food down on that table. I went back to the kitchen but there was no food there. Returning to the room, I saw Larry, rooting around in his record closet. I saw Jenny, in her place, waiting to be served, and Judy was sitting on the foot of the bed, engrossed in her makeup case. Perhaps too engrossed. If anyone was fooling with the food, it would have to be Judy.

"All right, come on, Judes, let's have the food." Judy's eyes came up from the mirror, all innocence. "What food?" I stared at her suspiciously, my fist on my hip, gentling the saucepan in my hand. "Hey, has anybody seen the food? I just put it down here, chicken, potatoes, and spinach. Now where is it?" Larry spoke up. "I haven't seen it," he said. Jenny said, "Look in the kitchen."

I went back for a second look at the empty burners. Nothing. I came back to the center of the room, still holding the pan. Judy was studiously drawing a line above her eyebrow, concentrating so avidly it made me notice the bedspread, which was drawn just an inch more than usual toward the floor. I bent and lifted it.

There, sending cheerful, innocent trails of steam up to the box spring, were the three serving plates. As I retrieved them, I heard Judy cackle with glee. She began bouncing all over the room, like a manic Ping-Pong ball.

"You should have *seen* yourself!" she hooted. "Oh, God, you should have seen your face, so serious, and so"—here she broke into an impression of Serious John—"'all right, Judes, where's the food?' and running around with that nn, *pan* in your hand . . ." She broke into her laughing squeal, producing an unearthly sound of pure joy. "You came out, and you did the nn, *longest* take"—she resumed her impression of me—"'okay everybody, let's sit d- let's sit' "—another squeal—"and with that pan in your hand . . . so nn, *bus*iness, oh you were all *bus*iness . . ."

I had to break up at Judy's exuberance and the kick she was getting. She milked the incident for all it was worth, going over it again, describing in detail the expression on everyone's face. "Larry didn't know *what* to think"—and reveling in my confusion—"you just kept standing there, with that nn, silly *pan* . . . walking into the kitchen and out again, and looking so nn, *bus*inesslike . . ."

She couldn't sit down to eat, she was so excited. The wheelchair had been forgotten. Judy was up now, doing a show for us as we ate, singing and prancing about to her own music.

"All right, Judes, fun time is over, now sit down and eat."

"Oh, going heavy on me, eh?"

"That's right, kiddo, it's Hitler time. You vill sidt down und eadt or you vill get no zupper."

Judy snatched three new potatoes from her plate and stepped back. "The Hollywood Palace presents—The Bonzini Brothers!" She threw the potatoes in the air and made juggling motions with her hands. The potatoes dropped with three soft *thwups* to the parquet floor. Larry gave a twitch of shock. Judy picked up three more potatoes.

"Judes—" I started.

"So fun time is over, eh?" Judy swung her right hand at my head, and before I knew what hit me, there was crushed new potato hanging out of my left ear. Then she went for Larry. With amazing speed and dexterity she stuffed a second potato under the top of his turtleneck sweater and mashed it in with the heel of her hand. Larry yelped and cringed away from her. I was bent to my left, like a swimmer clearing his ear, picking starch out of my Eustachian tubes. Judy had one potato left. "What about Jenny?" I said.

"Oh, no," she shot back, and came at me with her last potato. Straightening, I grabbed her right wrist in my left hand, blocking her swing, and—with my right hand—scooped up a mixed handful of spinach and sauce from my plate.

SPLAT! I whacked it all over the left side of Judy's face, and then I grabbed her nose with my creamy paw and began stuffing it into her nostrils.

Judy yowled, snatched whatever she could from her own plate, and mashed it into my hair, grinding it in, making sure my head was full of it. We were both heaving with hysterical laughter as I worked a fresh handful of sauce into *her* hair, beginning at the base of her skull and sliding up, massaging the back of her head with cream sauce. Vaguely, far off, I could hear Larry screaming at me, but I was laughing too hard to pay any mind. The two of us were a hideous pair of gooey-faced, spinach-strung monsters, dripping sauce onto Larry's Regency chairs, puffing with short barks of laughter.

I took Judy by the hair, bent her head back, and kissed her hard, through the cream, the spinach, through everything. Then I seized her hand and pulled her into the bathroom, where we stripped, giggling like schoolchildren. I turned on the shower, and we stepped in together. The water was warm, heavy and soothing. We did each other's hair, shampooing the rich lather in slowly and sensually.

We stayed in there a lot longer than we needed to.

WEDNESDAY, OCTOBER 30

Today started badly. We had an argument over the Ritalin pills. Since I'd been procuring them I'd been keeping them, doling them out as they were needed. No, that's not quite accurate. Doling them out as Judy asked for them, which was a different thing. That's what led to the fight.

It was noon and Judy asked me for Ritalin, four pills. Since she was accustomed to only two upon arising, it surprised me that she felt the need of a double dose today, when things seemed to be going so well. The whole curve of her life seemed to be on the upswing: Friday we were meeting Harold Arlen and the Lincoln Center people to discuss the benefit; it would be exciting and glamorous. Secondly, Judy had herself a new fiancé, one who seemed to care only about her comfort and happiness. Best of all, last night she had instigated the complete ruin of Larry's home. There was potato skin wedged between the floor and the bookcase, hairs of spinach were clinging to the picture frames, and there were stains on the Regency chairs that would never come out. By rights, Judy should be feeling wonderful, yet here she was asking for a double dose of Ritalin. The minute I asked why, she became harsh and abusive.

"Look, I'm not a fucking . . . child. I know how many pills I need."

"Judy, I don't know much about this stuff, but I do know that the fewer of 'em you take, the healthier you'll be."

"Oh yes? And how do you know that? Are you a doctor? Did someone appoint you my keeper? You know, I've been taking these pills a long time, buster . . ."

Oh, she was nasty; strident and unfriendly in a very serious way. Obviously, I'd pressed a nerve; this was a scene she'd played with many people, and here it was . . . cropping up again . . .

". . . with you," she murmured ruefully. "I thought maybe you'd be different. You're . . . sensitive. I thought perhaps you'd understand . . ."

"Judy, I'm trying to."

"Well, I'll tell you how you can help me: don't nn, *watch* me every minute, like you're my nn, *guard*ian or something. Let *me* keep the pills. It's . . . hu*mil*iating to have to come to you all the time, begging for them." Judy saw me look dubious. "I'm mature enough, Johnny . . ." she purred to me, caressingly. "I can use them correctly, I know how. Please . . . trust me."

So I did. If it was going to create such a rift between us, such a wedge, let her have the little plastic vial with the slate blue pills. It was my first compromise with what I thought was best for Judy. For I was afraid of alienating her, maybe losing her, and this made me weak, as the one who cares most is always weak . . . from fear.

The Draft Dodger audition was at a Hadassah club luncheon. Larry's mother was a member, and she'd suggested we might raise some money this way. It meant leaving Judy alone for perhaps an hour and a half.

We were halfway through the audition, when I got a call from Jenny: Judy had taken a fall in the apartment and injured her

eye. I was frantic. I wanted to leave right then, in the middle of
the audition. Larry pleaded with me to stay. I went back to the
piano and rushed through the songs, going from 33⅓ to 78 rpm.
It sounded like a Danny Kaye routine.

I drove back to the Sea Verge, running stop signs, panicking
pedestrians. Judy had a purple bruise above her left eye. She'd
slipped on the parquet floor and knocked her face on the edge of
the coffee table. We put a washcloth filled with ice cubes on it,
and I left to rent a car for the drive back to Manhattan.

When I returned, Judy was on the phone, trying to contact
her daughter Liza. Judy thought we might be able to stay at
Liza's apartment. But Liza wasn't there. A girl named Mary
Ellen answered. She didn't know where Liza was.

So Judy dialed Liza's father, Vincente, at Paramount in Hollywood, where he was directing *On a Clear Day You Can See Forever.*

When Vincente came on the line Judy turned the phone half
away from her ear and beckoned me over. I sat beside her and
listened to the couple that together had created *Meet Me in St.
Louis, The Clock, The Pirate,* and a very talented daughter; listened to them twenty years later:

"Vincente? It's Judy."

"Judy. Well. Surprise. How're you?"

"Oh, I'm all right. How's mmm, the picture?"

"Oh, you know. So-so. (pause) It's a picture."

"How do you like Barbra? Isn't she mmm, isn't she a wonderful—"

"Yes, a wonderful talent. Fine talent. The best." (pause)

"I'm . . . mmm, looking for Liza. Have you seen her?"

"No . . . no, last time I saw Liza . . . seems to me she was out
here in the spring. I think maybe she's in uh, Milwaukee, or
some such place. Seems to me I heard the two of them were
working somewhere. I think it was Milwaukee."

Vincente's tone was reserved. Not unfriendly, but guarded,
careful not to sound intimate, eager to be polite and to aid if he
could. But keeping his distance.

Judy called the Pfister Hotel in Milwaukee. Then the Century
Plaza in Los Angeles. Then Arthur Freed at Metro. I made a

mental note to pay Larry's phone bill this month. And Judy kept trying to reach Liza.

"Well," she said, finally, "we can drop by there. Maybe she'll be home. And . . . if she's not, we'll just tell Mary Ellen we nn, *need* the apartment."

Jenny gave me an urgent look and drew me into the bathroom. "Don't let her go to Liza's," she whispered.

"Why not? Listen, Jenny, my family's getting kind of uptight about us staying at home. If we can go to Liza's—"

"Liza has left strict instructions with her doorman. Judy is not to be allowed into the apartment."

"How come?"

Jenny looked down at the bathroom tiles. Once again she was revealing a family skeleton. "Judy and Liza are not on the best of terms," she said. "In fact, Judy's whole family finds it hard to put up with her, sometimes." She smiled ruefully. "Judy's been known to kick them out of the house. Anyway, we've got to convince her to stay away from Liza's."

THURSDAY, OCTOBER 31

We drove to New York, taking the wheelchair with us. When an item crossed Judy's path, it was hers by Divine Right. She was cheerfully amoral about what belonged to whom. Everything belonged to her, if she could get away with it. And she got away with the wheelchair. But she paid for it with a lost case of jewelry, which she was convinced Larry had stolen. "Well," she said, "I hope that stuff goes with his wardrobe."

It was Halloween, of all nights, and we double-parked by a stationery store, before we got on the turnpike. Jenny and I left Judy in the car while we bought goblin masks, and cross-eyed glasses, and tooth blackout cream and a lot of silly Halloween nonsense.

There was one ghastly mask—a hideous female face with horrid puffy features: a thick cherry red mouth, and blond hair the texture of cotton candy. Just the worst thing you can imagine.

"Judy will love it!" we cried, slipping on the masks, and we ran outside to the car.

But the car was gone.

Oh, Christ, I thought, Judy's driven to New York without us, and I'm responsible for the car. She'll wrack it up on the turnpike, I know she will. I found myself beginning to laugh and I couldn't understand why I should do such a thing. Then it hit me: if I had laughed, last night, at the destruction of Larry's apartment, I'd damn well better laugh now, tonight, stranded midway between Long Branch and Manhattan on All Hallow's Eve, probably owing the Hertz Corporation a new automobile.

And then the car appeared round the corner, with Judy's tiny, unseeing face behind the wheel.

"Judy!" I yelled, "over here!" I yanked open the door on the driver's side and shoved Judy over. She was breathless with anxiety.

"The . . . officer . . . he said I couldn't . . . nn, *stand* there . . . he . . . he made me drive around the—"

"We thought you'd be in Brentwood by now!"

"What . . . what's this stuff?" We tried on all the masks, as I headed for the pike, howling with laughter, throwing lines, a line for each mask. Then we traded them. Judy got the hideous blond number. She put on her faggot voice: "Now lissen, Gawgette, yew moind yer peas and kews, 'specially yer pees!"

And you can imagine what happened at the toll booths. We never stopped in an exact change lane. Oh no. Goofy paid the attendant a quarter while "Gawgette" screamed questions at him: "Lissen, is this the way to Tsoronto? We're going tsew a christening!"

And Judy would jam her foot on top of mine and send us zooming off down the turnpike.

FRIDAY, NOVEMBER 1

Jenny and I rolled Judy, hunched in the wheelchair and staring out from behind the "Gawgette" mask, into Marjorie's bedroom. It was one o'clock in the morning. My mother gasped with fright at this terrifying apparition and leaped from her bed. Judy bounced out of the chair and hopped in under the covers, draw-

ing her knees up to her chin and grinning like a gargoyle. "Hoy!
Oy'm Gawgette!"

Home again.

Three P.M. Harold Arlen arrived first, with two red roses
folded in tissue, one from him and one from his wife, Anya. Judy
was in the bedroom, putting herself together.

"You can take them back to her," Mr. Arlen suggested.

"Oh, Mr. Arlen, I know she'd prefer to have them from you.
Can I get you a drink? Fruit juice? Ginger ale?"

"Mmm well . . . maybe a ginger ale."

As I filled the glass in the kitchen, my foot tapped in anticipation. Harold Arlen, the man who wrote "One for My Baby"
for Fred Astaire, who wrote "Happiness Is Just a Thing Called
Joe" for Ethel Waters. No one who knew the best show music of
the past forty years could fail to have boundless admiration for
this most original of American composers.

I handed him his glass, marking his fastidious dark pinstripe
and the colorful striped shirt with French cuffs. His prominent
mustache and his polished shoes, together with his self-effacing
manner, indicated a contradictory personality: a shy show-
business figure.

He was admiring our spacious living room. "This is a co-op,
isn't it?" he said, choosing a chair.

"Yes, it went cooperative about ten years ago," I answered,
but my mind was elsewhere, filled with a thousand questions,
questions about numbers cut from shows and pictures, questions
about various directors and lyricists—how did Yip Harburg
differ from Johnny Mercer, for instance? That would fascinate
me. I decided to plunge right in.

"Mr. Arlen, how did—"

"You know, rents in this town must have increased nearly
twenty percent in the past five years," Arlen remarked.

"Yes, it's terrible," I concurred. Who cares? The others were
arriving any moment. I was lucky to have this time alone with
Arlen. There was so much to ask him. "Mr. Arlen, when you—"

"My rent is simply staggering," Arlen went on, "you wouldn't
believe it." He looked round the room. "I live on Central Park
West, and my rent . . . what I pay for my apartment . . ." He

did some mental arithmetic, using the ceiling for his blackboard. "I'd say my rent has increased by some twenty-five percent over the past four years."

"Oh, New York apartments, I mean decent apartments, are ridiculously overpriced," I agreed. I let a beat go by. "I always wondered, Mr. Arlen, with Johnny Mercer—"

But the doorbell rang and ended my time alone with Harold Arlen. The two gentlemen I greeted were Henry Guettel, production supervisor for Lincoln Center, and Jay Blackton, a Broadway musical director. Introductions were made, pleasantries exchanged, and, after seeing both Henry and Jay had a drink, I went back to fetch the Lady.

She was in the bathroom, dressed only in a pair of panty hose. "Judy," I cried, "let's go, everyone's here, they're waiting for you. Harold's out there, he brought you some roses."

"Johnny, I can't go out there like this."

"Well, throw something on, a pair of pants, anything."

"Oh, Johnny . . . not for *Har*old."

"Judy, this isn't a performance, we're only discussing the tunes and setting keys for the orchestrator. Just put something on, anything." I threw her a pair of slacks. But you couldn't rush Judy.

"Just . . . I'll be there in a few minutes . . . tell them just a few more minutes."

So I returned to the living room and made small talk. I already knew Henry, and we talked about a mutual friend, Marvin Schofer, who was with the Boston Symphony. Then we discussed the show. It was an annual benefit held in Philharmonic Hall for the George Junior Republic, a school in upstate New York. In addition to Arlen, they were honoring Vincent Youmans and Noel Coward, but the entire second act would be devoted to Arlen's music. Eight other performers were involved, including Bea Lillie, Howard Keel, and Leslie Uggams, all to be directed by Burt Shevelove. Judy, naturally, would have the star spot, and close the show with "Over the Rainbow," the tune that had become her signature.

Three other tunes had been suggested: "The Man That Got Away" and "It's a New World for Me," both from the film *A Star Is Born*, and "Get Happy," Arlen's first hit, which Judy had later sung in *Summer Stock*.

I glanced nervously at my watch. Fifty-five minutes had gone by, and we were beginning to feel uncomfortable forcing conversation. "I'll see what I can do," I said, and hurried back to the bedroom. Once again, Judy needed "just a few minutes." I trudged slowly back to the living room. "She'll be right out," I said.

Fifteen minutes later I turned in my chair and saw Judy's face peering around the hall door. She'd been standing there, listening to our talk. This, I learned, was characteristic of Judy; she loved eavesdropping on people to see what they were saying about her. Later, she adopted the habit of having me tape record business discussions from which she would absent herself. Afterward, she would listen to them.

"Judy, for God's sake," I said, springing from my chair and beckoning to her. The jig was up, she had been discovered. The men rose, and Judy entered the room and went straight to Arlen. Everybody did a subtle take as we saw she had no slacks on, no skirt, or anything, just a top and a pair of panty hose. She seemed to be saying "If I don't look like anything, they won't expect anything."

She and Arlen were in the midst of an affectionate hug.

"Hello, Judy."

"Johnny says you brought me some, nn, *flow*ers." Arlen bowed his head in self-deprecation. "Mmm . . . from Anya and . . ." He didn't even finish the sentence.

"How is Anya?" Judy asked with concern. "I hope she's well." And into Anya's health, and then recent personal history, then reminiscence and anecdote, a golf course story about "The Man That Got Away," and have you seen, and whatever happened to, and I think Sid's in LA, and all the time Jay and Henry are exchanging looks and sneaking peeks at their wrists. The three o'clock meeting is now into its third hour, and nothing has been accomplished.

It was an effort for me to break in—these were just the stories I wanted to hear—but I realized it was neither Henry nor Jay's place to interrupt, so I took the bit between my teeth and slipped between two sentences.

"Everybody's very excited about the benefit, Judy, and I think we've agreed on the tunes." I named them. "Now we have to set your keys," I went on, "and then Jay will go home and come back with four gorgeous orchestrations." I winked at Judy. After the performance, Lincoln Center was giving Judy those four gorgeous orchestrations, and, from this nucleus, she could build a new set. And Sid could go screw himself. I turned to Jay. "How many pieces, Jay?"

" 'Bout forty, I think, John." He consulted his notebook. "Yes, forty." I went to the piano.

"Now, we've been doing 'Man That Got Away' in B Flat . . ." I played the famous opening vamp and stopped abruptly. "Oh, Mr. Arlen," I said. "Would you . . ."

"No, no, no," said Arlen, waving at me with a keep-going gesture. "You go ahead." I cursed myself. I should never have touched the keys. I should have pretended I couldn't play. Then Arlen would be sitting at the keyboard now, and I'd get to hear him play the tunes the way the composer intended.

Judy tried "Get Happy" in two keys, but nothing could be determined, the voice wasn't ready to sing yet. It was only five-thirty P.M. To Judy, five in the afternoon was like seven in the morning to a person on a normal schedule.

Arlen sighed when he found "Rainbow" was in the key of A Flat. He'd remembered it in F, an easier key. "Mmmwell," he sighed, "I'll just have to practice." Arlen would be playing this song for Judy as the finale to the evening.

It was close to seven now, and I could hear my parents being quiet around the house. The three o'clock appointment was ending. Tunes had been set, keys noted, the running order tentatively determined. Jay and his arranger were coming back two days from now. There was general movement to the door, and then, somehow, "Last Night When We Were Young" came up in the conversation. I think Judy mentioned it as her favorite tune of Harold's. This was one song Arlen agreed to play, and I noted —as I watched and listened—a harmonic change I'd never heard before. Arlen was half humming the melody in his cantorial manner, and then, softly, Judy joined him:

"Last night . . . when we were young . . ." she sang.

Henry, Jay, and I stood there with three different attitudes: Jay, the musician, his head cocked slightly to one side, observing

Arlen's technique at the piano; Henry, the pragmatist, running late, discreetly masking his impatience; and me, the romantic, transfixed by the conjunction of these two unequaled talents, the creator and the interpreter. I was lachrymose.

It was getting to be a habit.

Tonight, after yet another triumph at Three, we went to Stan Freeman's house for a nightcap. Stan has a player piano, and he put on a piano roll of "Hello Bluebird," one of Judy's numbers. The roll began rinkety-tinking out the piano arrangement, and it caught Judy's interest. She peered into the small open window, examining the roll curiously, watching the punched indentations that programmed and drove the keys, touching the revolving cylinder with her fingertips.

Suddenly she shut her eyes. "This is how Helen Keller learned to play."

At the time, Stan was conducting for Marlene Dietrich, who was doing her one-woman show at the Lunt-Fontanne and this season was being referred to on Broadway as The Singing Hun.

Judy did a very accurate impression of Marlene singing "Falling in Love Again." Judy mocked what she felt was posturing and pretentiousness in Marlene and never missed an opportunity to deflate Dietrich's image with unflattering anecdotes. How she tripped on her entrance at the Café de Paris. How, at a party, she played a record of her European tour.

"There was no, nn, singing . . . just applause. She'd say 'This is Stockholm' and you'd hear . . . Yay, Yaay . . . Then she'd say 'And this is Bwussels,' and you'd hear Yay, Yaaay . . ."

Coincidentally, Dietrich lived in the same Park Avenue building we did. When we came home, after Stan's, we found a clipboard full of notes on a table in the lobby, left by Marlene for Stan to pick up. The notes outlined a new running order.

When Judy saw it she dug her nails into my arm. "Johnny, look! Oh, we've got to do . . . nn, something . . ."

There was only one thing to do. I took out my pen, and we began to annotate Marlene's running order:

1. Overture (shorten this—it's endless)
2. "Naughty Lola" (you've been doing this long enough)

3. "Falling in Love Again" (same old shit)
4. Closing (and about time).
It was one of Judy's happiest moments.

SATURDAY, NOVEMBER 2

Tim Bass had left an envelope. Tim had been Judy's lover and factotum for two years. He'd phoned before our Jersey trip, but Judy dismissed him scornfully and wouldn't speak to him. So I'd taken the call.

"This is Tim Bass, I hope you don't mind my calling, but I wanted to speak to Judy."

"I'm afraid that's impossible."

"Please don't misunderstand, this is strictly business. There hasn't been anything romantic between Judy and me for over a year. But there were—there still are—several projects that Judy should look into, and . . . well, I just wanted to talk to her. She knows what it's about."

"Tim, she told me to tell you she has nothing to say to you."

"But she should take advantage of these things before they get cold. Look, can I just drop off some stuff at your place?"

"Fine."

So here it was, a manila envelope, ten by thirteen inches, delivered, Marjorie said, by a very presentable young man. Mom thought he looked like a "Yalie."

Judy refused to acknowledge anything concerning Tim. He was through, finito, *ausgespielt*. But here was the envelope, addressed to Judy, care of Meyer, and marked "Dated material—Urgent!" Inside was a bizarre assortment of memorabilia, an accumulation of two years' work on Tim's part, and a poignant mixed salad of incipient business ventures and tender mementos. Jumbled together in the envelope were plans for:

A. A chain of Judy boutiques, to feature a line of Judy sportswear, Judy cosmetics, and a Judy coloring songbook (you are the editor and selector with color-in drawings of you from your most famous—or favorite—shots).
B. A Judy nightclub.

C. A movie with a cameo part for you—screenplay enclosed (with or without song, as you prefer).

And similar ideas. Tim had commented at the bottom of the page:

"All involve good money, *in advance,* directly to you, plus profit percentages to you. None involve me."

And there was more:

1. A glut of bills, receipts, and financial statements from hotels, limousine services, a jeweler, a garage, and an optometrist.
2. A letter from Judy's Boston attorney advising her that a California storage company was about to auction her furniture unless charges were paid.
3. A copy of a letter from Tim to Mr. Wong of the IRS, stating that he, Tim, had pawned two of Judy's rings at her request, and that she was the sole recipient of the money.
4. A bookkeeper's ledger of expenses incurred by Tim on Judy's behalf, carefully detailed. Over a two-year period (1967–1968), these expenses amounted to $58,815.62.
5. A statement signed by Judy acknowledging her debt to Tim of some $19,000 covering both cash outlay on her behalf and Tim's salary, presumably as her business manager.
6. A copy of a legal document instituting suit by Tim against Judy for the recovery of monies Tim claimed he was owed. The document was a summons.
7. A covering letter from Tim, written in red felt-tip pen on both sides of five green memo cards.

"Judy—in all fairness, these have been refiled by my new lawyer in New York, and, if our other projects get fouled up, I have no choice but to have him go ahead with them (as a matter of principle, practicality, and justice). You know this is the last thing I'd want to do, but if you try to get me out of the club, or some other way keep me in the awful condition *we* have both gotten "Tim Bass" into, then I have no choice. So, they will be served, if necessary, as soon as I realize that you, finally, really *are* as against me as I am being told by everyone now.

"For your own good and the children's, at least money-wise, *please* don't pass up the club—you can make a lot of money and finally realize a dream. And you really should call Barney Sackett—his projects are between you and him and his rich friends (not me) (unless you should want me there, but I know you won't) and you can make an awful lot of $ there, Judy, just for yourself, and have some fun.

"I'm going away for a few weeks, maybe months. I'll see Stephen, Tommy, Ben, & my family now and then to see if anyone has called, so if you want anything, just leave a message, ok?

"Believe it or not, I am your friend—always will be—and want the very best for you—the 'Judy at Midnight Mass' is still very real to me, and although I am jealous as hell of John (and the way things seem to be quickly headed romantically)—if you are happy now, I am glad. I'm not. Love, Tim.

"PS The two summonses attached are not being served yet—I still haven't let them—I only wanted you to realize the seriousness of the situation. Love, Tim."

Well. Quite a package. I went back and reexamined everything. I needed to sift the implications of this material, let it take shape in my mind. Oh, and I had missed something: on the other side of the letter to Mr. Wong about the rings was a note from Tim, in his red pen.

"This is the letter they want—should I send it or shall we be friends? (Remember, *I* promised you'd have the rings for your club opening!) PS Make sure the IRS doesn't find out about all the money you've gotten under the table—like the recent CMA check for $8,000 for residuals, or the 25¢ I gave you once, etc.— or they can get nasty—"

Hmm. Tim was doing his best to be nice, while still eager to recover money Judy owed him. The tone of his note was gentle, appeasing, and loving, though his time with Judy had both impoverished and debilitated him. Had I not been blinded by my infatuation, I might have discerned, from the clues provided by Tim's Rosetta Stone of a packet, the faint outline of how my own situation with Judy could turn out.

Obviously, Tim and Judy had begun on a wave of romance and ended, two years later, beached on a parched shore of hostility and recrimination, she scorning and reviling him, and he suing her for over fifty-eight thousand dollars. Wasn't there something to learn from this?

Jesus, *fifty-eight thousand dollars*. I flipped through the ledger again. Hotel bills, limousines, cash, tips, more cash, medicine (I knew what that was, the goddam Ritalin at ten bucks a throw), transportation, more cash, money to Lorna, money to Joey, money to people I didn't know. For the first time I saw in dollars and cents how much it took to support the Legend known as Judy Garland.

And the torch had been passed to me in the Legend relay. Where was I gonna get the cash to see this through? This very minute I owed the Hertz Corporation eleven dollars I barely had in my checking account. I'd been living free since they tore down my apartment building and I'd moved back home again. You know how it is, you move back, and your rent's free, and your food's free, and your laundry, and you start treating yourself to clothes and suddenly you have no money. You have less to spend than when you paid rent and food and laundry. Maybe you start borrowing.

As Judy was making up before Three tonight, I asked her whether Marjorie could come in to watch the process. My mother had confessed a desire to sit in on one of Judy's makeup sessions; she admitted she might pick up a few pointers. After all, at M-G-M Judy had undoubtedly learned all the tricks in Wally Westmore's catalogue.

Sure, Judy said, come on in. So my mother sat beside her, watching, as Judy did her face. During the hour or so Mom spent with Judy, I wandered in and out, keeping Judy's drink fresh, noodling at the piano, giving little thought to what Mom and Judy might be talking about. I certainly never envisioned a chat between a mother and her prospective daughter-in-law.

I was walking down the hall from the living room, approaching the bedroom, and I overheard my mother asking Judy about her father.

"Is he still alive, Judy?"

"Oh no . . . he's dead. He daid now."

"What did he, uh, do for a living?"

I had to stifle a guffaw of uncontrollable laughter. My mother was quizzing her son's girl friend about her family background —and it was Judy Garland.

SUNDAY, NOVEMBER 3

The Candy Store was a "wrinkle bar," gay terminology for a place where older men can make contact with younger ones. Downstairs was a bar, for cruising, and one flight up a piano, for listening.

Upstairs, too, was a tiny, cluttered office, and it was here that we visited Tony and Luigi tonight, after Three. I am not giving their correct names, and you will see why in a minute. These were the men who wanted to open the nightclub Tim Bass had mentioned. They had a large operation behind them, with a lot of capital, and the deal sounded attractive: Judy would lend her name and prestige to the room and appear every once in a while. Not often, opening night and maybe a few times more in the next several months, when she felt like it. If she agreed to this, Judy would be given five thousand dollars under the table, as an advance. She would not have to declare it. Later, Judy would get a percentage of the room's gross, also off the record.

It sounded appealing, the only thing that worried us was the possibility of an unsavory association. Though I have to admit Tony and Luigi started off as a lovely pair of gentlemen. Tony, diminutive, with glasses, in his early forties, led us into the office and ordered drinks. "So, Judy. How you been?"

"Oh nn, *fine*, Tony. We just got back from New Jersey."

"New Jersey. Eh, we got friends in New Jersey, anh, Luigi?" Luigi smiled and nodded sagely. When he spoke his voice was an emery board.

"You know, Miss Garland, we been busy. We got a spot all picked out for you. Very elegant. On the East Side, just your style. Sixty-third Street. A nice place."

"Sure, sure," Tony chimed in. "Judy knows we been working. We gonna do the right thing by her, Judy knows that. Soon as Judy okays the location, we'll get with Mister Bass—"

"Oh, Tony, Mr. Bass is mmm, no longer *with* me."

"Sure, Judy, whatever you say. Forget Mr. Bass."

"Mr. Bass and I have . . . parted, nn, *com*pany."

"Eh, is he bothering you, Judy?" Tony looked to Luigi. "He's bothering you, we can make him stop that. Oh, we can make him stop that very fast." Tony put his hand on top of the phone. "You want me to make a call?"

In my mind I saw a vision of Tim Bass at the bottom of the Hudson River, his eyes staring upward, his hair swaying in the water like willowy wheat, his feet stuck in a cement block. Judy was smiling amiably, as if Tony had just suggested a country weekend. Sure, why not?

"No," I jumped in, speaking up for the first time, "there's no trouble with Mr. Bass. He's just out of the picture, that's all."

And that's how Judy got out of the nightclub business.

MONDAY, NOVEMBER 4

"It's time for you to start working again," I had said to Judy on the ride back from Larry's. "Let's get you a concert."

"Sid has my nn, orche*stra*tions . . ." Judy demurred.

"We'll get new ones. All we need is ten more."

"Oh, Johnny . . . the nn, *IRS* will take the money . . ."

"They'll let you keep some of it. I'm getting in touch with an accountant, we'll work it out. Come on, let's call CMA and have them line up a date."

But Judy didn't want to deal with CMA, though she had just reinstated them as her agency. "It wasn't nn, *fair*," she'd complained to me. "They nn, *dangled* my royalty check in front of me and made me drop the *suit*."

Judy had withdrawn from a joint lawsuit against CMA in return for an eight-thousand-dollar-royalty check. Her partner in this suit was Sid Luft and his production company, Group Five. Judy didn't like them either. "They've tied up the rights to everything I own, my records, my TV series, my nn, *kids*. I think they have the rights to my nn, reincar*nation*."

Judy didn't like anybody. Finally, she agreed to let me call Ken Roberts, an independent booker who "is a little more *sensitive* than these nn, *flesh* peddlers."

So today Ken came over and spent the afternoon. Ken was willing to accommodate Judy, who didn't like playing those huge "stadiums, and nn, *arts* centers and nn, *bowls* . . ." "Okay," Ken agreed, "let's book you into smaller houses." There was the Academy in Philadelphia, the Kleinhaus in Buffalo, Symphony Hall in Boston.

Judy wanted to play one-night stands, rather than week-long engagements. "I'm a sprinter," she said. "Not an en*dura*nce runner."

"Done," said Ken. Also, he said, he was willing to give Judy a guarantee of five thousand dollars per concert, something another booker would shy away from, given Judy's record of irresponsibility.

In addition, he was willing to lay out the cash to publicize these performances. He obviously liked Judy, and, most importantly, trusted her, putting his money where his mouth was.

What he said sounded good: Judy could make fifteen thousand dollars for a weekend's work. Judy was nodding affably, agreeing to everything. I was taking it all down on a legal pad, trying to evaluate the numbers. I knew nothing about the booking business. I figured Judy would speak up if something was out of line.

And then Judy said something illuminating. "I'm glad I'm stupid," she said, with a tentative smile. "I just want to work."

I realized then that Judy wasn't involving herself with the mechanics of all this, with the figures or the houses or the gate or the percentages. She was just happy to be given a stage somewhere, she didn't want to talk business. She abdicated any involvement in this area. "Just let me be an *artist*," she said. This talk was for the menfolk, over brandy and cigars. Talking business was unfeminine.

"It's not for nn, *la*dies," she said.

TUESDAY, NOVEMBER 5

The inscrutable Mr. Wong rang the bell promptly at two P.M. today, accompanied by his associate, Rosen, a slim glum-faced man in his thirties who looked like the kid in your sophomore high school class who was good at trigonometry. Mr. Wong was almost jovial in contrast, a stocky Oriental in a dark suit with impeccable manners. I liked him on sight, even though I knew his mission was to squeeze blood out of Judy. His attitude was one of dogged determination. It was his job, as a collector for the IRS, to track down Judy and her ex-husband, Sid, who'd been leading him a merry chase for years. Less than two weeks ago, at Richard Stryker's, Wong and Rosen had met with Judy and Tim Bass to discuss the debt. Now, confronted with a new business manager (me), they had to start all over again.

I heard Rosen mutter something under his breath about new business managers every twenty minutes. He was tired of running uptown from Church Street every week without seeing any progress.

Luckily, my accountant, Aaron Schecter, was with me. Unluckily, he'd been caught in traffic, so, instead of arriving an hour before Mr. Wong, as planned, he arrived with him, giving us no time to fill him in on the background. He'd be flying blind, as I was.

All I knew was that Judy owed the government a lot of money, that these guys were out to get it, and that Aaron and I somehow had to save as much as we could of whatever money Judy might earn in the future.

I seated them all at the table in the dining room, Aaron and Wong at the head and foot, Judy and Rosen facing each other across the middle.

"Are we to understand, Miss Garrand, that Mistah Bass is no longer your representative?" Mr. Wong inclined his head inquisitively toward Judy.

"Yes . . . that's right. Mr. nn, Meyer . . . and Mr. mmm . . ."

"We'll need power of attorney," said Rosen.

"Yes," Mr. Wong affirmed. "In that case we will need a power of attorney from you to these gentlemen, authorizing them to act in your behalf."

"I have it," said Rosen, and dug a form out of his briefcase. Judy signed it. Mr. Wong then produced a printed list of questions.

"Now, Miss Garrand, we need to know some facts: have you any assets on hand? Any cash reserves, for instance?"

"I have about three hundred dollars," Judy replied. Mr. Wong made a notation. "Do you have any items of value, like works of art, or jewelry?"

"Well, you know about that. You've nn, *pawn*ed my rings. Mr. Bass gave you the tickets."

"Yes, Miss Garrand. Is there any other jewelry?"

"No, there isn't. It's gone, you've taken it all." Mr. Wong consulted his sheet. "Now, in nineteen sixty-three, you are listed as the president of Kingsrow Productions. Were you the president?"

"Yes, the company was in my name. And, I believe, Group Five." Kingsrow was the company that produced Judy's TV series.

"We have a list," Mr. Wong continued, "of expenses incurred by Kingsrow Productions, in your name. The items include six filing cabinets, four electric typewriters, four desk chairs, one automobile, stationery in the amount of eight hundred dollars—"

"All that was disposed of, sold by Sid," Judy said fiercely. "Why don't you go find Sid? Why don't you find the person who really owes you this money?" I could see she was growing fitful and upset. Mr. Wong spoke to her in a kindly fashion.

"Please, Miss Garrand, bear with us just a little longah."

"Go ahead," Judy murmured pathetically, "take it, take everything. I don't care."

There was a silence as Judy put her hands to her face, covering her eyes. I decided I would break it.

"Look, I'd like to establish now whether or not Miss Garland can work and keep the money she earns," I said. Rosen picked up on this instantly. "By no means," he said firmly. "Any future income will automatically be attached."

"Then what's the point in her working?" I argued. "And, if she doesn't work, how do you think you'll ever get any back taxes?"

"John," said Aaron, warningly, "there are other possibilities."

I turned to Aaron. "Like what?"

"Like an offer in compromise."

"Good, let's examine it. But I do want to get straight about the work."

"We will allow Miss Garland to keep a percentage of her earnings," Rosen conceded.

"How much?"

"That depends on the job."

"What does that mean?"

"Different percentages for different jobs."

"And what about her expenses? Arrangements, copying costs, musicians, uh . . . gowns, agency fees—"

"These will be taken into consideration."

"All right, let's say she makes five thousand dollars—" Rosen interrupted me irritably. "Look, Mr. Meyer, we're not here to bargain with you. I cannot quote figures on suppositions. You come to us with the job and we'll tell you how much Miss Garland may keep."

Unexpectedly, Judy began to scream. "Oh, I'm sick of it! Sick of it! I can't listen to it anymore!" And she ran from the table.

There was a confused pause. I was beginning to see that Judy was crazy like a fox. We were all looking at each other. Then Aaron started talking. He said that, despite Judy's outburst, she was as eager as the IRS to get things in order; that we had to determine what kind of reparation Judy would be able to make, after her responsibilities for past debts had been assessed; that an offer in compromise might be a possibility. He asked for another meeting, the date of which was to be set after he'd talked it over with Judy and Mr. Meyer.

Wong and Rosen seemed to think this was reasonable. They needed only one thing more: Judy's signature on a document stating that Sid had collected all monies from the sale of the Kingsrow car and office equipment. This would absolve Judy of any financial responsibility vis-à-vis Kingsrow.

I took the statement into the bedroom. Judy was sitting on the bed. "Are they gone?"

"They're going. They just need one more thing." I held up the paper. "You have to sign this so you won't be held—"

"I'm not signing anything. Every time I sign something I get into trouble. Everybody's always putting a piece of paper in front of me and saying 'Sign this and everything will be all right' and then Mr. nn, *Wong* marches in and tells me I owe him four hundred thousand dollars. Well, I'm not signing any more nn, *pa*pers."

"Judy, please . . ." I explained the statement to her, how it would release her from being held responsible for Kingsrow's debts, but Judy wouldn't sign. It was as if she was getting back at Mr. Wong for the willful agony he was causing her.

I tried cajoling her, then I tried threatening her. Finally I said "Look, I don't give a fuck, I'll go back and tell them you won't sign this, and that you're responsible for all the Kingsrow stuff."

So Judy signed, at last. But my *God*, it was a battle.

Later this afternoon, after Wong, Rosen, and Aaron had departed, my publishers, Bob Colby and Hector Stratta, arrived, to simultaneously court and audition Judy. These men were forming a new record company, Blue Records, and signing a prestigious artist like Judy would be a coup for them—if she was in voice and could be counted on not to be in Australia on the day of the recording session.

They were an unlikely pair, Bob and Hector; Bob played the courtly Mississippi gentleman while Hector (Ettore) was the volatile Italian, excitable and demonstrative. They were enthusiastic when Judy sang "Hate Myself" for them and then "It's All for You," the Shelton Towers ballad that Judy had now adopted as our love song. When Judy got to bar four of "Hate Myself," I saw Bob and Hector exchange the look of gold miners who have just tapped into the mother lode.

Judy, in turn, made much of Bob's English adaptation of "Free Again," a recent hit for Barbra Streisand.

"Oh, did you do that? It's nn, *mar*velous." She went on effusively about how impressed she was with the translation from the French. Judy had a way of flattering the male ego that was feminine without being coy. Of course Bob lapped it up like hot fudge sauce.

"And I'm so pleased at the idea of nn, re*cor*ding again."

"We're aiming for quality, Judy," Bob said. "We want to get the best arranger, the best musicians . . ."

"Mmm . . . Mort Lindsey is a . . . fine arranger."

Bob and Hector exchanged a glance. They were currently pushing Michel Legrand. We debated the merits of various arrangers for an hour, but by the end of the afternoon we'd agreed on three things: 1) Judy was to receive a recording contract with Blue Records. She would record exclusively for them. 2) Upon signing this contract, Judy was to receive a twenty-five-hundred-dollar cash advance, nondeclarable. 3) The first two songs set for Judy's debut on the Blue label were to be "Hate Myself" and "It's All for You."

The meeting was over. Judy hugged the men good-bye; she was forthcoming that way; if she liked you, she hugged you. As she scampered happily back to the bedroom, I stood in the foyer, waiting with Bob and Hector for the elevator. They were trying hard to contain their excitement, but it was a losing battle. Bob stamped his foot on the carpet.

"She sounds so good, so togethuh," he crowed enthusiastically.

"Oh, she's good, she sounds good," Hector echoed.

"She does just a hell of a job on 'Hate Myself,' a *hell* of a job." I basked in the heat of their enthusiasm. As the elevator door closed on them, I could feel the vital surge of healthiness and productivity in this week of appointments and meetings, of setting wheels in motion. Get the taxes cleared up, sign a record deal, get new orchestrations, set the concert dates. Free the Lady to be the best she can be. Judy was feeling up, emanating energy and talent, intelligence and humor. And me, I never felt stronger or more capable.

It was a sensational feeling.

WEDNESDAY, NOVEMBER 6

Jay Blackton reappeared with his orchestrator, a gentle, reticent man named Jim Tyler who was going to notate the music on his oversize pad of score paper. Once again, Judy kept them waiting while she cosseted herself in the bedroom. Once again I urged her to appear.

"I just need a nn, *few* more minutes . . . can you start? And I'll be there . . . soon . . ."

I returned to the living room with some trepidation. These guys were knowledgeable musicians, while I play purely by ear. Nevertheless, I sat at the piano and plunged ahead, just as if I knew what I was doing.

We began with "It's a New World," a song that has a fragile, spun-glass verse, or introduction. This verse cannot be overpowered by too much orchestra. "Maybe just guitar," I suggested.

"You know," said Jay, "we have a guy who plays terrific harp."

"Yeah, what about doing it with harp?" asked Jim.

"It's fine with me, but I better ask Judy, just to be sure."

Judy readily agreed to the harp, but she still wouldn't come out of the bedroom. Finally, in her singular stutter, she asked "Would it be, nn, all *right* if . . . why don't you . . . bring them back here?"

And so I did, leading Jay and Jim down the long hall to the disordered bedchamber. Judy had climbed under the bedcovers, hiding her undress and now, like some convalescent child regent, was ready to grant an audience.

I brought in the tape recorder, and we listened to the tunes on the original sound tracks, Jim sitting, his pencil poised, carefully attentive to any remarks.

"Get Happy," for instance, was from *Summer Stock*, 1950. Hearing the strict, on-the-beat tempo, Judy scowled. "This is kind of nn, *square*," she said. "Let's make it mmm . . ."

"*Hipper*," I finished, "not so fifties." Jim nodded. Judy and I interrupted the even, winding revolution of the reels to sing fills and stings in our own newly created, plosive musical vernacular, using the syllables "dah" or "vop" to signify rests or syncopations. As in the second chorus of "Get Happy":

"Forget your troubles, come on get (vop! vop!) happy (vop!)
Chase your cares away
(Vop! vop! vop!)
Hallelu—get happy . . ."

It took nearly two hours. We returned to the piano to go over some harmonic changes, and when Jim left he was supplied with tapes of all four songs, plus the Overture, which he was to reconstruct from today's notes.

That evening, Judy and I went out for what we'd planned as a romantic, candlelit dinner at Orsini's, reputedly one of Manhattan's top restaurants, which it would be, if only the food matched the candlelight.

But all through this supposedly tender repast we couldn't help giggling, gleefully and loudly, about how we were euchring Lincoln Center out of two thousand dollars' worth of free orches-

trations, and about how Sid would shit when he saw Judy working again.

Judy and I kept shushing each other, because Orsini's does its
utmost to create an atmosphere in which provocative sexiness
can flower. You're supposed to dash right from your zabaglione
into the sack.

But we were unable to contain our raucous chortles, and the
other couples in the restaurant, busily groping each other under
the table, were soon casting grimaces of annoyance in our direction. We were breaking the mood.

I finally had to give Judy a grope of my own, to quiet us
down. A throng of grateful lovers heaved an audible sigh of relief.

THURSDAY, NOVEMBER 7

We can't avoid hospitalization. The foot refuses to heal. Judy's
hobbling about, she can't wear shoes. Also, we have to get out of
here, my parents are starting to panic, and the bedroom is beginning to close in again. My mind is made up. For all these
reasons, we're going to the hospital.

"No! I won't! I hate nn, *hos*pitals. I've been in so *ma*ny of
them."

"Judy, it'll never get better, you'll get gangrene like Gregory
Peck in *Kilimanjaro* and they'll have to take off the whole leg."

"Well nn, *let* them. Maybe the leg can do some concerts.
Maybe we can book my leg into the Palace . . . see if *it* shows
up."

Judy tried all her tricks. She tried to divert me, she played
anger, she played poignancy, she played at being sullen . . . and
finally gave in.

"Just for a few days, Judy. Till the skin grows back."

"Well, only if I can go to that one on . . . you know . . . it's in
the sixties, next to that nice French restaurant . . ."

"French restaurant in the sixties. Would that be Quo-Vadis?"

"Mmm, no . . ."

"The Colony?"

"No."

"Voisin?"

"Yes! That's the one. I was in there once, and I had all my food sent in from Voisin."

"Honey," I cried, "you can have your meals flown in by mallards from Maxim's."

The hospital Judy meant was the Leroy, on East Sixty-first Street. It was characteristic of Judy to choose this place, for the Leroy is the black sheep of hospitals, allegedly the last stop, the end of the medical road, a repository for doctors who've lost their licenses and can't get on a tramp steamer to the tropics. Judy always sided with a helpless, vulnerable underdog. And so she chose the Leroy.

But it's not easy to get into a hospital, did you know that? You can't just go up to the door and say "Hey, I'm bleeding, I'd like to check in here." You can't even be admitted by your doctor unless he's affiliated with the hospital.

"All *right*," I said patiently to the voice on the switchboard, "give me the name of one of your doctors, and I'll call him."

"Sir, we do not release the names of our staff."

"Oh, Christ, all right, give me Doctor Smith."

"We have no Doctor Smith, sir."

"Give me Doctor Jones, Doctor Brown, Doctor . . . Rubin." How did I know what doctors were at the Leroy? Then she did a really nice thing.

"Perhaps you'd like to speak to Doctor Klinger?" she said.

Doctor Klinger came over, looked at the foot, and phoned immediately to reserve a private room. He called Judy "honey." Of the doctors I dealt with during my months with Judy—and there were more than a few—Dr. Harold Klinger, of the infamous, notorious Leroy Hospital, was the kindest, most perceptive, skillful and accomplished physician I met.

Close to fifty, slight, with a goatee and a brisk manner, Dr. Klinger was sensitive not only to Judy's physical condition, but to the emotional tremors that caused her dysfunctions.

Nurse Marsden, petite, starched, and English, installed Judy in Room 1103. For a hospital it wasn't bad at all; the walls may have been institutionally green, but there was a nice intimacy about it, almost cozy, and Judy settled in happily, having decided to be pleased now at all the fuss, pleased to be the baby, pampered and coddled.

As long as she wasn't being deserted.

"No, baby, I'll be right back. I'm just gonna run up to Voisin to get the menu."

Voisin, a temple of haute cuisine, was four blocks up Madison Avenue, and very snooty. They wouldn't deliver. The maître d' was cold, disdainful. Even when I mentioned Judy's name. Maybe it was my sneakers.

"Okay then—I'd like you to pack a meal up for me."

"Yes, we can do that. Just tell the chef what you want, and we'll have it ready for you. But you must pick it up."

"I'll be back for it."

I handed the Voisin menu—blue, with white statuary—over the sheets to Judy. We did forty minutes on this menu.

"What's nn, 'volaille'?"

"Italian pop song. Voh-laye-aye . . . whoa ho ho ho . . ."

"I thought this place was French."

And so on. Forty minutes. Judy decided on veal Orloff, with pommes parisienne, braised celery, and endive salad with garlic dressing, an order of garlic bread, and "nn, maybe a nice piece of . . . *Brie* cheese, for dessert."

I called the order in to Voisin's chef, Leo, and, an hour later, stuck my face in to pick it up. Leo had packed the food in separate foil containers with tops, each one marked. The bill came to twenty-two fifty.

I told the cab to wait, dashed in, grabbed the food, which Leo had put in a Jack Frost sugar carton, hopped back into the cab, and circled around Park Avenue to the Leroy.

We spread the meal down that rectangular hospital table that goes across the bed, and went at it like starving cannibals. Delicious. Judy was pouring vodka into her hospital fruit juice—I still don't know how we got away with that—and I was keeping my Meursault chilled in the fridge down the hall. This was indeed the ultimate in hospitals. I saw now why Judy had insisted on the Leroy. We kidded around until ten, an hour after curfew. Finally Miss Marsden chased me out.

FRIDAY, NOVEMBER 8

CAMERA MOVES IN ON: My legal pad. It is covered with notes to myself.

1. Call ABC-Paramount (Larry Newton). Does he have rights to next record?

There was a possibility that Judy's next recording might be bound contractually to this company. As Judy observed, people were always giving her papers to sign. I had to clear this up before we could sign our agreement with Bob Colby.

2. Set appt. Begelman.

I had to meet with David Begelman of CMA, Judy's agency, and see what I could get him to do for her.

3. Get train—F.A.O. Schwartz.

Judy told a story about an accident on the *Train Bleu*, the crack Paris-Lyon express, which had crashed and killed a hundred and sixty people. Those who found this tale neither humorous nor instructive were referred to as "heavy furniture." You hadda be there, I admit, but when Judy told it, this story was hilarious. So I was going to stop by Schwartz's and pick up a little blue model engine. I knew Judy'd howl when she saw it.

4. Colony.

Oh yes. Today I had to stop by the Colony and pick up *that* menu. We'd order from them tonight. And the next night Caravelle, and then Lutèce, and Chauveron. The town's top restaurants catered to the Leroy. What a sybaritic, Lucullan idea. Tonight I was going to drink a Graves, a Smith Haut Lafitte.

I reached the hospital about three-thirty, but Judy was not in her room. Out for testing, Miss Marsden told me. So I tossed the train on her bed, and taped the menu to her door. On it I wrote: "Do you want to eat here tonight? I adore you."

We did order from the Colony, repeating the Voisin procedure. It was cheaper this time, only eighteen-fifty, because the Colony had no garlic bread. I began to reconsider my gluttonous

fantasy of the afternoon; at this rate, we'd use up all our money
in two weeks.

I was going to have to get some cash from somewhere.

SATURDAY, NOVEMBER 9

Cash. As a songwriter, you belong to one of two licensing or-
ganizations—ASCAP or BMI. These outfits log the performances
of your songs on radio and TV and collect your royalties, which
they disburse to you, minus their fee.

I was with BMI, in their Musical Theater program. BMI gave
money to writers they considered promising, to keep them from
signing with ASCAP. The man in charge of writers at BMI was
Ron Anton, who took a paternal interest in his protégés, and was
often in the office on Saturdays. When I told Ron what was happening, and with whom, he was first astounded, then excited,
and finally concerned.

"My God," he said, "it's unbelievable. What are you going to
do with her?"

"Well, one thing I'm doing with her is recording my songs.
She's gonna cut two of them for Bob Colby and Hector." I knew
it would please Ron to hear that someone in the rather ivory tow-
erish theater workshop was actually getting his songs out on
the market.

"But Ron . . ." I continued, "I'm gonna need some money." I
stopped. "I know I've already collected my advance for the year
. . ." Ron looked at me levelly. "How much do you think you'll
need?"

"I don't know. Enough to see this through."

So Ron let me sign next year's contract a year ahead of time,
and I walked out of BMI with a couple of thousand dollars. I
could never have made it through the next six weeks without
that money, and Ron, it's all your fault. Bless you.

I had another idea, a way not to get, but to conserve money.
If I were smart (and I was) there should be ways to parlay
Judy's name into free merchandise. Tim Bass had been able to

extract cash up front on the promise of Judy's endorsing boutiques, clubs, lines of cosmetics. Why couldn't I?

So first things first. I called Voisin's and asked for the manager.

"Mr. Lubitsch speaking."

"Good afternoon, Mr. Lubitsch, this is John Meyer, we spoke the other night. I ordered a meal for Judy Garland, she's at the Leroy."

"Yes, Mr. Meyer. Was everything satisfactory?"

"Yes, Miss Garland was very pleased. She intends to order dinner out every night for about a week and from the same restaurant. In fact, Leonard Lyons is printing this item in his column, that Judy Garland has dinner sent up each night from the Colony, or Chauveron, or wherever. Naturally, Miss Garland feels that whichever restaurant she chooses should be happy to provide the food gratis, without charge, in return for the publicity."

I heard Mr. Lubitsch purse his lips. "Now, the Colony has already agreed to this arrangement," I lied, "but Miss Garland so enjoyed her meal the other night—Voisin *is* her favorite New York restaurant—and she was so hoping it could be you."

I stopped. I felt as if I were running a gauntlet. There was silence on the other end of the line. Then Mr. Lubitsch said: "Excuse me a moment, Mr. Meyer," and I waited, thinking about the pack of arrant nonsense I'd just spread all over this guy. The Colony had agreed to no such arrangement, and neither had Leonard Lyons. I did know Lyons slightly, through his son Warren, and this would be a perfectly legitimate item. But I couldn't force him to print it. I remembered Churchill and thought Jesus, what'll I do if I win?

Mr. Lubitsch was back. "Ah, Mr. Meyer, how many meals did you say would be involved?" I estimated it quickly. How many could I get away with, what would the traffic bear? I had said a week.

"Oh, seven or eight," I said.

"Well, Miss Garland has always been a good customer," Lubitsch told me. "And I think we can take care of it." I grinned with glee.

"Thank you, Mr. Lubitsch." Careful, I warned myself, don't
sound *too* excited.

"But Mr. Meyer . . ."

"Yes?"

"You will ask Miss Garland to go easy, please? The other night
she had quite a dinner."

"I'll see to it, Mr. Lubitsch." Sure, I thought, just the bare es-
sentials—appetizer, entrée, salad, dessert, and could we carry
the coffee out in a Dixie cup?

I must say, Voisin was lovely. They packed us a fresh meal for
a week. And surprise, when I called Leonard Lyons, two days
later, to report the item, he'd already heard about it. He'd been
to Voisin the night before, and Mr. Lubitsch had spilled the
flageolets. The item appeared a day later in the *Post*: "Judy Garland has her meals sent up from Voisin while she's recovering
from a minor foot injury at the Leroy Hospital."

SUNDAY, NOVEMBER 10

"I found the cameraman who shot *Star Is Born* on the nn,
unem*ploy*ment line. His name was . . . Sammy Leavitt . . . for
some reason our first cameraman didn't work out, and I remembered Sammy from nn, *some*where . . . but I couldn't find him.
We checked with, you know, the ASC and everyone . . . and
then, one day . . . one of the dancers said they'd seen Sammy on
the line at nn, unem*ploy*ment . . . so, the next Tuesday I went
down there . . . and nn, brought him *home* . . ."

It's Sunday. I've brought the tape recorder down to entertain
Judy. Playing her old sound tracks triggers a series of reminiscences. Stories of those golden, fruitful days at Metro, the studio
days when they needed product, when they made three hundred
pictures a year, when there were so many talented people doing
such fine work.

Like Orson Welles . . .

"He . . . used to come over at nn, three in the morning and
recite nn, *Shakes*peare. You know, we had to get up pretty nn,
*ear*ly in those days to get to nn, *make*up . . . and, at three

o'clock I'd answer the door, and there would be nn, Orson, in a *cape*. His chauffeur would announce him, and he'd nn, *march* in, without a word, and start doing Macbeth in my living room. I finally had to say, nn, '*look*, Orson . . .'"

Or agent Irving (Swifty) Lazar.

"I named him 'Swifty,' you know. That's my name. He fell out of a plane once, in Gander. We were refueling. In those days, when you flew to Europe, you stopped in nn, *New*foundland . . . and they'd open the door, to let in some fresh air, but they wouldn't pull up the nn, *stairs* . . . and Swifty had been asleep, and . . . he thought we'd landed in *Eng*land, so he got up and . . . just stepped off the plane . . . we looked down, and there was his silhouette . . . in the snow."

Or Tony Martin.

"He couldn't nn, *walk* . . . in tempo. He was supposed to sing 'You Stepped Out of a Dream' and simply nn, *walk* across the stage . . . in time to the music. He couldn't do it. He ruined nn, take after *take*. Finally, the dance director said 'okay, just shoot him from the waist up' . . . and he got down on his knees and took the backs of Tony's ankles in his hands, and nn, *marched* him across the stage . . . in tempo."

How glorious to see Judy flower, with just a bit of care, and a simple, controlled environment (she was down to four Ritalin a *day!*). To see Judy revitalized, weaned from her compulsive dependencies on drugs, alcohol, late hours. There is no reason in the world why she can't be a sane, cogent person, who knows what's good for her, who responds to treatment, who needs so little, really, to be her best self. Just the absence of disorder, just calm, and balance, and proportion, and then the oppressive cloud lifts, and she's that warm, funny, glamorous female who also happens to be the world's greatest musical performer, and who, as Cole Porter remarked, would be so "Easy To Love."

"Come on over here," Judy said. I couldn't get much farther over. I was already lying on the bed beside her. We shared a kiss, then another. "Baby . . ." I murmured. Judy gave me a wink.

"Come on," she said. I glanced stealthily at the door. Outside our little cocoon it was nine-thirty in the evening. Visiting hours were over, and any moment Miss Marsden would be in to chase me out. Never mind. We'd chance it.

I dropped to the floor, snapped the back of a chair under the doorknob, and, struggling out of my clothes, zipped back into the sack with Judy.

Listen, they did it in *A Farewell to Arms.*

MONDAY, NOVEMBER 11

"Mcdgl Alley, charming split-level, 3½ rms, piano, sublet 6 mos."

We've decided to take an apartment. Repeat, an apartment. How we'll pay for it is yet to be determined, but today I went down to Macdougal Alley Mews (gas lamps and cobblestones) and saw the place described in this ad. It was exquisite, comfortable, and original. An English couple in the Diplomatic Corps was relocating to Washington. The rent was five hundred and fifty dollars a month and the lady wanted three months down.

I said Thanks, I'll let you know. I was looking for something cheaper. I followed two more leads from the New York *Times,* and then decided it would be easier to put myself through the genteel humiliation of a Pat Palmer interview. Pat Palmer is a rental agency, and they insist you come in and talk about it, but you're really there so the lady can look you over and make sure you qualify for placement. Are you the caliber of tenant Pat Palmer can, in good conscience, submit to her exclusive clientele?

Well, truthfully, no. A free-lance songwriter who keeps late hours, plays a loud piano, and is frequently behind in his rent—I am, let's face it, the least desirable of tenants. Add Judy Garland, and forget it.

Ah, but I can fool Pat Palmer. I came into the office as the ultimate conservative, navy pinstripe suit, Church shoes, French cuffs, and hair squared to the nth power. Mr. Establishment. I told the lady I was a feature writer for Time, Inc., looking for a three-month sublet, please, in a decent neighborhood. Like to pay about three hundred a month. I did not mention Judy.

TUESDAY, NOVEMBER 12

It worked. Pat sent me down to see four rooms on East Thirty-fourth Street. A new high rise by the river. A woman named Eleanor is vacationing in Europe for three months. Perfect. She wants four hundred a month, which is steep, but . . . there's a piano. Well, it's lovely, I said to Eleanor, but I really can only afford three hundred. Tell you what, said Eleanor, I'll throw in my housekeeper, Manuela. I nearly took the place right then and there. Manuela is Judy's name in *The Pirate*.

WEDNESDAY, NOVEMBER 13

Mickey Rooney called today, from California (I know, said Alice, it gets curiouser and curiouser). He rang Park Avenue, and I told him to phone the hospital later, about five.

"The hospital? Hey, buddy, what's wrong with her?" His feisty, bantam personality shot through the wire all the way from Los Angeles.

"Nothing serious," I said. "She has a bad foot, we're fixing it up."

" 'Cause I got some big plans for Judy, fellah, and I need her in shape."

"Well, you can reach her at this number after five, okay? I know she'll be glad to talk to you."

"N . . . no, darling . . ." Judy said to me. "Th . . . there was never anything nn, ro*mantic* between Mickey and me . . ."

It was five o'clock at the Leroy. Judy was sitting up in bed, telling me about Mickey.

"Oh no, he never even . . . *look*ed at me . . . he was too busy with women like nn, Barbara *Hut*ton . . . you have to remember, he was the biggest . . . I mean there was *no*body bigger than Mickey, women used to nn, *hurl* themselves at the windows of the limousine . . . and we were doing something like nn, *ten* shows a day . . . it was exhausting, we were the big-

gest thing in the *country* in nineteen-forty . . . of course Louis
B. did his best to nn, *keep* it from us . . . but after a week of
these vaudeville shows, with the people simply nn, *crushed* into
line, it did begin to dawn on us that maybe we . . . weren't such
a nn, *dud* after all . . .

The phone rang. Judy and I looked at each other. She made a
quick gesture to the instrument. "You take it," she said.

"Judy, he wants to speak to you."

"Take it," she insisted. I picked up the receiver. "Hi, Mickey,"
I said. "This is John."

"Hi, pal. You got my girl?"

"She's right here." I held the phone out to Judy, and she
pulled me down on the bed to listen with her, sharing the
receiver as we had with Vincente Minnelli.

"M-Mickey?"

"Judy, how ya doin'?"

"Well, I'm in the nn, *hos*pital."

"Your pal told me. What's wrong with you?"

"I've got nn, *lep*rosy."

"See if they can save your legs, will ya? You're gonna need
'em. You're going into partnership with me."

"I am?"

"Judy, I been talking to my business manager, he's setting the
whole deal up. It's a beautiful idea, just beautiful. But we need
you out here, so I'm gonna arrange everything, transportation, a
place to stay, if you need to be in the hospital okay—we got one
of the best right up here in San Francisco, a major clinic with
drying out and everything, and Judy, you don't have to worry
about the bills, I'm taking care of everything—"

"M-Mickey—"

"—because this beautiful idea is gonna change your life, Judy.
I don't have to tell you, you probably heard, but I been asleep
for the past six months, just wouldn't come outta the house,
wouldn't get outta bed, just wouldn't face things, Judy, but it's
all changed now, thanks to Ozzie, this guy can turn lead into
gold, honey, and this is no jive, he told me, Ozzie said, well, you
gotta open a school, you and Judy . . . and when he said that it
was like the things fell from my eyes, darlin', just fell from my

eyes, because it means you and me together like the old days, hoofin' it side by side, all across the country, like Fred has, a whole chain of schools, the Mickey and Judy Schools of Musical Comedy, for the kids, honey, Ozzie's got it all worked out, partners, fifty-fifty, after the initial investment comes back, but I need you out here, honey, you gotta be with me, so I'm sending you a ticket, it'll be in tomorrow's mail—"

"Mickey, nn, hold the *phone* . . ." Judy finally interpolated. "I don't want to come to California . . ."

"Oh not right away, not right away," Mickey said. "I'll mail the ticket, take a week or so, where do you want me to send it?"

Judy suddenly gave me the phone, and I gave Mickey the Park Avenue address. "Okay, pal," he said, "I'm sending Judy a ticket, you make sure she's on whatever flight she decides to take. Don't mess up now, this is gonna be important for her."

"Whaddya say we give her a couple days to think about it, okay, Mickey?"

"Know what I'm gonna do? I'm gonna have Ozzie call and explain the details, the nuts and bolts of it. You'll see it's the biggest thing Judy could do at this point in her career, the biggest and the best. I'm gonna have Ozzie call."

I hung up and looked at Judy, wondering how this bolt from the blue was striking her. She was shaking her head in a bemused way.

"I don't want to go to . . . nn, Cali*for*nia," she said.

THURSDAY, NOVEMBER 14

All day Thursday Mickey's phone call bothered me. As I saw another apartment, as I bought six pairs of panty hose, as I tried to contact Larry Newton at ABC-Paramount—I kept thinking maybe it wasn't such a bad idea. If Mickey Rooney wanted to take Judy under his wing, if he wanted to give her a partnership in a freshly capitalized business, maybe Judy should take it, maybe it *would* be the best thing she could do. Mickey had certainly known Judy longer than I had, he'd know how to handle her. God knows, his resources were a thousand times what mine were. Maybe I should make her do it.

But something inside me didn't want to. A lot.

FRIDAY, NOVEMBER 15

"Oh yes, I had a nn, con*sum*ing passion for Ty Power . . . but I was so nn, *shy* . . . and we worked for different studios. So I found a book . . . it was called *Violets for Margaret,* it was one of those *Portrait of Jennie* type things where the lovers go back and forth over the nn, *cen*turies, and finally, you know . . . have to *part* . . . oh, it was dreamy . . . and I went to nn, Mr. *May*er and said . . . would you buy this for me? and he told me, well, Judy, I'll think about it . . . but I knew I had him . . . Louis B. couldn't nn, de*ny* me, if I was in the room, he just kind of *mel*ted . . . and I thought, Well, when we own this book, I'll get Mr. Mayer to borrow Ty Power from nn, *Fox* . . . and one night, David (Rose) and I were giving a party . . . and the doorbell rang and . . . nn, I *had*n't had the nerve to invite him . . . you know, I barely nn, *knew* the man . . . but there he was on the doorstep . . . and he said, Forgive me, but I saw your lights on and I wanted to bring you this book . . . I think it might be something we could do together . . . and he handed me a copy of *Violets for Margaret.*"

It was time for me to leave the hospital. I bent and kissed Judy sweetly, then passionately. She held me very tightly. "Johnny . . ." she whispered drowsily, for she'd been given a sedative, ". . . how would you feel about nn, a*dop*ting a child . . . ?"

SATURDAY, NOVEMBER 16

At eleven this morning there was a run-through of the Lincoln Center show. As Judy's representative, I sat in the empty orchestra and watched Howard Keel and Leslie Uggams rehearse their Arlen songs.

Burt Shevelove, who was staging the evening, wasn't bothered by Judy's absence. "What's the problem?" he asked me. I was standing with Henry Guettel. "She'll come out and she'll sing." Henry looked dubious. Not having his cleanup position star at rehearsal concerned him.

We've got twenty-four hours to go.

At seven I picked Judy up at the Leroy and brought her uptown. Dr. Klinger is allowing his patient a leave of absence from the hospital, granting her special dispensation to have dinner with my family. Herbert is cooking a loin of pork.

Our stereo equipment is in the dining room, because Marjorie won't let Herbert disturb her design scheme in the living room. I put the recording of *A Star Is Born* on the turntable, and, as Herbert was ministering to the pig in the kitchen, Judy began performing in the dining room. The song was "Lose That Long Face."

"Nn, they *cut* this number . . . after the picture opened . . . and, I must say, I did the dance of the *world* with two little newsboys . . ." Judy began demonstrating the dance, hoofing on the carpet. "Go lose that long face . . . that long face—" she sang. My mother was enthralled. I stuck my head into the kitchen.

"Pop!" I whispered urgently. "Come *see* this." Reluctantly, spatula in hand, Herbert came to the dining room door, and stood, impatiently, as Judy ran through the number. Thousands of people, from film historians to fans, would have given anything to be present for this moment, but all poor Pop could think of was, Is the pork basted? He smiled and nodded and went back to the kitchen.

SUNDAY, NOVEMBER 17

It was one-thirty in the morning. "Time to go, baby."

"Oh, Johnny, no . . . don't make me go back . . . let me stay here . . . please . . . with you . . ."

"Honey, I can't. You heard Dr. Klinger. You were supposed to be back at ten. He's been damn nice giving us this long."

I was adamant. Judy had to return to the hospital; it was a question of justifying Klinger's trust. Pouting all the way, Judy let me take her downstairs, and we caught a cab. Judy sat beside me, tense and unhappy.

Back at the hospital, I tried reading aloud to Judy to relax her. I've found my reading often has a soporific effect on people. I dimmed the lights, tucked Judy into bed, and began intoning *Nicholas and Alexandra,* a biography Judy had begun. I found myself reciting the facts concerning the crown prince's hemophilia. It was putting me to sleep, it ought to do the same for Judy.

I glanced at her in bed. She'd taken a Seconal, her head was on the pillow, her eyes were closed. I let my voice trail off, getting softer and softer . . . and, finally, I stopped, letting the silence unwind into the room, to mix with the sound of Judy's regular breathing. I sat quietly for a minute, which became two . . . which became three. Stealthily I rose, my tongue in my teeth, and crossed, catlike, to the door.

"Johnny . . ." Judy was up like a crack, quivering and urgent. "Johnny, take me back uptown . . . I'll never get to sleep here . . ."

"Honey, I *can't,* you're not allowed to leave the hospital."

"Then Johnny, stay with me, please . . . you've got to." Her supplicating tone would have melted granite. "Don't leave me alone . . . I'm afraid . . ."

"But Judy," I said, puzzled, "you've been alone every night for a week here." I looked at her with a dawning realization. "Is this because the benefit's tomorrow?" She nodded, mutely.

"I . . . always have to keep nn, *prov*ing myself, again and again, over and over . . . I always have to be better than the last time . . ."

"Judy," I said gently, "don't you know how very good you are? You're just the best, the very best there is. You don't have to prove anything . . . all you have to do is go *out* there . . . you've got them before you even open your mouth. They love you. You could *shit* on the stage and they'd love you." I held her to my chest. "Judy, please, you mustn't worry so." I could feel her trembling.

"Don't leave me alone," she repeated. I gave a sigh of despair.

"All right, Judes. What do you suggest?" Judy thought it over.

"Well . . . nn, maybe you could stay here . . ." She looked at the chair, then at the bed. Great, I thought, just let me place an order for breakfast.

"Okay, tell you what." I rose. "I'm gonna take a walk for a while, but I'll check back to see if you're still up, and, if you are, I'll come get you and take you back home." Judy clutched my hand.

"No, no, you won't, I know you won't—"

"Baby, I promise."

"Will you promise me? You won't just leave me here?"

"Darling, I give you my word, my solemn word of honor. I promise." I went to the door slowly, without making any sudden movements. "I *promise*," I said again. "I'll fix it with the switchboard and call you." (This would defeat the purpose, of course, but I had to get out of there *some*how.) I blew her a kiss and shut the door behind me.

In the lobby I told the girl on the board I'd be calling in an hour and had to be put through to Miss Garland. Then I went out onto Madison Avenue in search of a cab.

It was three-thirty in the morning, chillingly cold, and not a cab in sight. I walked down the avenue as far as Reubens. Reubens was closed. In my mind I was giving Judy an hour to get to sleep. I hoped she wasn't waiting up for the call.

Jesus, it was cold. All I had on was a light suede jacket. Where were the cabs? I started walking, hands in my pockets, shoulders hunched against the wind, squinting down the street for a taxi—hell, a bus would do. I crossed a block west to Fifth, hoping to catch some hotel taxis by the Plaza. I passed the General Motors Building, under construction. It looked impressive. If I were a laborer on that building, a riveter or something, I wouldn't have this problem. I huddled momentarily in a doorway to escape the wind.

Forty minutes had passed when I saw the yellow light moving east on Fifty-ninth Street. He was off duty, of course, taking the bridge to Queens, but I talked him into a detour. Make it worth your while, I told him, from the side of my mouth. Since I'd met Judy, everything was melodrama, a B picture, the world was a parody, a distillation of a thousand silver screens.

When I got home it was time to call Judy. It was against regulations, but the switchboard put me through, because, you see,

I'd told them I'd be calling. If you warn someone ahead of time, you could rob Tiffany's. Oh, yes, you're calling about the burglary. Go right up, the gems are expecting you.

"Judy? Are you asleep?"

"Johnny . . . you called . . ."

"I said I would, didn't I? I don't break my promises."

"Johnny . . . please . . . come and get me . . ."

"Honey, have you tried to sleep? I mean, really? I bet you stayed up waiting for me to—"

"Johnny, please, *please* come and get me . . . I can't . . . I'm . . . I've tried, I really have, honestly . . . don't leave me here, Johnny . . . please . . ."

I thought about it. If I disregarded Judy's plea, I'd be up all night worrying about her anyway.

"All right, Judy. I'll be down in fifteen minutes. Be ready." I went down the hall and opened my father's bedroom door as silently as I could. I extricated the truck keys from his pile of bills and loose change. Herbert stirred uneasily.

"Mwuh . . . wh're you doing?"

"Keys," I said, and heard him shift unhappily against the linen.

Judy was ready, dressed in a beige suit. We threw on her mink, packed her makeup case, and closed the door to her room. As we stood by the elevator the night nurse asked what was going on.

"Miss Garland is released for the evening," I said.

"I wasn't notified of this."

"Well, you can check with Dr. Chester," I lied. "He authorized it."

"I'm sorry, we cannot release a patient without written authorization. I'll have to check this." She picked up her phone. I pressed the elevator bell again. Where *was* the goddam thing? It was taking a year.

"Give me Dr. Chester, please."

The seconds ticked by as I prayed for the elevator. The night nurse was waiting for Dr. Chester. I won. The door sighed open and I shoved Judy inside.

"Just a minute," the night nurse said. "This is against—" Her phrase was sliced in two by the closing door. Yes, it was melodrama. This was our second movie escape: first, the Prison picture at Richard's, and now the Snakepit picture at the Leroy. The night nurse calls downstairs to a white-coated, grinning butch matron. She throws a straitjacket over Judy—no, no, let me GO! Aaaannhh, aaaannhh—CUT TO CLOSE-UP: hypodermic needle entering vein, oh God—

The elevator doors slid apart. The only person in the deserted lobby was the girl on the switchboard. She smiled pleasantly.

"Good night," she said.

But even uptown, in the familiar security of our bedroom, Judy found sleep impossible. Even with another Seconal. She was too keyed up, too overwrought. This night's sleep was shot to hell. Forget it. And I'd counted on facing the benefit fresh and alert. About six-thirty in the morning, with the daylight, Judy finally was able to relax enough to let *me* catch a few hours' sleep.

At noon I gave Judy four Ritalin, and gladly. Today I wasn't going to deny her anything within the bounds of reason. I saw now why she was so erratic as a performer. She was terrified, scared out of her mind.

"Think of Merman," I told her. "Just think, What would Ethel do?" Henry called around twelve-thirty. "What is your ETA?" he wanted to know.

"We oughta be there about three," I said. Factoring the increased anxiety time with the normal two-hour dressing period, three seemed about right. I was learning to gauge the quirks and idiosyncrasies of Judy's mechanism.

We arrived at three-twenty. In addition to the primping uptown ("Marjorie, may I borrow this nn, *pin?* Larry is wearing all my *jew*elry"), we had to stop by the hospital for Judy's gown, and then stop at a drugstore for an Ace bandage (for the heel) and then a final stop at a delicatessen for a bottle of grapefruit juice to go with the vodka we were bringing. We were in the cab for forty minutes.

As we drew up to the State Theater, the cab's door was opened by agent Irv Squires of CMA, who announced himself and extended a helpful arm to Judy. I threw the dress across his arm, Judy's heavy sequin-studded mother of a dress, the one that had cost twenty-two dollars to clean.

I resented Irv, on Judy's behalf, as a representative of the agency that habitually ignored her, but as soon as they heard she was doing something independently—like this benefit—they crawled out of the woodwork.

"Yah," I greeted him shortly. "The red makeup case and the shopping bag." We started off, leaving him to bring up the rear. The effect I'd hoped to achieve—the Star swooping in before a wave of lackeys—was somewhat vitiated by Judy's game foot. She was not in top swooping condition.

We advanced slowly, Irv puffing along behind like a native bearer. "You look wonderful, Judy," he called. Judy didn't hear him.

"Yah," I said.

We became involved with a Kafkaesque series of doors, elevators, and corridors. It's impossible to negotiate the labyrinth that is the backstage area of Lincoln Center unless someone leaves you a trail of breadcrumbs.

We emerged, at last, into an immense orchestra rehearsal room, where Jay's band was running through the music for the final time before the show. As we came in the door, all heads did a discreet half-turn, and you could hear the rustle of contained excitement. There she is, there's *Judy*, look how *small* she is, how *frail* she looks, has she lost *weight*, is she in *shape* . . . ?

As Judy advanced into the room I lingered in the corner by the door, prudently stashing the shopping bag with the vodka. I didn't want the bottle displayed, didn't want these dishy, fringe-of-show-biz gypsies being smug or forgiving.

The rehearsal had stopped to accommodate Judy's entrance. Arlen and Henry Guettel each came forward to greet her, and she kissed them both. Two stools were brought to the conductor's podium, one for Judy and one for me. Jay stood, smiling vaguely, waiting to get back to work. Jim Tyler was sitting to our right, at a long table covered with duplicate trumpet parts, lyric sheets, and copies of the show's running order. I suddenly felt a great affection for Jim and Jay, for these two professionals who had put themselves out, endured the waiting, made concessions and deferred to Judy's whims and crazinesses without a murmur. They belonged with the tacit brotherhood now, not fans, not part of the cult, but, like me, at one with those who felt for Judy, admired her, and rooted for her.

Jay lifted his baton, and Judy's overture rang out like a carillon. And now, with no stopping for corrections, and in the larger room, the music was lithe and springy, bouncing off the walls like a hard rubber ball. It was Hollywood studio time. Connie Salinger, the M-G-M orchestrator, would have been proud.

From her stool, Judy took up "The Man That Got Away," and, as she sang, with no microphone and without moving, the entire room fixed on her, irised down and zeroed in on her as if she were a magnetic field. Stagehands and dancers from next door, involved with another show, had crept in silently and were lining the walls, listening, paying tribute, for this was an event. Just getting Judy to rehearse was an event, for she rarely did. When she did a concert, her conductor rehearsed the band. Judy might come in to sing one or two songs and get the feel of the house. So, although she was only singing four songs, Judy was showing up on time and running them down, like a no-nonsense, no-temperament pro.

It made me so glad. This was the way things were going to be.

Something was distracting me. It was the pianist—he was winking at Judy. He was a fine musician, he played with flourish and taste, but he kept smiling at Judy, seeking some kind of recognition or approval. It bugged me. I leaned over to Henry. "Hey, tell the piano player to stop winking at Judy." Henry did a take, flashed a quick look at the piano, and bent to the pianist's ear. The poor guy wrinkled his nose and applied himself studiously to the keyboard.

After she'd sung "It's a New World," Judy turned to me. "Mmm, may I have some nn, *grape*fruit juice?" I smiled at her innocent tone.

"Sure," I said, and beckoned to one of Henry's youthful production assistants. "Could we have some ice?" I went to the corner and made Judy a surreptitious drink. From the bag I took two of the piano-conductor parts I'd been given, and, returning from delivering Judy's drink, I sat down beside Harold, who was momentarily alone.

"Harold," I said, a little stiffly, for I was still uncomfortable using his first name, "before I add my status as friend to that of fan, may I do something very fanlike? Would you sign this for me?" And I gave him the sheet of "New World."

Harold very nearly blushed. "Mmmwell, my goodness," he said, and modestly accepted the pen I was offering him. With great precision, he wrote this legend: "Dear John—with deep appreciation—Harold. 11/17/68." Composers always date whatever they write, I don't know why.

"Thank you, Harold," I said, "and, if I may, there's a friend of mine, Larry. He's a great admirer of yours, and Judy kind of ruined a couple of his chairs. If you could just sign this one to Larry? Tell him to have his chairs cleaned. He'd be thrilled."

So Harold took "The Man That Got Away" and inscribed a direction to Larry: "Dear Larry: have your chairs cleaned. Love, Harold Arlen 11/17/68."

Five P.M. Music rehearsal is over. We're going to the dressing room in Philharmonic Hall, some distance away. In all innocence, Henry asks me, "Where is Miss Garland's car?"

I swallowed a burr of guilt. Henry's given us two hundred and fifty dollars for expenses such as a limousine. But we've kept the money and arrived by cab.

"Uh . . . we didn't bring one," I had to say.

So one of Henry's production assistants brought a car around and delivered us to the temporary haven of a cloakroom, until our dressing room was free. Joan Sutherland or somebody was in there now.

Joan was out by six. The room, though small, was tastefully done, with a nice sofa, a dressing shelf with a mirror, and a spinet piano. From our shopping bag I withdrew a bottle of Burgundy, opened it, and gave a glass to Bill, the production assistant, and Gene, our hairdresser.

Gene was English, about twenty-two. He'd studied in London with Vidal Sassoon and had come from Bendel's to the Leroy yesterday, to give Judy's hair a cut and a touch-up. The gray streaks were gone now, Judy's hair was the color of charcoal. With his large leather satchel, Gene reminded me of Gunga Din, except, instead of water, he carried combs, scissors, and a dryer. He and Judy retired to the bathroom for a quick set and comb-out.

Judy was too strung out to think of food, but I was ravenous.

I called Herb Evans, across the street, and ordered dinner sent over. As I hung up the phone, Judy entered from the bathroom, a towel about her shoulders. She coughed twice.

"Johnny . . . I think I'm losing my voice . . . I'm afraid it'll go before I nn, get *on* . . ."

God, I thought, is it like this every time she performs? She was okay for the shows at Three, I recalled—of course, this was a much grander event. Tickets to this thing were a hundred and fifty bucks apiece.

Before Judy could get too frantic I called Dr. Klinger. Okay, said the doctor, we'll give her a throat spray, a cocaine derivative, it'll freeze her vocal chords temporarily. I'll have the pharmacy deliver it.

About half past seven my dinner arrived, and I was devouring it when Gene and Judy emerged from the bathroom for good. I grinned when I saw her. Judy tried to grin back, but her heart wasn't in it.

"Mmm, Melican soldier like Japanee girl?" she ventured half-heartedly. Before I could answer, there was a knock. I opened the door and there, standing before me in dinner clothes, was Richard Rodgers, president of Lincoln Center and dean of the Musical Theater, the composer responsible for *Pal Joey, Oklahoma!,* and *The Sound of Music.*

Judy jumped to her feet, nearly getting the point of Gene's teasing comb in her eye. "Dick!" she cried happily.

"Hello, Judy," said Rodgers, warmly. They embraced. Judy introduced me, and I introduced Gene. Rodgers and I had met before, but he didn't remember. He had a way of acknowledging an introduction—a short nod—as if he wanted to get past it. Judy and I sat on the sofa, and Rodgers straddled a chair, ingratiatingly. I wondered if this were a social visit or a business call. Was Rodgers being friendly or was it a courtesy call on behalf of management? Probably a little of both.

"I think the last time we were on the same bill together was at Jules Glaenzer's house," he said. Judy smiled in reminiscence.

"Yes, with the two nn, *sol*diers. Tell Johnny." And Gene, I thought, conscious of the small slight.

". . . and Gene," Judy added, reading my mind. I could have kissed her.

"Well, one night during the war," Rodgers began, "Judy and I were both dinner guests at Jules's. And after dinner we were gathered around the piano singing, when a ring came at the doorbell. Now Jules, who was the perfect host, went to answer it himself, and there, standing in the street, were two buck privates and their dates. Just a couple of servicemen, out for a good time. They were a little tipsy, they'd heard the music, and they wanted to join the party. They were just drunk enough to ring the bell.

"'Well, by all means, you come right in,' said Jules, and he took them to the sofa, and sat them down, and brought them all a drink. And Judy sang a song or two and I played the piano. It was just a party to them. They had no idea who we were. But they were having a *wonder*ful time.

"And after a while Jules said to them, 'Do you know who's been entertaining you?' They said, no sir, they didn't, but it sure sounded awful pretty. 'Well,' said Jules, 'this is Mr. Richard Rodgers, and this is Miss Judy Garland.' Well, of course they were astonished. My name didn't mean anything, but they'd all seen Judy. They were practically speechless. And they thanked Jules very politely, but as they were leaving, one of them sighed, and kind of shook his head, and Jules said, 'Why, what's the matter?'

"'Well, we've really had a terrific time and thank you very much,' said the soldier, 'the only trouble is, when we get back to the base . . . nobody's gonna believe us.'"

Rodgers smiled broadly, and Judy laughed, and Gene smiled, and I said, "Aah, that's lovely." I'd formulated a scheme.

"Mr. Rodgers, we were just singing one of your songs last night," I told him. "One of your loveliest, I think—'Boys and Girls Like You and Me.'"

"Oh yes," said Rodgers.

I went to the spinet and played the first four bars. Rodgers drifted over. Judy was standing in the center of the room.

"Dick," she said tremulously, almost shyly, "would you . . . would you help me nn, warm *up?*"

Rodgers sat on the piano bench. I bent to his ear. "In G," I said. So Rodgers played, and Judy sang, just as, years ago, they had played and sung for two enlisted men and their girls. I was watching Rodgers' fingers. Composers are notoriously bad pianists (except for Gershwin), but to hear one play his work is always illuminating, for you hear the music with his heart, and often you can pick up a fuller intention.

Rodgers, in fact, played capably, paying attention to the keyboard. He was doubtless unused to playing the song in the key of G. As Judy sang, I gave up trying to absorb anything technical and simply leaned against the wall, listening to Judy, bathing in the moment.

I mentioned another Rodgers' tune Judy knew—"Why Can't I?"—and he played that one for her, too, leaving out a harmony my ear was accustomed to hearing. Fascinating. In our living room Arlen had missed a chord in "Last Night When We Were Young." Composers who read and notate music often need the sheet in front of them. The notes are out of their mind, and they need to be reminded of their creation. Since I can't read, I'm forced to remember everything.

And now Judy was fumbling for the title of yet a third Rodgers' tune. It was irritating her that she couldn't think of it.

"Oh, you know . . ." she said. "The song that lady with the nn, *leg* made such a fuss about . . ."

"Oh," said Rodgers, "you mean 'With a Song in My Heart.'"

"Yeh-heh-ess . . ." Judy smiled. Tonight she was the lady with the leg. Judy fumbled through this lyric without really knowing it, but when she got to the final phrase, I thought her voice was going to blast out the walls: "With a song in my heart . . .

For . . . you!!!!"

The last notes of any Garland rendition are spaced for maximum effect, and they come at your head like a hardball. Watch out.

And then it was over. "Dick, Dick, thank you, thank you for warming me up . . ." And Rodgers was rising, kissing Judy, and through the door in thirty seconds. Judy widened her eyes and jabbed at the closing door with a childish finger, screwing her shoulders up into her neck.

"Do you know how nn, *hard* it is . . ." she whispered. "I mean he's just imp*o*ssible . . . he *never* sits down at the piano . . . *no one* can get him to play . . ."

"Well, you did."

"*We* did," Judy corrected me, smugly. "And nn, we de*serve* it."

Stepping into the elevator that would carry us three flights down to the stage level, Judy looked ravishingly, radiantly beautiful. In fact, she looked sexy. She was in her pink sequin gown, which had long sleeves and a thin slit of décolletage. Her makeup was dramatic, the huge, dark eyes highlighted by her pale, powdered cheeks, the hair setting off that incomparable face in a short brush cut. She had an air of action-packed chic. She was a svelte dynamo.

And she was vibrating like a tuning fork. "Johnny . . . I'm terrified . . ." She seized my hand and I squeezed firmly.

"Honey, you look gorgeous . . . and you're gonna be great." We stepped out of the elevator and picked our way to the wing, Judy clutching my hand, and dragging the gown's short train behind her. The performers and stagehands in the wing parted deferentially, in quiet awe. A chair was brought and Judy sat down, placing her plastic cup of vodka by her feet on the floor.

Burt Shevelove put an arm around my shoulder. "Now, after the applause there'll be Judy's overture. Judy will take her place here"—he indicated the back of a flat—"and kind of slide out in front of it."

"What? What am I doing?" Judy's voice was sharp and anxious.

"Here, baby, see?" I said soothingly, "You'll be behind this flat here, and, when the time comes—"

"How will I know when?"

"We'll tell you," said Burt.

I stood behind Judy's chair and cupped her chin in my hand, firmly enough to make my presence felt, but without smudging the makeup.

"I love you," she said.

"I love you, and you're going to be wonderful."

Harold came up behind us, and I stepped away to let them have a moment together. I found myself beside Henry.

"The evening seems to be going very well," I said cheerfully. Henry gave me a guarded smile. He was obviously relieved to see Judy downstairs and ready. I remembered the film clips of Judy that were primed to roll in the projection booth upstairs. These were in case of Judy's defection. Henry's smile told me he still wasn't sure Judy was going out there. Boy, she had scared Henry good.

The overture started, and Judy took her place behind the flat, her back to the audience. This was it. At the climax of the music, Judy shot out her right hand, palm twisted toward the house, and, after giving them this tantalizing glimpse of sequined wrist and outstretched fingers, she swung out before them, Zap!

There was a gasp of recognition: my God, it's Judy! Judy Garland. Is it really? She looks fantastic! Christ, I didn't know she was gonna be in this show, shh shhh hush, she's singing . . .

The applause subsided, and Judy was into "The Man," singing to a total hush, to complete, rapt attention. And this was not her cult, these were hundred-dollar-a-ticket fifty-year-olds, as intent upon her as the most misty-eyed fan.

And oh, she was good. She was exciting that night. I watched from the wing, seeing her in silhouette as the hot white spotlights burned my cheeks. Before Judy began "New World" she commented on these lights. Shielding her eyes with her hand she said "Mmm, could you make that . . . a bit . . . you know, really, it's like an *X ray* . . ." And they gave her something softer, more ballad, and she did the song. It's my personal favorite, and, as she finished, I was wiping back the tears, and so were those around me.

In the second eight bars of "Get Happy," Judy ran a quick, involuntary hand through her hair and shot Gene's careful coif all to hell. She was alive and electric, and when she brought Harold onstage for "Over the Rainbow" ("Harold and I have a nn, *casual* acquaintance . . ."), the applause was an alloy of respect and admiration for each of them.

Harold sat on the piano bench and Judy gave him a look of solemn inquiry. "Now . . . what would you like to do, darling?" But everyone knew what they were going to do, and when they did it, Judy kneeled by the piano bench and sang it directly to Harold.

> "Somewhere . . . over the rainbow
> Way up high
>
> There's a land that I heard of
> Once in a lullaby."

The song that made her famous, I was thinking. I wondered if it still represented something to Judy, or if repetition had worn away its mystique. And then I thought how exceptional this whole adventure was, and how incredibly lucky *I* was to be given this intimate chance to help, to touch, to know Judy, to run with the rainbow, to keep it polished and lighted and glowing for our moment together. And no matter how long or short that moment might be, I told myself, it was here now, it was mine, and while it was I'd give more of myself than I ever had to anything. Maybe I could expand it, stretch it, push it beyond the rational boundaries of time or space or human capability. These were my impulses, unformulated, inchoate, but strong as the smell of ammonia nonetheless. I was determined to give this experience its head, and not to be hamstrung by anything.

> "If happy little bluebirds fly
> Beyond the rainbow
> Why, oh why—

"Thank you, Harold," Judy said.

> "—Can't I!"

Harold's tears were dropping on the ivory—his fingers literally slipped off the keys. There was a surge of tumultuous applause, as Harold fairly leaped from the stage in acute embarrassment. You can imagine how this very private man felt with fifteen hundred people watching him cry.

I was the first person he bumped into offstage (I literally don't think he could see where he was going). He hung on to my shoulder.

"She'll say any goddam thing," he said.

Back in the dressing room it was Triumph Time. Irv Squires was ecstatic. "Ah, she was fantastic. Judy, you were fantastic, sweetheart, here, lemme help you with that." He was breathless with excitement. Everyone was. Judy had taken us all to a new level of existence, where the air was rarefied; she'd made us all breathe oxygen.

"Lotta people out there tonight," Irv kept saying, "a lotta people. Earl Wilson, I told him, sure she's ready to work, the agency has a lotta bookings lined up. And Jack O'Brian—"

The tiny dressing room filled with congratulations; Arlen and his wife; Rodgers and *his* wife; Gloria Vanderbilt, Anton Dolin, major celebrities, minor names, but no fans this time, for it had not been announced.

In the midst of this glamorous confusion, my mother came backstage with her escort, Bob Hall. Herbert had elected to stay home. When Judy saw her, she cried "Marjorie!" and gave her a big kiss. Everyone wondered who Marjorie was.

Excitement crackled through the room. It was another comeback. In miniature, perhaps; she'd only sung four songs, but it sure looked as if the Lady was together again. She had been in control, assured, and (you almost took it for granted) brilliant.

"Well, are we celebrating?" It was Irv, ready to spend some of CMA's money on Judy. But we had promised Dr. Klinger Judy would be back at the Leroy no later than one this morning, and, after our unorthodox behavior last night, this was one commitment we had to keep. After all Dr. Klinger had done for us, I wasn't going to disappoint him.

"Because I think the lady deserves a drink, don't you?"

Of course she did. She had been magnificent. "Okay," I said, "let's go for a fast one." I turned to Judy. "Wanna make it Clarke's?" Judy giggled, remembering Jake LaMotta.

"Who do you suppose we'll run into tonight?" she asked me.

"Max Schmeling," I said, under my breath.

MONDAY, NOVEMBER 18—12:30 A.M.

Clarke's was full, a Sunday haven for the restless, the unattached, and the just plain hungry who know it's the only place in town they give you Béarnaise sauce with your hamburger. Jake LaMotta wasn't in tonight, so our entrance, at least, was peaceful. In fact it was gay and hilarious, cresting on the evening's triumph.

We were five: me, Judy, Marjorie, Bob, and Irv Squires. I brought an extra chair to our table just in time to hear Judy say to Irv, "Okay, now what about this agency of yours?"

"Aah, Judy, they're gonna be so thrilled. When I tell him what you did tonight, David will flip his—"

"Yeah, yeah, what ab*out* David? Where is David, anyhow?

The doll. Isn't he a doll? Would you like to know something? I can't get David on the phone, that's where David is." She took a sip of vodka. "I want to know what CMA is *doing* for me."

In the space of five seconds, Judy had done an emotional turn-about, from the triumphant and acclaimed star to the grieving bit player. Irv's tone was pacifying, placating.

"Honey, I, personally, had to turn down three bookings for you. One in Chicago, one in Philly—"

"And what about the apartment?" Irv looked at her warily.

"What apartment?"

"The one CMA keeps for its clients. I have no place to live, did you know that? I'm imposing on the generosity of nn, *Mr. Meyer*"—she gestured to me—"and his mother." She turned to Marjorie. My mother smiled painfully.

"Judy . . ." Here Irv reached across the table and put his hand on top of hers. "We all want to do whatever we can for you."

"You do? Well, you can start by getting me some money. Git outta here and git me some money now." Judy gave a short, bit-ter laugh.

"Sweetheart, anything you want you can have. We only want to get you—" Irv stopped abruptly. He had almost said Back on your feet again or Functioning again or something that would have been equally tactless. My mother was squirming in her chair. She and Bob exchanged a significant glance.

"You know, Mr. Squires," Judy continued, oddly formal, ". . . without me there wouldn't *be* any CMA. I built that agency. David and Freddie were two guys in a phone booth before I came along. Now they don't take my calls."

"Judy," Irv countered, "everybody thinks you're the greatest. What you did tonight—"

"Yes, but Mr. Squires, what am I going to do *tomorrow* night? Everybody thinks I'm such a nn, *Legend* . . . do you know sometimes I sit home, just praying for the phone to ring?" She looked round the table. "I'm broke, Mr. Squires, I don't have a penny. Not a copper. I need, nn, *work*. Now is your agency going to get it for me or not?"

My mother half rose from her seat. "Perhaps we'd better—"

"No, no, sit down, Marjorie. Let's hear what Mr. Squires has to say." Poor Irv looked like a caged badger, wondering how he got into this.

"Look, Judy, all I can say is that CMA wants to do right by you. Nobody wants to see Judy Garland back on top as much as I do. I don't know if you remember this, but a long time ago—back in fifty-six after the second Palace engagement—I booked you into Symphony Center in Chicago. I've always thought you were the greatest. And, believe me, there's nothing the agency wants more—"

"Then let's see some money," Judy said. "I need some money. Right now. I'm broke, buster, and I need some money. I have to pay the IRS."

Irv looked at her helplessly. I caught my mother's eye, and with a jerk of my head indicated that she should leave. My mother rose, and so did the men.

"We've got to be going," said Bob.

"Nice to've met you," said Irv, shaking hands.

"Take care, Judy, and thanks for a wonderful night." Bob helped my mother into her coat amidst an awkward silence, and they threaded their way out of the room. Judy waited until Irv and I were back in our chairs. Then she tore into him again.

"I just signed with CMA for another three years, you know, and if they think—"

"Okay, look," I interposed, "this is neither the time nor the place. Irv isn't responsible for these decisions, anyway. Later on this week we'll meet with David and iron it all out." I rubbed Judy's shoulder. "Now we've just had a wonderful evening, where you performed brilliantly, where everybody thought you were magnificent, and where you even got Richard Rodgers to play rehearsal piano for you, so let's have a drink on it, okay? We'll straighten all this out later on."

Judy chortled. "Wasn't Dick's playing, nn, rotten?" she said. She was perfectly willing to be guided back to cheerfulness. Beside me I felt Irv breathe softly out in relief.

It was raining when Irv dropped us off on Park Avenue. Judy simply would not go back to the hospital, though we had promised Dr. Klinger. Judy cooed and curried me in her devastatingly winning way, and I gave in, as I always did, as I always would.

Hymie, the ancient doorman, didn't want to open the revolving door for us. He wanted us to come in through the double doors, which were exposed. I shouted at him viciously, from under the rain-drummed canopy. "Goddamit, Hymie, don't argue with me! Open the revolving door!" Terrified, Hymie did. I was amazed at myself. This was the third time in a week I'd been overbearingly impatient, rude, and unfeeling with somebody. What was happening to me?

At ten-thirty in the morning Marjorie knocked on our door. "Telephone." It was Dr. Klinger. Hadn't we promised to return Judy by one A.M. last night? Did we give our word so lightly? Did we realize it compromised his position with the hospital?

I felt terrible. "I'll have her back there no later than two, Dr. Klinger, I promise you." I hung up and shook Judy awake. "We've got to get back," I said. "They're screaming bloody murder."

Astoundingly, we made it to the Leroy by one-thirty. When we got to her room, two nurses, a thin one and a stocky one, were putting Judy's clothes into her suitcase.

"What's going on here?" I demanded.

"Supervisor's orders," said the stocky one. I lowered my voice an authoritative octave. "Does Dr. Klinger know about this?"

"We got word to have Miss Garland's things ready."

"We'll just see about this," I said. Judy's lip turned down. She was being evicted. "Don't you worry, darling," I assured her. "Everything's gonna be all right."

Dr. Klinger came into the room five minutes later. Judy had climbed back into bed, her favorite refuge. The doctor stood at the foot of the bed, as I sat by the window, tense and anxious.

"You know, Judy," he began, "when I let you out last night it was as a very special favor. We take a dim view here of letting a patient leave the building without being discharged. When I let you go it was with the understanding you'd be back by one o'clock, at the latest." He looked at her steadily. "You didn't get back here till one-thirty *this afternoon*." Judy looked down at her sheets, chastened.

"Dr. Klinger," I said, "it was my fault. I should have seen to it she got back on time." Klinger did not take his eyes from Judy.

"This hospital has every right to expect its patients not to treat it as a hotel. No matter who they are," he added, meaningfully. "We're not running the Plaza here."

"I know," Judy murmured, almost inaudibly.

"I want you to understand I thoroughly agree with the administration's attitude . . . and I was on the point of discharging you, at their suggestion." Klinger looked at me and back to Judy. "Do you know what stopped me?"

Nobody said anything.

"When I saw them packing your things," he said.

"Mr. Meyer for Mr. Begelman," I said to the receptionist. She punched a button on her phone console, announced me, nodded. "Mr. Begelman will be with you shortly," she told me, and I settled into one of CMA's French Provincial settees. The whole waiting room was done in French Provincial. Inwardly, I snorted. Flesh peddlers putting on airs.

David Begelman and Freddie Fields were smart; they had parlayed a single client, Judy, into a stable, then parlayed the stable into this agency. And eventually, CMA (Creative Management Associates) would merge with GAC (General Artists Corp.) and AFA (Ashley Famous Agency) to become the octopoidal ICM (International Creative Management), and David Begelman would go on to head a movie studio and forge other people's names on checks.

Last month Judy had dropped a legal suit she had pending against CMA, and re-signed with them for another three years. And now Begelman wasn't answering her calls, what kind of crap was that? The chip on my shoulder was assuming giant proportions. I looked at my watch. If Begelman keeps me waiting another five minutes, I thought, I'm walking, that's all. I stared at the back of the 10 × 14 manila envelope on which I'd listed the points I wanted to discuss with Begelman:

CMA's Responsibility	*Group Five*
$	Concerts—Carnegie, Philharmonic
Rehabilitation	TV shots
Music—get back	Laurette
Apt.	Records—ABC contract (?)
Lack of interest	Immediate cash

Beneath the envelope were two copies of this evening's *Post,* copies I'd picked up on the way over. Earl Wilson's column tonight featured a rapturous blurb about Judy's appearance at Lincoln Center:

> "Judy Garland staged another comeback. Keeping her promise, and well prepared, though limping slightly on an infected foot, Judy was a surprise guest star at Lincoln Center's tribute to Vincent Youmans, Noel Coward, and Harold Arlen.
>
> "In good voice, confident and self-assured, Judy was brought out by host Garry Moore, who said: 'Now here's a performer who's identified with Harold Arlen.'
>
> "Then she brought out Arlen. As she was singing 'Over The Rainbow,' she stopped in the middle of a lyric, knelt alongside the piano, and, with a bow that obviously touched the audience, said: 'Thank you, Harold.' Agent Irv Squires of CMA said there's plenty of working [*sic*] awaiting Judy, who seems ready."

A pretty girl with soft red hair looked out. "Mr. Meyer?" I stood up. "My name is Connie," she said. "I'm Mr. Begelman's secretary. Will you come with me, please?" Her voice was terrific, friendly but not intimate. The right balance. I wondered if Begelman would be as classy as his secretary.

Connie ushered me into a spacious office with a pair of large, black leather chairs facing an impressive desk. Between the chairs was a phone table with a built-in speaker, and to the left of the desk was another set of black chairs, one of which contained Irv Squires.

As I entered, I got my first look at Begelman: midforties, graying hair, soft features, almost flabby. Jewish, but not aggressively so. He was on the phone, leaning back in a swivel chair, but he rose instantly—though not quickly—to shake my hand and nod hello while he spoke.

I turned to Irv. "See your name in print?"

"No, I heard about it." Irv's eyes were eager. "Can I see that?"

I handed him one of my *Posts*. He turned to Earl Wilson's column. "Mmm," he said.

Begelman hung up, looked at Irv. "Earl Wilson," Irv said.

"Oh, may I?" Begelman's tone was polite but commanding. He held out his hand for Irv's newspaper. I saw Irv hesitate. He hadn't finished. Poor Irv, he was always getting the short end of the stick. "Here," I said to Begelman, and handed my second *Post* across the desk, which I now saw had Queen Anne legs. Begelman opened the paper and began to read, and I smiled. This was a happy beginning for the meeting: fresh publicity for Judy's success. It's occurred to me, in what's left of my objectivity, that CMA may be partially justified in throwing up its hands. She didn't show up for three concerts. She was fired from the set of *Valley of the Dolls*. When you listened to the dark side of the Legend, it was not the picture of a responsible, productive artist. I was glad to have Earl Wilson as ammunition.

"Marvelous," said Begelman, closing the paper. "Irv tells me she was terrific."

"Like the old Judy," said Irv.

"Yah," I said, casually, underplaying. "She was pretty good all right." I smiled sympathetically at Irv. "I'm sorry she gave you a rough time last night."

"Oh, listen . . ." said Irv.

"Mr. Meyer," Begelman began, "we want to do everything we can to help Judy. I say this sincerely. No one cares more for her, or takes more of an interest in her than we do. If Judy's ready and . . . able to work, we'll be the first to applaud. We have only a sincere desire to help."

"In what way?"

"Well, Irv here . . ." he indicated Irv, who took the ball.

"I've hadda turn down at least three bookings for Judy in the past month," said Irv. He extended an explanatory palm to Begelman. "John heard me say this last night. They wanted her at Symphony Center in Chicago, Orchestra Hall in Philadelphia, the Music Center in LA . . ."

Begelman took it back. "Of course we're in a tough position as far as concert dates go, because she doesn't have any orchestrations."

"Mmm," I said, noncommittally. I was determined not to let Begelman get away with anything.

"Now Ben Freeman, her lawyer—have you met Ben? Ben tells me he can get her orchestrations back if she'll just do one concert, for a fellow named Marelli. Marelli claims she didn't show at a concert he booked for her."

"Is that true?"

"That's not the point, darling—" said Begelman, and stopped as he realized he didn't know me well enough to call me "darling" yet. This was only our first date.

"May I call you John?" he asked me. I smiled inwardly. "Go ahead," I said.

"Anyway," Begelman recovered, "the point is not whether she did or didn't do the concert, that doesn't matter. What matters is, can she get her orchestrations back? Now, I don't know where Ben stands with this guy Marelli—"

He swiveled round to his phone and buzzed Connie. "Get me Ben Freeman in Boston." He swiveled back to face me. "But you see, John, without orchestrations we're helpless."

"You know, David," I started deliberately (if he could call me John I could call him David), "for an outfit that calls itself Creative Management you're vastly uncreative (was this me talking?). All right, maybe you're hung up for a while with concerts. What about other areas?"

"Like what?" David eyed me suspiciously.

"Like records, like TV shots, like special projects. Judy wants to do a property about Laurette Taylor, a picture."

"John, a picture takes two years, just to get the names on a piece of paper. That project is at least nine months away, more like a year."

"My ambition," I said, "is to see Judy do another *Star Is Born*."

"That would be wonderful. I agree with you that Judy's career moves should have resonance. By that I mean . . . impact. The films had resonance Carnegie Hall had resonance. But right now . . ." He paused, looked at the ceiling. "Frankly, John, I don't know a record company in town that'll touch her."

I couldn't help bristling defensively. "Well it just so *happens*," I said, "that I'm setting a record deal for Judy with a brand-new company. Which reminds me, I've been trying to find out from Larry Newton over at ABC whether they still have her under contract. Do you know?"

"I can find out." He buzzed Connie again. "Get me Larry Newton at ABC-Paramount." I had to admire the way he moved; he was right on top of it.

"But we're talking about *cash*, John. What Judy needs now is immediate *cash*, to put a roof over her head, make her feel like a lady again. And the quickest way to get cash is concert dates."

Irv spoke up. "We're talking ten thousand minimum, John."

"Would you like to hear what Judy thinks?"

"By all means." Begelman leaned across his desk with an attentive smile.

"Judy thinks you should give her some money." Begelman's smile became a puzzled grin. "Give her some money? What do you mean?"

I took a breath. "What I mean is, when Count Basie signs with Joe Glazer for three more years he gets a fifty-thousand-dollar bonus. When Judy Garland signs with CMA for the same period she gets bubkes, not dollar one. She thinks you should give her some money."

The puzzled grin became a little tight-lipped. "Now listen," Begelman said, "I don't like that at all. I'm just as good at my job as she is at hers. And if Joe Glazer has to give Basie fifty thousand dollars, then he's a hell of a lousy agent. Who told you that, anyway?"

"It's in this week's *Variety*," I said. "You got a copy here? I'll show you."

"Look, I'll tell you this here and now," Begelman said, his voice rising sharply, "if she can get another agency to give her fif—to give her *anything*—to go with them, we won't stand in her way. She can have a release from her contract. My honor as a gentleman. Irv, you're a witness to this." He was breathing a little heavily. "And if you want to bring anybody in I'll be glad to repeat what I just said, in front of them."

I craned my neck back toward the door. "George," I called. Begelman laughed shortly. "I mean that," he said.

"Look," I said, "let's not get upset."

"Who's upset? Irv, am I upset?"

"Look okay to me," said Irv.

I was beginning to sense how to get to David Begelman. "Hey," I said, "all I'm saying is, you've got a valuable property here, why let it languish? Judy can make a lotta loot for CMA, let's see what we can do with her, okay?"

The phone buzzed and Begelman punched in. Connie's voice came over the box. "Mr. Newton has left for the day, Mr. Begelman."

"Right. Thank you, Connie."

"Oh, and David, another thing: Judy complains she can't get you on the phone, that you avoid her calls. It's a small thing, but you know how much emotional security she needs . . ."

"Well, that's funny . . ." David's expression was pained. "I'm certainly always ready to talk to Judy whenever she calls. I don't know why she should feel that way."

"I think it's because your secretary says 'just a minute, I'll see' and then comes back with the news you're not available, and it kind of sounds—"

"Of course, of course, it sounds like a brush." He buzzed again. "Connie, would you come in, please?"

Connie came in and Begelman told her never to put Miss Garland on hold. "If I'm out, just say so."

"And maybe where you can be reached," I added.

"Yes, Connie, that's a good idea. Just tell her 'Mr. Begelman is at the Dorchester,' and give her the number, or Acapulco, or wherever, but don't let her get the impression—" Connie nodded. "I understand." She left the room. I glanced down at my envelope, spotted the notation 'Apt.'

"Now what about this apartment?"

"What apartment?"

"Yes," said Irv, "she hocked me about this last night." I was a little uncertain of my ground here, but I didn't want to lose the momentum I was generating. "Apparently," I began, "CMA keeps an apartment for its clients, and Judy thinks she should have access to it."

"An apartment for clients?" Begelman's brows went up. "No such animal. CMA maintains an apartment for its *staff*, its executives. Herman Frey is in there now, from the coast. If she wants to move in with him . . ."

Okay, his round. I was afraid of that. I got off the apartment quickly, saved from greater embarrassment by Ben Freeman's call from Boston. Ben's broad, New England accent came through the speaker with a metallic ring.

"Ben," said Begelman, "I'm here with John Meyer, who's acting for Judy, and he wants to know about the Marelli deal."

"Does he have the five thousand dollars?" Ben didn't know he was on the air.

"Well, I wish you'd explain that to John, he's sitting here now." Begelman indicated the phone by my chair and I picked up the receiver. "Hello, Ben," I said in my most authoritative, deepest stud voice.

"Hello, Jahn. Here's the deal: Marelli waants to produce a concert with Judy, and then give back her orchestrations. He says he can get them. Now, in return, he waants twenty-five thousand dollars, plus two percent of Judy's gross earnings for the next year. We might be able to whittle him down to one percent, but, in my opinion, it's hardly worth it." He paused. "Are you with me?"

"I'm listening," I said cautiously. I had no idea whether these figures made any kind of sense. I was jotting them down on the envelope.

"I've advised Judy to grab it," Ben continued. "These orchestrations are worth close to a million, and, if you think of it in that light, she's getting off very inexpensively. But there's one catch. Marelli waants five thousand down as a guarantee against the twenty-five, and Judy doesn't have it. Judy's funds are very limited."

"Yes, Ben, and that reminds me." I looked at Begelman. "May I do a little private business here?" Begelman nodded, began to rise, looked at me questioningly. Did I want privacy? No, no, I motioned him back into his chair. He pressed the phone to his ear.

"Ben, Judy tells me you owe her a financial statement. She hasn't received it yet."

"I know, Jahn." Ben's tone was apologetic. "I've been in Europe, and I just haven't gotten to it. First thing tomorrow, I assure you. I've been abrahd."

"Well, I hope you had a good time, Ben," I said, for Begelman's benefit, putting just the right amount of acidity into my voice, "but can we get it out?"

"First thing tomorrow."

"First I've heard about this, Ben," Begelman said.

"All right," I said firmly, feeling I had to make a decision, any decision. "I think we'd better pursue this Marelli deal. It's the only—"

Suddenly Begelman sneezed. Right into his receiver. Ben, thinking it was me, said "God bless you." I, knowing it was David, said "Gesundheit." Begelman said "Thank you." I glanced up at him. He was wiping his nose. I stifled the laughter that was bubbling up in my throat. Judy would fall on the floor when I told her. Now where was I?

"John seems to think this Marelli thing can work out," said Begelman.

"Look, we could fight it. We could take them to court," Ben said. "And by the time we won—and, incidentally, there's no guarantee of that, not by any means—but, assuming we did, a year would be gahn and we'd have spent the same money, roughly speaking, on lawyers' fees. The important thing is—"

"You're right, Ben," I said, decisively. "Can we get in touch with Marelli?"

"I'll try him right now. Can I call you back?"

"We're here," said Begelman.

"Look forward to meeting you, Jahn."

"Me too, Ben."

"Will you be in Bahston in the near future?"

"Very possibly."

"Well, I look forward to meeting you. Say hello to Judy for Martha and me both. We both send our love."

"I will."

We all hung up. There was a pause. Then Begelman spoke. "It's the best thing."

"It's the only thing," I said. "We've got to get the lady working again . . . it's where she belongs." Both men looked at me. "I know she's a lot of headaches," I continued. I wanted to *win* this man, wanted to make a convert of him, make him share the fervor, make him really *work* for Judy. "I know she's probably your most difficult client. I know up to now she's been undependable and aggravating. Well, that isn't gonna happen anymore. From now on, Judy Garland is gonna be not only a great artist, she's gonna be the most responsible, dependable, pro*fess*ional in the business. This is a God-given talent, and we've got to protect it. I mean, this isn't Wayne Newton, this is only the most fantastic, greatest, most talented performer ever born, and . . . if it takes a little more effort, a little more time . . . sacrifice . . . well, it takes it, that's all." I felt the back of my tongue begin to fill my throat. "Because . . . she's just the best . . . the very best there is." I had to stop, before I dropped tears on the black leather upholstery. I realized I'd just made a speech. I rose from my chair.

"And that, gentlemen, is all I have to say."

Begelman stood and came round from behind his desk. "And very well said, too." He looked at me appraisingly. "Are you a lawyer?" he asked me.

"No, a songwriter. Why?"

"You handle yourself very well."

"I shouldn't even be doing this," I said. "I wouldn't do it for anyone else."

Begelman extended his hand. "We'll be in touch," he said.

Part Two

❋ ❋ ❋

Boston

TUESDAY, NOVEMBER 19

We're catching the three-thirty flight to Boston, where Judy has an apartment. "Flight" is the operative word here. Judy is checking out of the hospital, and we cannot go back to Park Avenue, my folks won't have it. Judy is too much of a disruption.

It's just as well, we would soon smother there. It's time for a change of scene.

By one o'clock I was harried and rushed, with too much unfinished business, too many calls to make: Ken Roberts and Bob Colby and my lawyer, and I'm sitting in a phone booth at the hospital getting Judy checked out. We've got to get going.

My final call was to Begelman. He's lunching at the Oak Room, Connie tells me. Plaza nine three thousand. I had him paged.

"David, listen, it's John Meyer. We're going to Boston, I don't know for how long—"

"I think we have that number."

"I just gave it to Connie. Now David, I'm getting into this pretty deep, and I want to know—"

"We appreciate this, John."

"What I want to know is, if we need it, will CMA advance us some cash against future appearances?" The buzz of the Oak Room got louder. "John, let me just say this: if we have Judy's signature on a contract for a concert appearance, you will not find us, ah, unyielding."

"Because I don't know how long our money will hold out."

"Keep in touch, John, let us know how things are progressing. Have a good trip." The way David spoke reminded me of Richard Nixon. It was not reassuring.

I sped back to Park Avenue to pack Judy's bags. On the way upstairs the elevator man winked and told me there was a blonde waiting for me. Who the hell—? Oh my God, Susie Zisko, from Newark, a twenty-year-old co-ed who'd been in a show of mine. A month ago I'd told her she could stop by today and say hello. I'd completely forgotten.

"Susie! Hi. Listen, come give me a hand."

I pressed her into service immediately, throwing her a pile of worn panty hose and telling her to pick out the serviceable ones. Susie couldn't believe it. Judy Garland!

"How are you getting to the airport?" she asked. I hadn't thought about it. Cab, I guess.

"Want me to drive you?" she said, sweet and eager and hoping. Why not? We dragged the luggage downstairs, Judy's two red Samsonite valises, plus a Valpak and hatbox, my suitcase and briefcase. We filled the backseat and trunk of Susie's beat-up old Valiant.

Judy was having trouble checking out. The Leroy wouldn't let her go without a final determination of her medical coverage. This had been going on for a week. As a member, Judy's expenses should have been insured through SAG (Screen Actors Guild) but she'd let her dues lapse, so maybe we should contact AFTRA (American Federation of Television and Radio Artists). It was a terrible mess. The hospital bill came to eleven hundred dollars, plus there was Dr. Klinger's fee, and it was nearly two o'clock.

Susie gave a little gasp of disbelief as Judy hopped into the front seat beside her. It really *was* Judy Garland. Judy said "Well *hello*, Susie . . ." and it was lucky Susie had the activity of driving in which to channel her excitement. Judy smiled at her affectionately as Susie's loquacity filled the car.

"I'm playing Abigail in *The Crucible* at Newark State and listen, Johnny, could you come and see it? It's gonna be next week, Friday and Saturday, and oh dear, how long are you gonna be away?"

Judy instantly became the sympathetic mother. "Now, Susie, I promise we'll get him back, if we have to put him on . . . nn, *roll*er skates."

"Oh, Miss Garland . . . could you come too?" Susie hardly dared to ask.

"Well, if nn, *Johnny*'s going, I'm certainly going, too."

"Eeee!" Susie was so overwhelmed that she threw herself into Judy's arms.

American Airlines squeezed us a quart of fresh grapefruit juice to go with our ever-present pint of vodka. They put it in a plastic container, and we drank it all the way to Massachusetts.

On the flight up I taught Judy to play Pass The Trash, a vari- ant of seven-card stud. Judy was a poker player, and today we inaugurated the tradition of "The Pot"—a little black purse full of change which grew fat over the next three weeks as it collected each day's nickels, dimes, and quarters. We never played with chips, only coins. No pennies allowed.

As we strapped ourselves into the seats Judy said, "Why this big rush to Boston?"

"I just felt it was time we got away."

"Herb and Marge didn't want us back," she said, with painful accuracy.

"Ah, Christ, I just wanna get out of New York," I sighed, try- ing to keep my voice casual as the plane taxied down the tar- mac. I'm always a little anxious till we reach forty thousand feet.

We pillowed into the sky, Judy looking out the window, not buying my story, gathering energy to play being hurt and in- jured. But the answering pressure of her fingernails in my palm told me she was too busy being nervous about takeoff.

Judy was as big a chickenshit flyer as I was.

At Logan Airport we tried to rent a car, but neither of us had a credit card, and you know how they are about that. You gotta have plastic money. However, despite her caution, the Avis girl was eager to rent to Judy.

"I see. Well, Mr. Meyer, do you belong to a company whose credit is guaranteed with us?"

"I'm sure I do," I replied instantly. "How about Warner Brothers-Seven Arts?" My first principle, you'll have gathered by now, is that Necessity Is the Mother of Invention.

The Avis girl handed me a blue volume the size of Peru's phone book. "See if your company's listed in there," she said.

The book fell open to the S's. The first viable name I spotted was Screen Gems, Columbia Pictures, 711 Fifth Avenue.

"Here," I said, pointing to the name and address. The girl took it down assiduously on the rental sheet, and ordered us a Buick sedan.

Gliding along Storrow Drive at a moderate speed (Judy didn't like to go over forty mph) I took a breath of the cool exhila- rating air. Here was Boston, a clean white page, ready for the creation of a new adventure. I had friends here, and I felt I could handle whatever came up. I had the intelligence, the knowledge, and the instincts to make the right decisions. I was getting Judy together. I was the custodian of a precious human phenomenon and in control. I felt an immense sense of destiny.

Nearing Judy's apartment, I pulled up at a pharmacy in Kenmore Square. We were running low on Ritalin, the vital essence. Twice in New York I'd had the opportunity of getting some but didn't want to interrupt the momentum of our departure, knowing how the least incident could deflect Judy from her course; with Judy, if the steak is cold, there goes Europe.

I turned off the ignition. "Oh," Judy said, "this isn't a good place. They're bastards here."

"We'll see," I said.

The druggist seemed friendly enough as I handed him the three prescriptions. In addition to Ritalin, Dr. Klinger had prescribed Darvon, a painkiller, and Seconal, the sleeping pills.

But, as Judy had warned me, this was a drugstore that observed the letter of the law. I hurried outside to the car. Judy was playing the radio. "What's your doctor's name here?"

"Wh . . . which one? You could try nn, *Fletc*her . . ." I found Fletcher's number and presented it to the druggist, but—at seven P.M.—there was no answer. I tried my sigh of resignation and impatience and I tried my wheedle; but nothing worked. It was no dice.

"You see?" Judy chided me as I slid back behind the wheel, "I *told* you. Now let's go to the nn, *good* drugstore."

The good drugstore gave us all three prescriptions without so much as a raised eyebrow. Sensational. Everyone should have this drugstore on the corner. They'll even deliver.

Ninety-eight Seconal? Yessir, be there in ten minutes. Are you sure that'll be enough?

Well, how many do suicides usually take?

Oh, between fifty and sixty. How many in your party?

Just one.

Judy lived in the Prudential Center apartments, a complex of three high-rise buildings, the Fairfield, the Boylston, and the Gloucester. Judy had three and a half rooms in the Fairfield.

Bedroom, living room, kitchen. Not bad, and plenty of closet space, but I was annoyed by the water taps. The bathroom faucet had a knob you pulled out for Volume and dialed left or right for Hot and Cold. The kitchen sink had a throttlestick you bent forward for Volume and moved left or right for Hot and Cold, but you never could get the coordinates where you wanted them—the right Volume at the right temperature.

For two sixty-five a month Judy was privileged to enjoy not only twenty-four-hour doorman service, but also the Prudential's compulsory air-conditioning system—two positions, On and Off. The windows were sealed, you couldn't open them. It made me claustrophobic.

Downstairs, we had a cavernous, multilevel garage, and a shopping mall. Grocery market, cleaners, travel agency, liquor shop, everything.

Judy had furnished the place in Early Eclectic. The bedroom featured a Spanish chest of stained mahogany with a matching headboard that was across the room from the bed. The headboard stood, alone and majestically, in the corner, while the standard, fifty-four-inch double bed (which it was meant to crown) sat nakedly against the far wall.

Atop the chest were the following items: a twelve-inch Panasonic TV set (black and white); a dozen bottles of assorted perfumes, colognes, lotions, and suntan oils; packets of bobby pins, clips, and pocket Kleenex; tubes and jars of skin creams and unguents. Standing incongruously in the midst of this detritus was a small, silver-framed color shot of Judy and John F. Kennedy.

In the living room, a picture window faced the door as you entered, and through it you could view a Lord & Taylor's on the other side of the plaza. The floor to the left of this window was littered with liquor cartons, a nonfunctioning record player, and three plaid suitcases, the cheap kind, sitting with their tops open, like eager mouths waiting to be fed. In the cases were clothes, some Judy's, some her daughter Lorna's. The cartons were filled with papers: a Bible, concert programs, reviews from newspapers, contracts, tax statements, and an IOU from Sid to Judy for "ten thousand dollars to be deducted from this week's gross."

By the entrance to the kitchen, which was on your left as you entered, was a white ice-cream table with wrought-iron legs accompanied by two matching chairs with red vinyl seats. Set against the opposite wall was a round maple table with a Formica top, and four chairs.

Beneath the window, running the width of the room, was an ugly blue sofa with brown wooden arms and brass studs where the fabric joined the wood. Judy's definition of people as "heavy furniture" came from this sofa.

By current American standards, the Fairfield is a luxury building. Which means the walls are just thin enough so you can hear your neighbor's voice . . . but too thick to make out what he's saying.

This evening we went to dinner at a restaurant named Amalfi with my pal Marvin, who worked for the Boston Symphony. I hadn't seen Marvin for a year, and we played a prank on him. I told Judy to call him at the Symphony offices and announce herself only as "Judy."

"Marvin? Hi. This is Judy."

"Judy?" Marvin knew two or three Judys.

"Yes. How are you?"

"I'm fine . . ." said Marvin hesitantly, trying to place the voice. "Where are you?"

"Oh . . . I'm in nn, *town*. At my apartment. I'm with Johnny." Judy kept Marvin going for ten minutes. He was sure he knew that voice from somewhere.

Later, at Amalfi's, Marvin and Judy got into a discussion of music—the new rock as opposed to the classic show tunes of the forties. Marvin maintained the kids weren't interested in show music, just rock.

"Well, not nn, *all* kids . . ." said Judy. "A lot of those kids come to see *me* . . ."

"Yes, but Judy," said Marvin pontifically, "that is rather a tribute to your magnetism as an artist rather than to the music you sing." Marvin was being gallant, but he has a tendency to talk like this, professorially.

"No, I think you're wrong . . . the kids are coming back to the really good music . . . Cole Porter and Harold Arlen . . ."

Judy and Marvin locked horns on this, and halfway through

the discussion I saw Judy turn off, as sharply as if someone had pulled a switch. Then and there she decided that Marvin was opinionated, academic . . . and pedantic.

WEDNESDAY, NOVEMBER 20

Okay, let's get things organized. First, we unpack. This'll be my closet and this one'll be yours. I'll take these two bottom drawers. Now, what do you want to do about this dress?

"Mmm, that's for cleaning."

"The sequin gown."

"In the closet."

"This beige top."

"That's, nn, *Lorna's*."

"Okay, we'll make this Lorna's case. All Lorna's stuff goes in here. How about this skirt?"

"Oh . . . there's a matching jacket for that . . . it's around here somewhere, unless nn, *Larry's* wearing it. It needs a cleaning, don't you think?"

I called the cleaner downstairs, and he came up and collected thirty-two dollars and eighty-five cents' worth of cleaning. I mean when Judy had her clothes cleaned, she had her *clothes cleaned.*

Okay, the unpacking was done. Now a maid, to sweep, wash, and straighten up. Do you know a maid service, Judy?

"Let's look in the nn, *Yellow Pages.*" Judy was very big on the Yellow Pages. In fact, she'd found her present attorney, Ben Freeman, through the Yellow Pages.

I dialed Miss Mary's Maids. Miss Mary herself informed me, with polite hauteur, that she couldn't fit us in till next week. Next week! I was stunned.

"Look, Miss Mary, I'm not enrolling my child in private school here, I just wanna get the house cleaned."

"Ah'll see if one of mah girls wants to work extra, but ah can't promise you."

"Miss Mary," I said, quietly, "this is for Miss Judy Garland."

There was a slight hesitation. "Miss Judy Garland?"

"That's right."

And of course we got service immediately. Judy's name worked magic in situations like this. As I put down the phone I wondered whether I'd eventually come to resent it. John Meyer can't get a maid, but Judy Garland can. It had bothered me the night P. J. Clarke's had opened up, after hours, because it was Judy. I shrugged to myself. Listen, what the hell, if it gets us what we need, gives us an edge. But still . . .

Judy herself was extremely sensitive to this; my position in relation to her, my sense of identity, of self. She was on the watch constantly to preserve it, to keep me from ever being considered Mister Judy Garland, or worse, Judy Garland's escort. In public, she was always deferential.

"And this is Mr. Meyer," she'd say. Never John, or even John Meyer. Always Mister Meyer. And when decisions needed to be made:

"Well, whatever nn, Mr. *Meyer* . . ." and she'd gesture toward me, which was my cue to say, "Yes, let's," or "I really don't think so," and then turn to Judy, "Unless you really want to?"

This was perhaps the most feminine thing about Judy, the way she related to a man, perceptively realizing that he needed to stay in enough control to keep his dignity, which could be threatened a thousand times a day.

Never once did she forget this—and never once did she err.

Sometime in the midafternoon Annie Bryant came over and took down sketches of seven more songs to orchestrate for Judy. Annie is a tall, sweet-natured, warmhearted girl who—at the time—was a student at the Berklee College of Music. Annie now arranges and composes for her own jingle house, but, when I met her in Boston, she was barely nineteen.

For nineteen she was a damn accomplished musician, and, as we sat on the ugly couch, with no piano, working out modulations and tempi from tape recordings, we developed an instant affection for each other. There was no pretension about Annie, and music was the major part of her life.

"That's basically a G seven," I said at one point, "but let's flat the fifth, okay?"

Annie grinned up at me from her scorepad. "You want me to add the thirteenth?"

And Judy said, "Oh, you nn, musicians with your secret nn, *code* . . . B minor sixth, G fifteenth, E twenty-eighth . . ." Somewhere in her amazing life, Judy had befriended this shy, awkward prodigy, and Annie was doing these charts as a favor to Judy, whom she adored. When they were finished, Judy would be able to work. Anywhere.

THURSDAY, NOVEMBER 21

At two-thirty today we put the broken record player in the back-seat of the Buick. We planned to drop it off at a repair shop after doing some shopping at Jordan Marsh. Judy's kitchen desperately needed equipment.

In the housewares department it was young married time for Judy and John. "Well, which pattern do *you* like, dear?" "Mmm, I rather fancy the green." The saleslady couldn't figure us out. Judy was doing her deferential act, and I was doing my expansive, oh-what-the-hell-if-you-like-it-buy-it act. I didn't know whether to feel like a boyfriend or a sugar daddy.

Herbert's cooking training came in handy when we got to kitchen utensils. I remember selecting a Peugeot pepper mill over another one. I still have it. Altogether, I spent one hundred and eight dollars and sixty-nine cents, and this is what we bought:

    a. a set of dishes (service for four)
    b. a set of silverware (stainless)
    c. four glasses
    d. four place mats
    e. a saltshaker and pepper mill
    f. four dish towels
    g. a dish rack
    h. a spice rack
    i. two casseroles
    j. a salad bowl (with fork and spoon)
    k. a tray
    l. a set of spices

    m. two pot holders

    n. two rubber spatulas

    o. a trivet

and, p. a corkscrew.

About four-fifteen, Judy pooped out. Too much walking around, her foot was bothering her. "Would you mind if I went downstairs and nn, *wait*ed for you in the cocktail lounge?" she asked me. "I think it's called the . . . mmm, Brass Lantern."

"Okay," I said, "I'll meet you there."

I was writing the check when I noticed our saleslady looking around for Judy. "She's gone downstairs," I said. The woman's face fell. "Oh dear . . ." she hesitated, "I wanted to ask her for an autograph. Do you think she'd mind?"

"Of course not. Give me your name and address and I'll have her send you one."

I went downstairs to the main floor, but there was no sign of a cocktail lounge called the Brass Lantern. I asked directions and was told it was in the Annex across the street. But, standing before the Annex directory, there was no Brass Lantern listed.

I went out to the street and collared a passerby. Yeah, it's two blocks down. I walked the two blocks and found the Brass Rail, but not the Brass Lantern. I turned back to Jordan Marsh, re-tracing my mental breadcrumbs . . . please . . . the Brass Lantern . . . it's a bar . . .

There was a coffee shop downstairs called the Brass Lantern, and okay, it's supposed to be a bar, but let's take a look and yes, by God, this is it, not a bar but a coffee shop, all you can drink here is *hot chocolate* for chrissake, and Judy is shaking and in the early stages of delirium tremens. "Where *were* you?" she cried.

"I couldn't find the place . . . I kept looking for a *bar* . . ."

"There's not a nn, *drop* to be had here . . . and"—Judy lowered her voice—"everybody's been nn, *pestering* me."

Indeed, a small crowd had collected and was getting closer. I took Judy by the arm and shepherded her protectively out of the store, saying, Not now, I'm sorry, Miss Garland doesn't feel well, I'm sorry, not now.

In the car we were hit with a nasty surprise: the hi-fi unit was gone, stolen from the backseat. Shit. I started the engine. Judy had only one concern. "Let's get to the nearest nn, *bar*," she said.

We drove through the alley onto the next major thoroughfare, and found ourselves in a commercial district seemingly devoid of bars. There was a stationery store, a fabric store, a luncheonette. No bar. I could feel Judy beside me, beginning to quiver. I took turn after turn, looking for some cheap neon sign that said CAFE or BAR or CHICKIE'S PLACE or ROADHOUSE . . . whatever. Ninety seconds passed in silence, and now I'd have settled for a sign that said LIQUOR, a package store, a bum in a doorway, *anything*.

Finally we saw our salvation—a Polynesian lounge, the South Seas. Lanai time, with plastic palm fronds and garish island murals on the wall; it was a dive, yes, but were we glad to see it.

Judy ordered a double vodka martini and began to relax. It seemed as if we'd weathered a crisis, come through a monsoon, an earthquake, some terrible trauma. And what had happened? Nothing. We'd gone without liquor from afternoon to early evening. With Judy, everything became intensified. The tiniest incident or attitude was magnified out of proportion. It was a life of hyperbole, like being high all the time. It was a bitch to keep up with Judy's emotional pace, but if you could cut it you functioned at your peak capacity. Judy was like a walking line of cocaine.

Now, through a pair of plastic straws we were sharing a Scorpion, one of those tropical, rum-based concoctions that comes in a gourd, with a gardenia floating in it. Judy had asked that vodka be substituted for the rum. "Rum makes me nn, *sleepy*," she said.

I suddenly noticed I was ravenously hungry. You had to watch out with Judy not to let hunger creep up on you. Judy sometimes went a day and a half without eating. I looked at my watch. It was nine-thirty.

"Hey, I'm starving," I said. "Let's get out of here and have some dinner."

"I'm having a good time," said Judy. "Why don't we order some spareribs?"

"No, I don't want to eat here."

"Well, could we just stay . . . another ten minutes?"

"Okay, it's nine-thirty. At nine-forty we go." The Scorpion was affecting me, and I needed to drive. Suddenly I saw that characteristic, mischievous expression come into Judy's eyes. It was the look she'd had before she hit me in the ear with the potato.

She pointed to a coatrack by the door, which had been hung with several coats and one small hat with a Tyrolean-style feather in it.

"I'm not leaving," she told me deliberately, "unless you put on that hat and coat and walk out." I stared at her. I knew she meant it.

"Aw, come *on*, Judes."

"I mean it," she said, with a finality that brooked no argument. It was so bizarre. Judy, totally flippant about anything serious, became all business when involved in her fun.

I said something futile about not being silly.

"Well, *I* don't care if we stay here all night. Nn, *you're* the one the nn, *food* isn't good enough for here . . ."

I was just smashed enough to say to myself, what the hell. " 'kay. Have it your way." I rose, went directly to the rack, slipped on the coat she'd indicated, slapped the hat on my head and returned to the table, which I pulled out for her. "Let's go," I said.

Without smiling, Judy got up, and I helped her into her mink, keeping my eyes on the floor. I knew there were three people in the room, a large, heavyset man drinking by himself at a corner table, and a small Chinese and his American girl friend on stools at the bar. The coat was tight on me, and anyone observing me would have seen a very uncomfortable guy. I felt like I was straitjacketed.

We walked carefully and slowly out of the place, Judy dragging behind, trying to prolong our exit, trying to get me into trouble. Nobody said a word.

We walked to the restaurant's parking lot, Judy in her mink and me in my new coat and Tyrolean hat. "You look very nice," Judy said, approvingly.

I put the car in drive and rolled the few feet from the lot to the restaurant entrance. I put the shift in park and jumped out.

"Unh unh unnhh . . ." Judy cautioned me, realizing my intention. "Don't be a rat fink . . ."

I bounced back into the South Seas. Reentering the dim bar, I approached the corner table. "This your coat?" I asked the heavyset guy. He shook his head dully. He was beyond speech.

That's a relief, I thought. I tapped the little Chinese on the shoulder. "Yes?" he inquired politely. I was taking off my new attire. "'S been a mistake," I muttered. "I'm sorry." I set the hat and coat on the bar stool beside him. His girl friend gave me a strange look.

When I got back to the car, Judy had buzzed up the windows and locked the doors. There she sat, arms folded, smug as a Cheshire cat, staring straight ahead of her down the street. I knocked on the window. Mmm mmm. Judy shook her head. She jabbed her finger in the direction of the restaurant. It was definitive: I wasn't getting back in the car till I returned in that poor guy's hat and coat. She wasn't budging.

I stood there, perplexed, on the sidewalk. The Buick's motor was humming quietly, sending a visible shimmer of carbon monoxide into the chill November night. Well, I thought speculatively, there are two ways out: I can stuff my handkerchief into the exhaust pipe and asphyxiate her; or I can get the hat and coat.

With a sigh of resignation, I plodded back into the bar. Again I approached the tiny Chinese. Without a word, I took his coat from the bar stool and began to put it on.

He turned around on the stool. "Hey . . . that's my coat." I put his hat on my head. "I'm afraid I'm going to have to have your hat and coat," I told him, in a reasonable tone.

"Beg pardon?"

"Look," I said, taking my pen from my breast pocket and grabbing a cocktail napkin, "give me your name and address and I'll send these back to you."

The tiny man didn't say anything. He looked at me with total incomprehension. His girl friend was frightened now; she thought I was some kind of nut. Maybe I was.

"Just write down your name and address," I repeated. I proffered the pen and the napkin.

"I beg *pardon*," the man blurted, finally. "These are . . . *mine*." I spoke as slowly and distinctly as I could. "Yes, I know.

Would you come outside and explain that to my girl?" I asked him. "She doesn't understand that these are your clothes."

"Has my name inside," he said. "I show you." He reached toward me and tried to expose the lining of his coat.

"I *know*," I said, understandingly, "but would you please explain it to my girl? She happens to be Judy Garland."

"Judy Garrand?" His eyes opened incredulously. The whole thing was a dream to him.

"Yes," I said, and propelled him by the arm off his stool and out the door, his girl friend following a suspicious six paces behind.

As we approached the car I asked him his name. George Lee, he told me. I knocked on the window. Judy was grinning from ear to ear, unable to suppress her delight in having provoked this incident. She buzzed her window down.

"Judy," I said grandly, "this is Mr. George Lee, a great admirer of yours."

Mr. Lee was flabbergasted, He rocked back on his heels with surprise. "Ah . . . Miss *Garr*and . . ." was all he could find to say.

Judy extended a regal hand. Mr. Lee grabbed it and held it as if he would never let go. Kiss it, schmuck, I thought, and you'll get your coat back. But Mr. Lee merely stood there in awe-stricken silence.

Judy picked up the cue. "Mr. nn, *Lee* . . ." she said, in a manner the Empress Eugénie might have envied, "we've become quite nn, at*ta*ched to your clothes."

"Yes, Miss Garrand, but . . . ahhhhh . . ." Mr. Lee was completely lost. He was floundering and overwhelmed. He didn't understand the put-on. He still thought there was a legitimate mistake somewhere, and that, if we talked it over logically, it could be sorted out.

"Is *my* hat and coat," he said.

"*Yes*, Mr. Lee," said Judy, completely poker-faced, "but we nn, *need* them."

By this time I'd left Mr. Lee's hat and coat on the hood of the car, and managed to slip back behind the wheel. I saw Mr. Lee's face light up with an idea. I think at last he caught the spirit of the moment.

"Okay," he exclaimed, suddenly elated. "Tell you what: I give you hat!" And with that he plucked his tiny Tyrolean hat from the hood and dropped it right on Judy's head, jumping once in the air with a giggle of delight.

I know an exit line when I hear one. We drove off in a blaze of laughter.

We parked by a seafood house on Boylston, the Half Shell.

During dinner we started talking with the adjoining table, and ended by picking them up—a married couple, Jim and Lois, and their pal Dick, who was in Boston on business. We were laughing with this trio, so Judy and I agreed, through a tacit series of squeezes, to continue our evening as a quintet.

Our next stop was a Turkish belly-dancing room, the Casbah, where Judy persuaded Lois to join in the terpsichorean gyrations on the floor. Lois, normally conservative, let down her hair and did a mock-lascivious, charming dance for us.

We wound up the evening at an after-hours bar known as Napoleon, where Judy overwhelmed everyone by singing her two new Meyer numbers, "Hate Myself" and "It's All for You." Judy made me sing them first, so she could fix the still unfamiliar lyrics in her mind.

Of course she was the highlight of the evening, and the five of us rode out of Napoleon on a wave of enjoyment. It was four-thirty A.M. as we hailed the final cab of the night. Earlier, we'd deposited the Buick in the Prudential garage.

Since we were five, Dick hopped into the front seat, and Judy perched on my lap in the back.

Dick was cheerfully tight. "We'll drop you," he said expansively. "It's on our way, I'm at the Hilton." He threw his arm across the back of the seat, revealing an expensive-looking timepiece under his cuff.

"I wonder what time it is," Judy said, reaching out and sliding Dick's expansion band over his thumb and fingers. "Hmm, four-thirty . . ." she murmured, squinting down at the watch. "Weren't those nn, belly dancers *amazing*? What con*trol* . . ."

"Incredible," Lois agreed. "I don't know how they do it." Beneath her, I felt Judy slip Dick's watch into the pocket of her mink. Oh, not again, I thought.

As we stepped from the cab I had the impulse to confess: hey, Dick, she's got your watch, and listen, it was just a gag—she thought it might go with Mr. Lee's hat.

But I kept quiet. It would have been too shameful to admit that Judy was serious about copping the watch, even as a gag.

Upstairs, I slipped off my jacket, rolled up my sleeves, and waited. Judy was undressing when the knock came at the door. It was a confused and befuddled Dick.

"Uh, 'scuse me . . . 'deither of you guys see my watch?"

"Your watch?"

"Yeah." He glanced uncomfortably around. "'Tseems to be missing. Lois says she thought Judy might . . ." He left the sentence unfinished.

"Judy . . ." I called from the door. "D'jou see Dick's watch?"

An adorably innocent Judy peeked around the corner of the bedroom door, a towel clutched to her bosom.

"Dick's what?"

"He's lost his watch, Judes. Have we seen it?" A look of extreme concern from Judy, eyebrows furrowed, trying to recall. "Nn, no, I don't think so . . ."

"Well," Dick said, shifting feet, conscious he was intruding on a bedtime scene, "if you happen to run across it . . . I'm at the Hilton." He shut the door morosely.

I turned from the door. "Judy . . ." I said reprimandingly. Judy gave her little girl giggle.

The goddam watch was a Patek Phillipe. The next day I dropped it off at the Hilton desk.

FRIDAY, NOVEMBER 22

My grandfather Leo had voiced a common concern: why doesn't she go to her friends? Surely, among the rich and powerful people she knows there are some who could help.

Sure. There are lots of them. Like Mickey Rooney, for instance. What happened to Mickey and his offer? Judy spurned it, by finessing it. She never called him back. His offer didn't coincide with her plans.

Other people she antagonized, alienated, or betrayed, like her children. She'd behaved so badly to Liza that her own daughter didn't want her in the house.

And some she was simply too proud to ask. It was too painful. It was begging.

At seven this evening I called Harold Arlen in New York and asked him for eleven hundred dollars to pay Judy's hospital bill.

I told him Judy was too ashamed to ask him in person, which was true, and that I was calling without her knowledge, which was not true. Judy was sitting right there beside me, sharing the phone, listening.

"Well," said Harold, that kind and generous man, "you send me the bill, and I'll speak to my man . . . and we'll see what we can do about it."

SATURDAY, NOVEMBER 23

Dearest Judy

You may have your ups and downs but to me you will always be the Queen Of Them All. When you sing I feel as though I have lived and died at the same time. There will never be another like you, Judy. Please make some more appearances and please some more records. I have every record you ever made.

> I will always love you
> Stephen Robbins
> Bronxville
> New York

The letters overflow the liquor cartons and are scattered about the apartment as well. Fan mail. Judy gets it by the ton, enormous amounts, forwarded from CMA. I reproduce a few samples, unedited, with all typos and misspellings intact.

1. Fans and Well-wishers, like Mr. Robbins, sent simple, declaratory notes to Judy describing the effect she's had on their lives. Many of these were handwritten on the inner face of cards from well-known greeting card companies and often contained enclosures. This card, for example, was accompanied by an eight-pack of Life Savers and a Bible.

Wishing you
  A quick recov'ry
To perfect health and then

A hope that you
  Will never need
A get-well wish again!

STAY WELL ALWAYS

Dear Judy Please keep this Bible with you. I think it will
bring you good luck. This is the first time I
    ever wrote to a movie
    star. I know how lone some
    it is in hospitals, and I thought
    you would appreciate a card.

> An Admirer of Yours
> Portia McMahon
> 192 Framingham st.
> Waltham. Mass.

2. Requests. People ask Judy for everything from a photo-
graph, to advice, to an interview.

Dear Judy Garland:

  Would you please send me a picture of yourself. I would
like to receive a one of you very much.
There is one question I would like to ask you how did you
get into show business. What grade do you have to have. I
am in Grade Nine, when I leave school I always said I was
going to be an actress, I am not to bad at singing and I can
dance very good, and have a very good voice.
I am thirteen years old but will be fourteen the last of this
month. Thank you

> June Gabler
> Bonamsta Bay Wesleyville

Judy:

I understand you have an ulcer on your heel. Judy, could
you please tell me what you're doing for it, as my brother
has an ulcer on his instep that refuses to heal, in fact, he's

had it five years now and the doctors can't seem to do a thing for it. What medication have you been using? Any advice would be appesiated. Best regards

Kathy Marks
Shaker Heights
Cleveland

Miss Judy Garland
c/o Mr. Ben Freeman Esq.
83 Milk St.
Boston, Mass.

Dear Judy—

It was so exciting chatting with you on the phone. I called from Boston University School of Public Communication, where I'm in the journalism depertment working with Professor Tim Colodny. (He was formerly a senior editor with *Look* for 21 years). He edits all my material, and with his vast experience, I'm glad to have him "in my corner".

Enclosed is an article on Danny Kaye. I was only with the group for five days and was able to garner enough information, so that I'm almost finished with a second story about him. (Legally, I did not have to show him a copy before publication for I wrote nothing confidential, but, ethically, I felt I wanted him to see and o.k. it before it was printed, which I accomplished).

I should very much like to do a series of articles about you (over)

for either one or more national magazines and also for Associated Press. I shall only publish stories in periodicals of your choice, and, of course, you would have to approve of whatever I write or I shall delete it.

This is how I planned to start, if it is agreeable with you, for it is one of my favorite veracities:

"When a trout rising to a fly gets hooked on a line and finds himself unable to swim about freely, he begins with a fight which results in struggles and splashes and sometimes an escape. Often, of course, the situation is too tough for him.

"In the same way the human being struggles with his environment and with the hooks that catch him. Sometimes he masters his difficulties; sometimes they are too much for him. His struggles are all that the world sees and it naturally misunderstands them. It is hard for a free fish to understand what is happening to a hooked one."

Incidentally, I only write about people I'm interested in; I turned down many offers, for I'm a free-lancer, and the remuneration is not of primary importance to me, so that any arrangement you wish to make will be fine.

I've found you literally impossible to contact, so I'm sending this on to Ben Freeman, since I was recommended to him.

I wish you everything you wish for yourself.

Michelle

P.S. Please save this article on Danny Kaye for me, for I have very few copies, and since I know a number of prestige college presidents because of my affiliation with Women's Scholarship, (I'm a member of a ten-woman executive board)

I'm trying to get him any Doctor of Humanities Honorary degree which he greatly deserves. (Please keep this *confidential* for I don't even want *him* to know, unless it becomes a reality.)

3. Kooks and Wackos (usually religious).

Miss Judy Garland   oct 2—1968
(Personal & Private)

Dear Miss Garland:

Having been so unhappy so long and much trouble in your life, Do you really think this marriage will last and bring you a bright happiness. "I doubt It."

"Life's reflections are as mirrows", and in mine, I see your life, that's also the same identical pattern as mine.

I am more than a creative Realist, I'm a Scorpion with a

talent I haven't yet learned to control. Events seem to happen when I think or visit a particular place.

Yet Miss Garland I have nothing to offer a girl except honesty, consideration, Love, Effection and sincerity.

True I may sound like just another Kook who writes Fan Mail, but I've past that stage and Im on the Verge of breaking through my hardships.

At the moment Im a free lance Designer and Artist. Ive submitted some Drawings to the "Bart" project here and I have and exclusive building concept which I believe will be used throughout the world. These are only minor compared to the much talent still stored up inside me though.

You may have my handwriting analyzed to see if Im truthful or not.

What Ive yet to say will probably surprize you, but it will take place.

> 1. I see you proceeding to evaluate your life and in the process, marrying again.
>
> 2. Your career will take a new direction, and you'll be happy.
>
> 3. The man you marry will be considered short, dark and of Latin Origin.—in early 40.
>
> 4. Your health will improve due to a satisfied feeling, and Life will become easier.
>
> 5. You will add a venture to your style and it will provide you wealth of great volume, it will also reduce the work you now endire.
>
> 6. Many friends who have deserted you, return to gain your confidence—be aware of those that bare gifts.
>
> 7. Your doubts and fears vanish with a common man who speaks from your side.

I am not a fortune teller or an astrologer, as I said, I have a talent I haven't learned to control yet, but at times I find myself knowing whats ahead for others.

Seek the truth in your heart, for now at this time there's truly an answer to everything.

Im asking nothing for this letter, as Ive asked nothing from any one including Governor Reagan. Its my way of providing a service to humanity for being endowed with a gift.

My sincere good fortune to you.

Sincerely Yours
Kerry DiSalvo
1358-Beechnut Drive
San Bernadino Calif
94577

People wrote and invited Judy to collaborate with them on various projects, and business ventures. The following letter was handwritten in turquoise ink.

Vincenzo Buono
Member of National Association
of Securities Dealers, Inc.

Dear Judy—

I saw an item about your being in the hospital—and get the idea of writing to you about a very important matter. I believe this could enable you to make a great comeback in motion pictures—and also make a great deal of money.

The enclosed reports describe my proposition.

(Note: Buono's enclosure was comprised of ten typed, mimeographed sheets describing his literary output over the past thirty years; short stories, TV plays, ideas for screenplays, musicals, children's books, a collection of riddles and brainteasers, volumes of poetry, How To books, sports articles, comic books, cartoon features, an animated cartoon TV series—no area was left unexplored.

Buono felt that his stories, made into movies, could produce revenues comparable to those of *Maytime, Gone with the Wind,* and *Snow White and the Seven Dwarfs,* to name just three titles on a list of sixteen.

The enclosure pages concluded with this incredible paragraph:

"The Author believes that [the works] will compare favorably with the Works of Hemingway, Faulkner, O'Neill, Shaw; Hugo, Dickens, Scott, Tostoy [sic]; Byron, Keats,

Shelley, Browning, Tennyson, Milton;
Darwin, Newman, Ruskin; Hans Christian Andersen, Lewis Carroll,
Grimm Brothers;
Mark Twain;
Edgar Allen Poe;
Homer, Dante, Shakespeare, etc."

Buono's sheets attempted to interest the reader in financing all or any part of the works described, for production or publication. He also offered several of his manuscripts for sale. One of the titles was *From Bum to Billionaire*—price two dollars.)

The letter to Judy continued:

I've sent this to hundreds of people in all walks of life, all of whom have ignored it completely. Not one has asked to look at my material and judge the proposition on its merits.

It seems everyone thinks its a wild fantastic scheme, impossible of accomplishment—or a hoax or a fraud or a new con game! As a former army office, Graduate of West Point and classmate of General Wheeler in Washington. I don't think I could do anything like that.

As you can see, I'm trying to raise $5000 to carry out my Writing-Publishing Project. I'm willing to let the person who supplies this money share in the proceeds of the project up to $500,000.

It's probably not likely that you have the money available for this. So this is my offer to you: If you can find someone to supply the money, he'll make $500,000—and you $250,000—as your Finder's Fee.

I know that I can write as well as (list as above) and even Homer, Dante, and Shakespeare. While that may sound like a broad statement, I can prove it—through the partial writings I've already done—and which are available for anyone to see.

You could this money through me—by doing nothing— just finding a person with $5000 to put into this. Both of you would benefit even more than I've indicated.

You have a chance to benefit even more. Among the Dozens of Major Stories that I have some will fit you nicely

—to play the principal part. I can also write Special Stories just for you—as good as your best in the past—*Wizard of Oz, A Star Is Born,* or any others.

These would be good, wholesome stories, with universal popular appeal. They could make you a Reigning Queen again!

All you have to do is find this Donor. Have him get in touch with me—and I'll show him how all this can come true.

Hope you can do it, Judy—before someone else does.

Here's wishing you a speedy recovery!

Sincerely,
Vincenzo Buono

These letters are typical of the atypical people who wrote to Judy. I don't think Mary Tyler Moore gets the same sort of mail. Judy worked some strange kind of moon-madness on people, they felt a compulsion to reach out, touch, unburden their hearts to her.

I was fascinated by these startling windows into people's lives, and had no compunction about appropriating a clutch of these letters to study. Judy didn't mind. She never read them. But while I waited for Judy to complete one of her three-hour makeup jobs, I could open envelopes and see what colorful people there are in this world.

Today I ran across one, one out of hundreds, that compelled a response. Written in longhand, in ballpoint pen on a school tablet, the letter was addressed to CMA. It came from a grade school teacher in East Ivanhoe, Australia.

Dear Sir or Madam,

I was referred to this address by the letter enclosed. I am a teacher and have a class of 50 preps (pre grade 1 level) between 5 and 6 years old.

About six weeks ago, I told the children the story "Wizard of Oz" and as an activity allowed them to draw any of the characters To my amazement one child got up and suggested that they should send their drawings to Dorothy the girl with the nice singing voice Several of the children then talked about seeing Dorothy at the pictures, and the echo of sending them to her ran through the whole grade, before it registered with me what they meant.

The children tryed very hard, and some very good drawings were produced. I had a little talk with the, explaining that the girl who played Dorothy in the film is now grown up, and has children of her own and is a very busy person, because she is a world famous singer etc, but they were just as determined to send them to her.

Hoping to somewhat dampen their enthusiasm, I mentioned that the postage to America would cost a lot of money. Then a child mentioned his piggy bank, and before long all the children were telling me how they could go without their icy poles and lollies from the tuckshop etc.

I have never met with anything like this in my career as a teacher. I have been hoping and hoping during these six weeks that they would forget about it, but they haven't, so people suggested that I should write to Ed Sullivan etc. This I did, as well as to the "scarecrow" Ray Bolger. He wrote and told me he sent my letter onto a Freddie Fields in Los Angeles.

The children have done without their icy poles etc. and we have collected about eighty cents for the airmail postage. I haven't really approved of this, as some of them come from very poor homes and get about five cents a week to spend.

I was wondering, as the children seem so enthusiastic about this, if I sent their drawings to this address would they be forwarded onto Miss Garland personally and would she look at them.

As the children have saved for the airmail postage costs etc, and gone without their little luxuries, I feel it would be a shame to send them, if she wasn't to receive them personally. I feel to, if they could achieve their little desire it would be an incentive for them to improve in their work. Children at this age are easily upset deterred [sic].

I got really cross with them over it at one stage, but I had to assure them I would try as it affected their work They are not a (word indistinguishable) class, but there are some thing you just can't seem to explain to five and six year old children.

Hoping that I will receive some sort of answer to this letter. It is not very long until the holidays, and, after that, they will be starting the new year in grade 1 I myself, am transferring to another school and will be teaching at higher primary level grade 5 so I hope they won't be bothering the grade 1 teacher.

Thanking you,
Sincerely, (Miss) Methuny Viszler

PS Some of the children from wealthier homes have brought Miss Garland's records to school for show-time They all love her singing

Well, I was practically in tears by the time I finished reading this. I immediately wrote Miss Viszler that Miss Garland would be delighted to receive the children's drawings, that she should send them to 790 Boylston Street and I'd make sure they got to Judy.

It was my mission to make certain those fifty little Australian waifs had not drawn in vain.

SUNDAY, NOVEMBER 24

Today was spent on the phone, getting jobs for Judy. The first call was to England. After much wrangling with London information, we were able to track down an old acquaintance of Judy's, a booking agent named Harold Davidson. Judy told him she wanted to work in Europe.

Through the static of the overseas line, Davidson was sure he could command a top figure for Judy at one of London's leading nightclubs.

"You've got a *big* following over here, Judy," said Davidson, "and we've been too long without you. So if you'll give me a few days . . ."

Glad to, we said, left him our number, and hung up. Judy and I looked at each other triumphantly. We'd taken the law into our own hands. Who needed CMA? We could do it all ourselves.

Onward. I knew the producer of the "Merv Griffin Show," Bob Shanks, and I also knew who to contact at the other talk-variety shows in New York, the "Dick Cavett Show" and the "Tonight Show." I'd run into these guys at the Improvisation and around the business. I didn't even *need* to know them, all I had to do was call and say, "Hey, I can get you Judy Garland." I knew they'd jump at the chance.

These three calls we'd place tomorrow, when the people were in their offices. I turned to Judy, rubbing my hands together.

"Okay. Now. You wanna try something far out?"

"Wh . . . what did you have nn, in *mind?*"

"Let's call Sid and see if he'll let loose on those orchestrations." Judy looked at me with trepidation. "Oh, Johnny . . ."

"C'mon, let's take a stab at it. Maybe we'll just hit him right."

"I'd rather call nn, David *Begelman* and tell him I'm in Nome, Alaska, and to . . . nn, wire me *plane fare* home."

"We'll do that about four this morning," I said, "when he's asleep. But let's call Sid now." So we dialed his number.

They were divorced now, but for eighteen years Sid had been the main man in Judy's life, longer than anyone else. They'd had two children, Lorna and Joey, and Sid had been the producer of *A Star Is Born*.

There was a certain harsh familiarity to the conversation. Sid bitched about Mr. Wong, who was bugging him he said, "—all the way from New York, for chrissake. The bastard wants to attach my money. I can't take a job for over a hundred a week, that little fucker'll attach it."

Sid told Judy she should never have dropped her suit against CMA. "That's the one thing you had goin' for you, Toots." He called her Toots and Pally a lot. Never honey or baby or sweetheart. Toots and Pally. Sometimes Tootsie.

He told her she should not deal with Marelli, that Marelli could not lay his hands on the orchestrations. He had never heard of the Ben Freeman/Marelli deal, the twenty-five thousand plus two percent arrangement. "We never had a deal with them," he said.

Sid complained about having no money and about Wong's harassment. He was in bad shape, he said. He had expenses.

"Hey, how would you like to take the kids for a while, Toots? They're dyina see you."

"H . . . how are they . . . ?"

"They're fine. They get up, eight o'clock they're outta the house, goin' to school. You know. Healthy. No fuckin' around. I'm proud of them, both of them. They're real, normal kids."

"Well . . . that's good."

"They're better off with their father. But listen, Toots, I'm up to my ass in bills, I'm having a rough time of it. I gotta feed these kids, and then there's the house—"

"Sid, what do I have to do to get those . . . nn, orchestrations?"

"Judy, you don't want 'em. You start working and *bam,* the IRS is gonna come down on your tail like a ton of bricks. You know, Group Five paid fourteen thousand dollars for those orchestrations."

"Sid, why do you carry this nn, ven*dett*a against me?"

"No vendetta, I'm just saddled with a half a million bucks in back taxes, that's all. They're on my back and I can't move." Judy rolled her eyes at me. I shrugged.

"What about the furniture?"

"Listen, screw the furniture. I'm not paying any more storage charges. My kids have gotta eat."

It went on that way, an abortive, circuitous, unsatisfying conversation, Sid petulant and complaining, Judy helpless and frustrated.

And me, listening at Judy's ear. At one point Sid asked Judy her address, he was going to send something. Judy turned to me questioningly. What was the Prudential address? I dashed into the bedroom, grabbed a felt-tip pen, came out and wrote "790 Boylston" on the white telephone cradle in large characters. Judy, without her glasses, squinted down and recited the address. A few seconds after this she hung up. She looked at me skeptically. "Well, I nn, *told* you. You wouldn't listen."

"It was worth a try," I said. "You wanna watch *Sunset Boulevard?*" We lay down beside each other in the bedroom and watched Billy Wilder's masterful work, from the opening narration by William Holden's corpse to the final, terrifying, glitter-eyed close-up of Norma Desmond.

Judy saw how enthralled I was by this picture. I made several comments on the economy of the screenplay, the wit of the direction, the aptness of the casting. Judy gave me a bored look.

"You will admit that Gloria Swanson nn . . . over*does* it," she said.

MONDAY, NOVEMBER 25

We saw another movie tonight, *The Boston Strangler*, and something strange happened. A third of the way through the picture, Judy fell asleep. Tony Curtis was doing some extraordinary acting. I shook Judy awake.

"Hey," I said, "this is *good*." Two minutes later I glanced to my left and saw Judy dozing again. It puzzled us afterward.

"Maybe it was that double shot?" I suggested. Judy, girding herself to sit in a theater without liquor for two hours, had downed a giant gulp of vodka to prepare herself.

"Oh no . . . I wasn't the least bit . . . high."

"Just sleepy, hunh?" Curious, I thought. I did not put this together with Judy's reaction to Gloria Swanson.

Judy was not sleepy now, however. Now it was time to play. A couple to our right had been eyeing us furtively all through the film. They'd been noisy, in fact, and I'd asked them politely to keep it down. Now the man approached us. "I hope you'll excuse us," he said, "we didn't mean to disturb you."

"That's all right," I answered curtly.

"But, we did want to ask Miss Gahland . . . I have a restaurant up the street. Would she care to join us for a drink?"

Though Judy was normally wary of strangers and their invitations, she said Yes now and instantly. I guess she was thirsty.

The guy's name was Vinnie Toscano, and his restaurant was the Beef & Ale House. He sat us down at a big round table and ordered drinks. Vinnie had worked as a bartender in Las Vegas when Judy played Caesar's Palace, and there was much verifying of history.

"You wore a red cape with a white fur collah."

"Yeh-heh-ess, that's right . . . I did. A very nn, *tal*ented boy made that cape for me . . . a friend of Lem Ayers." Lemuel

Ayers, a brilliant designer, had done the set decoration on *A Star Is Born.*

"I always wanted to introduce that guy at a banquet," I told Judy, so I could get the chance to say 'Friends, Romans and countrymen—Lemuel Ayers.'"

Vinnie and the rest of the table didn't know what they were laughing at, but Judy's mirth was infectious, and they were happy to see Judy happy. Vinnie asked about Lorna and Joey, and this discussion of the kids led us to the Eternal Verities. Judy said her whole life was her kids. Vinnie said it's not what we are outside, it's what's in our hearts that matters, what we carry inside our hearts.

And Judy said, "And I've been searching a nn, *long* time . . ." She put her hand on my arm. "And, I've finally found someone who, nn, brings me *hap*piness."

Everyone looked at me. I felt I had to say something. "Judy and I are getting married," I said softly.

There was a buzz of surprise, and then congratulations all around the table. "You'll ahll come out to the house on Sunday," Vinnie announced. He ordered another round of drinks for the table, and a woman wearing glasses said What a shame Robert wasn't here.

"Nn, who's *Rob*ert?" Judy inquired.

"Oh, Miss Gahland, he idolizes you," said the woman in glasses. "He's got three scrapbooks of your clippings, and he plays that Cahnegie Hahll album all the time . . . Vinnie, go call Bobby."

Vinnie said it was one-thirty in the morning.

"Oh, Vinnie, he'd never forgive us. Go on, cahll him."

So Vinnie went upstairs and came down with Bobby, all dazed and sleepy, about fourteen years old, cute as could be, shy and quiet and awed. And Judy hugged him and told him what a man he was and made him blush and stammer, and Bobby, wherever you are, wasn't she great? Wasn't she just perfect about the whole thing? She wasn't patronizing, she wasn't abrupt, it wasn't a chore, she genuinely liked the kid, and Judy made a lovely moment of it and told him he'd better go back to bed now so he'd be fresh for tomorrow.

It was time to leave. As she rose from the table, Judy's eye was caught by the revolving clock above the bar. She tried to read what it said. "Buh . . . Budweiser ta . . . tastes . . . oh, I can't see a bloody nn, *thing* . . . I've lost my glasses." She turned to the woman with the spectacles. "Mmmmay I try yours?" The woman obligingly slipped off her frames and handed them to Judy.

"Oh, l-look," Judy said, peering from behind the lenses, "these are nn, *very* close to my prescription . . . may I have these?" she asked the woman. The poor creature looked around helplessly. The idea that someone would ask her for her eyeglasses was too staggering to comprehend.

"They're such an nn, impr*ov*ement," Judy was cooing.

The woman gave a half-resigned, half-cheerful shrug. "Go ahead," she told Judy, "take 'em."

Vinnie was squeezing my hand. "Jahn, if I can do anything fah you, either of you, ever, I want you to give me a ring. You know where I am. And remembah, Sunday you're coming out to the house."

He kissed Judy, and we went through the door. On the street, I suddenly had *déjà vu*. I remembered the Beef & Ale House.

"My God—" I cried to Judy, "I've *been* here. I had a fight with a girl named Betty about whether to eat here or not."

Judy bristled instantly. "Oh yes? Well, let me tell you about the restaurants I went to with Johnny Mercer: there was Scandia, and Chasen's, and several times we went to the Brown Derby." She turned and began walking ahead of me, up the street.

Wow, I thought. The mere mention of another relationship, and this is what happens. Okay, it may not be in the best of taste to talk of former lovers with your fiancée, but, in retaliation, Judy had hit me with the heaviest weapon in her arsenal. Johnny Mercer, the best lyricist in the country.

When Judy went for you, she went for you good.

TUESDAY, NOVEMBER 26

We got back to the Prudential about two-thirty in the morning. The apartment was depressing; in the kitchen, the sink was a mountainous sludge of caked skillets and greasy pots half-filled with water, and in the bedroom, sheets and blankets hung from the bed, and the open cases of clothes and papers spewed their contents to the floor. The cards in our poker deck had baked beans on them.

I surveyed the chaos. Merely freeing the bed for sleeping would require a half-hour's cleanup. It was truly dispiriting. Judy felt it too.

"Johnny . . ." she made a sensuous curve of my name. "Couldn't we go somewhere tonight . . . ? I know a place in, nn, *Cam*bridge . . ."

Go somewhere? My immediate thought was what will it cost us? My BMI bankroll was disappearing faster than I'd planned, what with car rentals and shopping trips to Jordan Marsh. Why spend money on motels when we had a perfectly decent apartment to sleep in? Tomorrow I'd call Miss Mary's Maids and we'd put the place in order. I could make the bed for tonight.

"There's, nn, *such* a lovely motel across the river, Johnny . . . with a marvelous view of the Charles . . . couldn't we go?" I looked at Judy, standing with her toes turned in, her hands clasped in front of her, being winning as hell. Well, I thought, we could use a change. It was time once more for that infusion of freshness which a new locale seemed to give us. We'd been in Boston a week, I remembered fleetingly.

I picked up the phone, located Judy's motel—the Fenway Cambridge. Yes, said the night manager, he could give us a room with a view of the Charles. Great. From Judy's hatbox we fashioned an overnight case, tossing in a nightgown, and some toilet articles. In her red makeup case we put three essential items: Judy's makeup, her jar of cranberry cocktail, and the ever-popular fifth of vodka. We were ready.

Downstairs, into a cab, and across the bridge. Judy sat inconspicuously on the couch in the Fenway lobby as I signed the register. "Mr. and Mrs. John Meyer," I wrote, thinking Wow, and all the way up in the elevator I was thinking Wow, until, opening the door to Room 612, thinking Wow hit me so hard I had to scoop Judy up in my arms, like the new bride she had instantly become, and carry her over the threshold.

I stopped by the bed. Without putting her down, I kissed her.

"Well, Mrs. Meyer," I said, "how does it feel to be married to the junior senator from Wisconsin?" But something in the way Judy was clinging to me stopped my kidding, and I thought, Yes, this is the real beginning of our honeymoon, a thrilling honeymoon that can last as long as we let it, as long as we work at it and care for it, we can keep this, I know we can.

Judy went to the window and looked out. She dropped her arm in a gesture of disgust. "What is it, baby?" I said. Judy shook her head.

"You can't see the river from here. You can't see a fucking thing." I joined her by the window. It was true. Below us was a view of three industrial buildings, factories, belching smoke from their stacks into the November night. If you pressed yourself into a corner and looked out obliquely, you could catch a tiny strip of the Charles, like a quarter inch.

Judy's lip was turning down like the tearful Margaret O'Brien. "Th . . . they said we'd have a nn, view of the *river* . . ."

"They sure as hell did." I sat on the bed, lifted the receiver, and waited a minute and a half. "Desk."

"Yes, this is Mr. Meyer in Room six-twelve. When I called earlier, you promised me a room with a river view. This room we're in has a view of the Krupp munitions factory. Now I wonder if you'd put us in the room we ordered."

"Wail, Mistah Meyah, that room is the best view we have of the rivah."

"You've gotta be kidding. You told me on the phone you had a room with a river view."

"I'm very sorry Mistah Meyah—"

"You mean to tell me that a hotel with seven hundred rooms doesn't have *one* that faces the river?"

"I'm very sorry Mistah Meyah."

I hung up. "They don't have anything." Judy was frowning. "Maybe this isn't the place . . ." she hazarded. "I think maybe it's the nn, *next* one up the road . . ."

My heart sank. "You want to leave?" Judy smiled at me, tentatively. "Would it be nn, all *right* . . . ? Do you think we could get our . . . money back?"

The warmth and softness in her face pushed against my iner-

tia. I grabbed the phone again. I counted twenty-two rings before the same Walter Brennan voice said, "Desk."

"This is in*tol*erable!" I barked. "Gross misrepresentation. I
should report you to the Better Business Bureau. On the phone
you distinctly promised me a room with a river view, and
now—"

"Mistah Meyah," said the helpless victim downstairs, "if your
accommodations are not satisfactory, we'll be happy to refund
your money."

"Good. We'll be down in ten minutes. Kindly call us a taxi."

I put the vodka back in the makeup case, and we rang for the
elevator. Stopping by the desk, I allowed the clerk to return my
check. He was too unnerved to recognize Judy.

"You may not know it," I told him, "but this is Miss Judy Garland, and she has been most displeased by her experience here.
We are definitely *not* recommending this hotel to our friends."

And we swept grandly out the door to our waiting cab. Except there *was* no waiting cab. It kind of ruined our exit.

We stood in the driveway, shifting from foot to foot, our
momentum broken. Though it was freezing cold, neither of us
would compromise the grandiloquence of our outraged departure by going back inside.

"You didn't tell him I was your wife," Judy said.

"What?"

"You should have told him we were married. It looks so bad."

"Oh, honey . . . I . . . I was so busy telling him off, I guess
the moment just didn't present itself."

"Well, I wish you had."

"I'm sorry, sweetheart . . ." The uncomfortable pause length-
ened into an uncomfortable silence. Judy was right, I hadn't
mentioned our marriage . . . and not merely because there
wasn't one. That didn't matter. I would gladly have lied, the
way I lied to druggists about Ritalin prescriptions, or to car
rental girls about movie companies. Lies were simply tools in the
game, an expedient. I accepted the idea of lying perfectly
readily, too readily, I guess, for just now I had lied to Judy. I
hadn't mentioned the marriage because I hadn't wanted to. And
at that moment I realized I was having second thoughts about
marrying Judy. Maybe it wasn't such a good idea.

And not ten minutes ago it had been wow-threshold-honeymoon-forever. I kicked the curb angrily.

"Where the fuck is our cab?"

Cruising down Memorial Drive I saw dawn creep over Boston, bringing the city into silhouette against the brightening sky. I opened the cab window and let the cool air caress my face, trying to sort out my feelings, trying to push back the intensity of everything, the pummeling intensity that threatened to implode my brain.

I concentrated on Judy's hand, warm in my own, and, gradually, I began to relax, to descend from my anxiety (these feelings were disturbing) till once again I could find the point where magically, blindly, Judy became the only woman I could ever love like this, the only woman on earth, the only woman ever born . . . and if she wanted to check into every motel in Massachusetts, it was okay with me.

Again I hoisted Judy across the threshold. In my mind, I saw myself carrying Judy over an endless procession of motel thresholds, sinking finally to my knees with Judy in my arms, singing.

"Oh yes," said Judy, once inside. "This is the place I meant." This room, in the Charter House Motel, did have a river view. It was behind the headboard of the bed. Now, if you drew back the curtain, you could get the blinding reflection of the six A.M. sunlight, right in your eye.

Judy came out of the bathroom with a water glass. "Is there . . . any ice?"

I was feeling a little drained. "Tell you what, Judy . . ." I said, "why don't you go out and see if there's an ice machine at the end of the hall?" I was flopped on the bed; even to talk was an effort.

Judy left the room, and I must have dozed for half an hour, because it was past seven o'clock when she returned, in consternation.

"Where were you?" I asked, sleepily.

"They don't h-have any ice on th-this floor . . ." Judy stuttered. "I had to go down to the nn, *eighth* floor . . . the other end of the hall . . . and I got nn, *lost* . . . and the fucking nn, *ele*vator wouldn't come."

Again we're in the midst of a crisis. Time for the jollies. I sum-
moned a fresh wave of energy. "Hey, let's do a bit: I'm the
crusading editor, and I'm exposing the corrupt political boss, Ed
Begley, right? It's the water supply, the kids' teeth are rotting,
and Begley is putting pressure on me to stop the exposé, and
you're my loyal wife, and you want me to back off 'cause I'm
gonna get hurt."

Judy looked puzzled. "I don't know this picture."

"Oh, sure you do—he's always . . . Hyenry Fahndah, and
she's always, uh . . ." I couldn't think who she always was.

"Jane Wyatt," Judy said.

"Right. Or Jane Wyman."

"Or Jane Greer. One of the Janes boys."

"Yeah, and she's always saying 'You know how Whittaker
works—do you want Tommy growing up without a father?'"

"Okay. You know how Whittaker works. Do you want Tommy
growing up without a father?"

We looked at each other. The wind seemed to have gone out
of our improvisation; it was limp, a fizzle. I'd killed it by
describing it too fully. But it had served its purpose.

I fell back on the pillow, slightly stupefied. The next time I
looked at my watch it was nine-twenty, and Judy was coming
out of the bathroom. She'd been in there bandaging her heel for
two hours. Through the mist of my drowsiness I reached out for
her, and she fell on her knees, her chest against the side of the
mattress. She seemed a little dazed.

I didn't know it then, but she was. She'd swallowed one of Dr.
Klinger's new sleeping pills, and it had taken immediate effect.
With my right hand, I seized Judy's left arm, trying to pull her
up next to me, but, in my torpor, I yanked at the wrong angle,
and inadvertently flipped Judy off the bed. As she fell to the
floor, Judy struck her head sharply on the edge of a marble
coffee table.

Her wailing scream of pain jarred me into quivering wake-
fulness. Oh, Jesus! I scrambled to her side. Judy was clutching
the back of her head and moaning.

"Judy . . . Judy . . ." I began rubbing her head, trying to
soothe the pain of the bruise, but something was wrong—it

wasn't a bruise. My hand came away warm, sticky with the dark blood that was seeping from Judy's lacerated scalp. Oh my God.

I stumbled to the bathroom, brought back a damp washcloth. Judy's short, gray-flecked hair was matting now, thickened with blood. Her moans were low, constant, and filled with pain. "Oh . . . oh . . ." she kept saying.

I had to get a doctor.

"Desk."

"This is Mr. Meyer in nine-fifteen. Is there a hotel doctor?"

"No, Mr. Meyer, but there's one at the medical center. Shall I ring him for you?"

"Please." I was connected to a doctor I'll call Brecher. He told me he could be over soon.

"What's soon?"

"Oh . . . I should say within . . . forty-five minutes."

"Doctor, this is an emergency. It's a serious laceration." I knew if I used the word 'laceration' he'd hurry. He gave me interim instructions: I was to keep her quiet with her head up.

Judy was still on the floor, moaning. I put my arms carefully under her thighs and around her back and lifted her to the bed. I put the two pillows beneath her head for elevation and yanked the covers down with three swift jerks. I pulled the blankets over Judy up to her neck.

Then I took a close look at her. Judy was semiconscious, whether from her pill or the injury I could not tell. She was moving her head from side to side in a jerky, convulsive way. The moans were still coming, but fainter now, and her breathing was shallow and—what was that medical term?—stertorous. Christ, what if she had a concussion? I pictured the headlines:

JUDY AND TUNESMITH IN MOTEL TRAGEDY

That was *Variety*. The *Times* didn't even mention me—

JUDY GARLAND ON CRITICAL LIST

Gingerly, I lay down beside Judy, careful not to jostle her. God, I was tired. Was it worth my while, I wondered, to nap for forty minutes? Suppose she fell out of bed or something? I felt guilty contemplating sleep with Judy dying beside me. I put my head on the mattress. It was uncomfortable without a pillow. Slowly, with a steady force, I pulled the corner of Judy's lower pillow out about six inches. I put my cheek down and slept till the doctor knocked on the door.

He was a real schmuck, this Dr. Brecher. He *hnn*ed and *hmm*ed over Judy for a while, and then announced he was going to *tape* her scalp together. Now, I'm not a doctor, but it seemed to me a two-inch gash in the scalp should be either stitched or clamped. Nonetheless, I did what Brecher told me to do: I lifted Judy from her bloody pillow, carried her into the bathroom, and sat her on the toilet seat, next to the sink.

Brecher began cutting hair away from the wound with a small scissors. He snipped tentatively at her head in a flabby, fearful manner. Maybe he was intimidated by his patient's renown. Maybe he saw his own headlines:

BRECHER SAVES STAR

Whatever the reason, I was thrown into an impotent rage, furious at what I considered Brecher's incompetence, yet powerless to do anything about it.

Judy was whimpering in pain, like a pitiful puppy. "It's all right, baby, I'm here," I said, squeezing Judy's hand. It didn't seem to help. Judy was crying louder now, in what seemed a dreadful agony.

Brecher's large, domelike head was bent ineffectively over Judy. He made a vague pass at her scalp with the scissors, nearly creating a new laceration. I lost my patience.

"Gimme that, willya?"

I grabbed the scissors and, as carefully as I could, began cutting Judy's hair. Her scalp appeared, a dead, fishy white. I wondered if I was going to vomit. I looked at Brecher. I wondered if he was going to vomit.

It took about half an hour. When Brecher's ministrations were complete, Judy was wearing a little white adhesive yarmulke. The doctor was washing his hands. Now, after it's over, the doctor is washing his hands.

"Uh . . . would you like to take care of my fee now, or shall I bill you?" he said to me.

Resentfully, I wrote him a check. "Now what about Ritalin, Doctor? Judy uses a mild stimulant—"

Brecher lowered his voice. "Positively no Ritalin, no stimulants, or drugs of any kind. And . . ." he glanced at Judy, lying on the bed, "it would be advisable not to let her take any liquor. We're dealing with a head injury here."

Very good, Doctor, I thought. You may take two giant steps.

"Now I've given her half a grain of sedative, and, in four hours, if she requires it, she may have another half grain. That is all she is to have. No other medication. Just keep her quiet and restful, and if you need me, call me."

"Thank you, Doctor."

An hour later, Judy was pleading for Ritalin. "Oh, Johnny . . . please . . . I'm in such pain . . ."

We have seen how hard it was for me to deny Judy anything. And now, in extremis, with her need so intense, it was almost impossible. Yet I could not give her Ritalin, the doctor had specifically warned against it.

"Try and make it through another hour, baby . . . just another hour."

"Johnny . . . please . . . I don't have the strength to stand the pain . . ." My mind saw Judy hemorrhaging, blood pouring from her ears and nostrils, because I'd given her Ritalin, forbidden Ritalin.

"Johnny . . . *please* . . ." Judy's voice was piteous.

"I don't think there *is* any, Judy . . ." I knew damn well there was.

"In my purse . . . the little heart box . . ."

The box Judy meant was her brass pillbox, shaped like a heart. People keep saccharine or vitamins in these. Judy used it for Ritalin and Seconal. I took her purse into the bathroom and opened the pillbox. Inside were three of the tablets, lying there innocently. Hard to believe these tiny spheres could kill you, could mix jaggedly with the sedative you'd swallowed, could set up an internal conflict and spill their battle out through your orifices, through your nose and ears . . . taking your blood, your life, with them.

Quietly, one by one, I inserted the tablets into the space between the sink stopper and the drain, not turning on the tap (the noise would give me away) but pushing them down with my finger.

I brought the empty pillbox back to Judy, closed. It was an effort for her to open the top. "Th . . . they're gone . . ." She stared blankly into the little box. "I know I had some in here . . ."

"I can't find any, Judy."

"Let me see my p-purse . . ."

I brought it to her, and Judy picked through her lipsticks, her steel comb, her crushed Kleenex, the tobacco shreds at the bottom. There wasn't any Ritalin.

She looked up at me disbelievingly. "Johnny . . . you wouldn't . . . lie to me . . . ?" The tail of her sentence curled upward, hopefully, hopelessly. Would she be glad if I were lying to her, or sad?

Two hours later Judy searched her purse again and found a solitary tablet tucked into the folds. Before I could stop her, she'd swallowed it. I waited tensely for the blood to spurt from Judy's ears and nostrils, but, to my growing amazement, Judy began to smile and talk with great animation. It must have been the emotional high Judy got from finally finding the pill, but there did seem to be an improvement.

I was glad she was better, certainly, but, as Judy talked, I found I could not keep my eyelids from drooping. Now that I knew she was out of danger I allowed myself to succumb to sleep.

I wasn't about to go through this alone.

"Vinnie? This is John Meyer. From last night, remember? Listen, Judy's had a slight accident, and I wonder if you could put her up at your place for a day or two . . ."

"An accident?"

"Yeah, she banged her head. It isn't really serious, but she oughta have someone to look after her a coupla days, and I thought maybe you could help out on this . . . ?"

"Well, Jahn, certainly I'd like to, but some of the folks ah coming out fa Thanksgiving . . . just a minute . . ."

Hand over the mouthpiece. Muffled exchange. You have to expect this, I thought, when you say things like If there's ever anything I can do for you . . .

"Jahn?"

"Yeah?"

"Maybe I can get one of the girls. Ah'll ask. You know, with Thanksgiving and all most everyone has plans . . . can I cahll you back?"

"Take my number. I'm at the Charter House."

Vinnie did get one of the girls. Mahgret, a waitress at the Beef & Ale House, came by at two-thirty this afternoon. I liked her the minute I opened the door. In her forties, with dark hair beginning to streak gray, a flat Irish face and a nothing-can-faze-me look, Mahgret was just what the doctor ordered.

We had to dress Judy and get her downstairs to Mahgret's car, a job that took us a good forty minutes. Judy, befuddled again and barely cogent (the Ritalin had worn off) insisted on sitting before the mirror. "I . . . l-look . . . *ter*rible . . ." she said.

"Well, Judes, I tell you what; I'll go downstairs and chase away the wire services, okay?" I was ashamed of myself for being sarcastic with Judy, but we had to get this show on the road. Still, Judy was concerned about her appearance.

"I . . . can't go outside . . . this way . . ."

I put her black floppy hat on her head to hide the ugly white patch of adhesive, and walked Judy out of the motel room. At the door, she hung back. "What's that bag?"

"We had bread and cheese in it, Judy, leave it." I set the makeup case and hatbox outside the door and rang for the elevator. I went back to fetch Judy, and, supporting her on my arm, coaxed her into the hall.

We were ten feet from the elevator, when it opened. I propped Judy against the wall and ran to get the makeup case and hatbox, which I threw onto the floor of the car. As the doors began to close, I stuck my hand inside and pressed the DOOR OPEN button, then dashed out to grab Judy and shove her into the car before the doors shut.

Judy was heading back toward the room. "Why should we leave that bread and cheese?" she said. Jesus fucking Christ, I thought. I grabbed the bag of bread and cheese. It was easier to bring it than to argue about it. I turned, and saw the elevator doors close on our luggage.

I don't believe this, I said to myself. I'm in a Jerry Lewis movie. The car had taken the hatbox and makeup case to the twelfth floor. I punched the bell, in irritation. The second car arrived, empty. I pulled Judy inside and delivered her to Mahgret in the lobby. Mahgret took Judy out to her car as I waited by the button, pressing furiously, trying to lure the first elevator down with our luggage.

Mahgret lived in the suburb of Ashmont, up two flights. I had to carry Judy up the stairs, she was too weak to walk.

On the stairs, Mahgret kept apologizing for her apartment. "It's noothing fancy now," she kept saying. She was afraid it wouldn't be ritzy enough for the movie star.

It was a pleasant, sunny apartment with many pictures of Ireland. "It's not mootch, but it's home," Mahgret said. "Now what can I get you to drink?"

"Oh no, Mahgret, we're fine," I said. Fervently, I prayed Judy would not make an issue of the drink. I had a vision of Mahgret watching us battle over the vodka bottle. Brecher had said no liquor.

"Would you like to hear some of Miss Garland's records, then?" Oh, perfect, I thought; Mahgret's a fan. She dragged an ancient Webcor phonograph out of a closet, and, after some tinkering, it functioned well enough to put on the *Carnegie Hall* album.

"I've always been sootch an admirer of yours, Miss Garland."

"Why don't you call me Judy?" Judy said. She was beginning to perk up. She sat on the floor and motioned us to do the same, opening her tiny change purse. "Mmm, let's play poker," she said.

I watched Judy critically as she dealt the cards. There didn't seem to be any ill effects from the Ritalin Judy had taken five hours ago. I had to concede that Judy knew herself best. And speaking of Ritalin, I thought, I'd better go out and get some; knowing Judy, she'd be yelling for it soon.

I left the two women playing five-card draw and went out to

the neighborhood drugstore, but, despite my fanciest verbal footwork, I was unable to get any Ritalin. Okay, never mind, I thought. I'll go home for some after dinner.

While I was out, Mahgret's friend Bill arrived and broke out the booze. Judy was having one now, a stiff vodka and cranberry juice, which she took with her into the bathroom. She was going to change and make up while Mahgret cooked dinner.

Ninety minutes later Judy emerged from the bathroom looking cheerful and lovely. She'd replaced her bloodstained blouse with one of Mahgret's sweaters and was in the mood to hear the *Carnegie Hall* album again.

As "Do It Again" began to play, Judy grinned and repeated the story of Kay Thompson's farting dog. Mahgret, putting a roast chicken on the table, nearly dropped the platter as she shook with laughter. The atmosphere became positively convivial.

Judy was talking of the early days at M-G-M; she talked about her mother ("She was the original . . . Wicked *Witch* . . .") and about writer/director Joe Mankiewicz, with whom she'd had a love affair. "Joe would use his pipe as a nn . . . *prop* . . ." Judy told us. "And . . . I remember, he . . . *hated* Tyrone Power . . . well, all the nn, *writers* did, because Ty was so wonderfully, nn . . . at*trac*tive . . . they used to sit around and . . . malign him . . ."

As I could have predicted, Judy didn't touch her food. Chicken and baked potatoes had been cooked for her, but strangers were present, and Judy preferred to tell stories. Sitting in Mahgret's kitchen, it struck me that Judy thrived on adversity, almost fed on it, in a way. It gave her something to rise from. Going from fifty to one hundred did nothing for her, but going from minus a thousand to plus ten pleased her. Then she still had the remaining ninety to conquer, and she could be the gallant, struggling waif. It was hard to play the waif's role when you were a success, and that was the role Judy was comfortable with, I realized. I remembered how Judy had behaved at Clarke's after her triumph at Lincoln Center, refusing to accept the idea that she'd given herself a boost. She was much happier now, as the injured chick in an obscure Boston suburb, wearing a sweater she'd borrowed from a waitress.

"I was performing in . . . Houston, and the nn . . . *Supremes* . . . were working in the same . . . block . . . and, one after-noon about . . . five o'clock, the phone rang in the hotel room, and they asked the nn, *gentle*man who was with me . . . might they come up and . . . meet me? And he explained no, he was sorry, but Miss Garland was . . . taking a nap . . . and . . . Diana Ross said, 'Well, can we just come up and watch her *sleep?*'"

Across the table, Judy's image began to blur. I suddenly felt so exhausted I thought I was going to slide off my chair to the floor. I was moving doggedly through the weight of my fatigue by a sheer effort of will.

Driving back to the city with Bill after dinner, the idea of an undisturbed night's sleep became irresistible. We were going to the Prudential to pick up some Ritalin, supposedly making the round trip back to Ashmont.

But Judy had been given a Seconal and was dropping off to sleep even as we'd gone down the stairs. What if I sent Bill back with the Ritalin and sacked out at the apartment? I could get a solid eight or ten hours' sleep and be more useful in the morn-ing. With luck, Judy would never miss me.

"Here," I said to Bill, handing him a vial of Ritalin, "don't let her take more than two of these every four hours. I'll be here, Mahgret has the number, but please don't ring me unless it's ab-solutely necessary. I'll call in the morning."

And I let Bill drive away.

THURSDAY, NOVEMBER 28

With a shudder of relief, I slipped between the sheets. Tired though I was, I couldn't resist reading a letter from Jenny I found on the floor by the bed. In the letter, Jenny assured Judy of her lasting love and affection and even included a poem she'd composed.

What was it, I wondered, that made people react this way, men, women, animals? People put themselves through the most outlandish contortions, they left jobs, broke friendships, deserted families for this woman. I mean come on, she's only a woman, isn't she, for all her originality? Pondering this, I fell asleep.

The buzz of the house phone woke me at three forty-five. "Miss Gahland wants you to call her."

Oh Christ, I thought as I dialed, here we go. The shit hits the fan. Mahgret picked up the phone. "Well, John," she said (oh, the poor woman, having to deal with Judy's tantrums in the middle of the night), "she got oop and she was hoongry, you know? So we heated oop the chicken, and she ate it, and she had a drink, and she wanted to know where you were. She wanted her pills, and I tried to keep them from her, like you said, but she said 'Don't tell me how to take pills, I been takin' pills since I was a kid.' She took four of 'em."

Terrific, I thought.

"She picked oop everythin' and put it in her bag," Mahgret went on. "She picked oop all the poker change. Wait a minute, here she is."

I could hear Judy asking Mahgret to close the door. "I don't want you people to hear this," she said, and then she came on the line. "Johnny . . . are you going to come and get me and nn . . . let these nice people go to bed . . . ?"

"Judy, please," I said, "be an angel and stay there just for to-night, please? Tomorrow I'll be over to get you."

Judy's voice turned hard. "All right, never mind. I'll take a cab."

She didn't take a cab, of course. She got Mahgret and Bill to drive her. On the way in she complained about the Jews, prompted by my "callous attitude." The Jews were lousy. They had all her money, Sid and Group Five. The Jews had always screwed her.

As I let her into the apartment she looked at me with injured scorn. "You like this hotel? Everything up to snuff? How 'bout something from room service?"

"Judy, you gotta understand—I am so tired I can hardly *see*." Judy gave me a withering look.

"I should have . . . exp*e*cted it. You walked out like they all do . . . when the going gets rough." She took a step toward me, and the move was oddly menacing. "Well, if you want to walk out, then *walk out,*" she spat at me. "Just fucking well pack up and get out, buster. I'm not running a hotel here."

Was she acting? Did she really view my spending a night without her as a betrayal? I tried to read the truth in Judy's flashing, hostile eyes. Her anger seemed frighteningly genuine. "Judy—" I started.

"You can just fucking well get out," she repeated, cutting me short. I breathed a deep, inward sigh. In a way it would almost be a relief. To lose the pressures, the anxieties, the uncertainties. She was telling me to go, and, if I did, that would be the end of it.

Okay, I thought, I'll go. If I hadn't been so debilitated I'd have packed and left right then. It was physically beyond me. I crawled back into bed and closed my eyes.

I slept uneasily till nine-thirty in the morning, and when I awoke it was Thanksgiving Day. Okay, I thought, thanks.

Judy had spent the remainder of the night on the "heavy furniture" couch in the living room. As I poured myself some juice in the kitchen, she moved silently about the apartment, toying with the poker deck, pretending to dust the ice-cream table. Not a word. Aloof. Distant. Finally I went to her.

"Are you still mad? You wanna give me a hug and talk about this?" Judy gazed at me coldly. "There isn't much . . . *point,* is there?"

So that was how it was going to be. Okay. It took me about twenty-five minutes to pack my bag. Judy watched me from her position on the couch. If our eyes met she looked away. I could barely believe she wasn't going to *talk* to me, that she would let me pack and leave and end our relationship like this, half bang, half whimper, totally inconclusive, arbitrary, recriminatory, bitter, and senseless. Was it really going to end like this?

I was looking for a pair of shoes. "In the bedroom," Judy murmured, without looking at me.

"You know," I said, "this doesn't make much sense."

Judy gave no sign of having heard me. She was looking out the window, at Lord & Taylor's rooftop. Well, okay. I was all packed and ready. I took my bag to the door and stood there, wearing my bewilderment like a shawl about my shoulders. All I had to do was turn the knob and leave. But I had this rotten unfinished feeling, this sensation of incompleteness was hanging in the air. I stared at Judy. Her head was averted, she wasn't going to say anything. I walked halfway back into the room.

"I just want you to know," I said, "that this has been the most profound experience of my life."

Judy did not respond. I stood there, like a jerk, waiting for her to say something, to resolve the incompleteness. Nothing. Not a word. I ran my hand through my hair.

"This is so anticlimactic," I said, "that it is almost unreal." Judy was a statue, posed by the window, eyes out. I walked to the door, picked up my bag, opened the door, and placed it outside. I turned to face Judy from the doorway.

"Well . . . good-bye."

Judy did not stir. I shut the door, carried my bag down the hall, and pressed the button for the elevator. I stood there for perhaps ten seconds, waiting for the car to arrive. Then I heard Judy's voice call to me from inside the apartment.

"Make sure you have a happy Thanksgiving!" she yelled. "Eat all your turkey, and don't forget the giblets!" She opened the door and slammed it shut with such violent force that I heard the fire extinguisher rattle in the incinerator closet. One vicious slam, with a crash of such volume that, were this a movie, all the neighbors heads would've popped out. Since this was real life nothing happened.

"And don't worry about me," Judy shouted from inside the apartment, "I'll get along just fine, buster, so don't worry about me, okay?"

The elevator arrived, and I stepped inside. I was in the Hotel Lenox, next door, calling Eastern Airlines, when I discovered I'd left my checkbook in the apartment. I had barely three dollars' cash in my pocket. I would have to go back.

I started to laugh. The people in the Lenox lobby stared at me curiously. It was too dumb, honestly; I'd made my final, dramatic exit. The Most Profound Experience of My Life, I'd told her. The door had slammed irrevocably behind me with the deafening ring of finality. And now I had to go back. Uh, listen, I forgot something.

Really dumb.

FRIDAY, NOVEMBER 29

The Carey bus from Kennedy Airport to Manhattan takes you through the most dispirited parts of Queens, the most disheartening streets of Astoria. Yet, at eight-forty this morning, watching the workers scurrying into the subway or opening up their bodegas, I caught myself envying them.

Yes, their heads were down, yes, they were urban cattle, squinting bleakly into another day of quiet desperation, driven by necessity toward their nine A.M. time clocks. I, on the other hand, had just descended from the most Olympian experience—a tempestuous love affair with a glamorous movie star.

But these rushing people, programmed and routined as they might be, were not walking around with an ice pick stuck in their heart.

It was over now, this Olympian affair, blown to pieces in a scene of painful recrimination, the partners blasted hundreds of miles from each other, the relationship in shards, irretrievably shattered.

That stupid bitch, that *stupid bitch,* I told myself. She ought to know by now what she demands of people. She ought to know they need a safety valve, sometimes, like a night alone to catch up on missed sleep, for instance. Oh, that stupid bitch. Well, she could find someone else to make the phone calls, to keep her laughing, to give her a jump in a hospital bed, let her try. She'd see. She can go fuck herself, I thought. *Look* at me, after doing *all that,* here I am out on my ass and back where I started with no career, no woman, and no hope.

Never mind. I tightened my lips in a wry, Bogart smile. I would get on with my life. I would forget Judy.

My mother sprouted tears of relief when she saw me come through the door. She embraced me so hard my bones cracked. I told her she didn't have to worry anymore, it was over, ended, never mind the details, we'd said good-bye, and I'm going to bed. I'd been up all night, huddled in the airport waiting room.

As I hit the pillow, I resolved to get back on a sensible schedule and to pursue a production of *The Draft Dodger* with renewed vigor.

The next thing I knew, it was five-thirty in the afternoon, and my mother was shaking me awake. "It's Judy," she said.

I got to the phone. "Judy?"

"Wh . . . where are you?"

"Well, where are you calling me? I'm in New York."

"Johnny . . . wh . . . why did you leave me?"

"I didn't leave you, Judy. You kicked me out."

"N . . . no, I didn't."

"Yes, you *did*, Judy." There was a pause.

"I didn't nn, *mean* to . . ." I sighed a long sigh. As hostile as I felt toward Judy now, I still could not be angry with her, and this made me disgusted with myself.

"Johnny . . . you deserted me . . . you left me . . ." I looked at the telephone cradle, trying to summon the strength to tell her to go fuck herself, which was what she ought to be told. I'd seen her manipulate people, pretend not to be able to read signs and stuff like that, and she damn well wasn't going to do it to me.

She was being kittenish on the phone now, tender and cajoling. I had to come back. She needed me. She couldn't get by without me. I told her I'd have to think about it. Maybe in a few days. I certainly couldn't come back now.

"What do you mean, you can't?"

"Just what I said, Judes, I can't."

"Why not? Why can't you?" Her voice held a cutting edge now. "Why *can't* you?" she repeated. She became abusive. I was a rotten bastard who didn't care about her. I was only using her to get my songs around. I was worse than Sid ever was.

Finally I hung up on her. She called back instantly with more of the same. Again I hung up. Again she called back.

"Priscilla," I said to my sister, "the next time she calls tell her I'm out."

Judy wouldn't accept this. "I know he's there, you bitch, now let me speak to him."

We let the phone ring forty-eight times. Judy literally chased us out of the house. Eventually, we went to the movies to see *Yellow Submarine*.

As I sat in the darkened theater, my foot up on the back of

the next row of seats, I felt I had escaped. It felt good to be free of that barely perceptible feeling of anxiety that, like the hum of a basement generator, had been with me since I met Judy.

SATURDAY, NOVEMBER 30

Priscilla and I got back home at twelve-thirty. There were three messages: Annie and Jenny had both called, and Marvin. Marvin's message was "The Legend is hysterical." Judy had phoned Marvin and told him I'd deserted and abandoned her and that he had to get me to come back. She'd said the same thing to Annie and Jenny. So they'd all been bombarding Marjorie with calls, looking for me. The messages were all the same: tell him to call me as soon as he comes in.

I called Annie first. Poor Annie, not yet twenty, had no idea how to handle the frothing Judy. She wanted to know was I coming back? What should she do? I called Jenny, who was wiser in Judy's ways, and told her to keep an eye on things and to calm Annie down. Then I called Marvin and told him to keep me informed.

By five A.M. Judy had lost control. From Annie, who had gone to the Prudential, I learned that the Legend had worked herself into a state of hysteria and had thrown a tantrum, beating her head repeatedly and violently against the wall; so violently, in fact, that her downstairs neighbor, Mr. Wayne, called the police. The police called doctors, and, by eight the next morning, Judy had been committed to Peter Bent Brigham Hospital.

It was late afternoon, and I had to decide: stay or go back. I talked with Larry. There was action on *The Draft Dodger*. An agent in Los Angeles wanted me to meet Norman Panama, a Hollywood director. There might be a film deal brewing and it would be a good idea for me to fly out.

"Jesus, Larry, I don't know if I can. Judy's in the hospital."

"John, haven't you proved to yourself that you can't help her? That woman is *murder,* and she's turning you into a wreck along with her. When was the last time you did any writing? When was the last time you could even re*lax?*"

"I know, Larry."

"And you wanna throw yourself *back* into the meat grinder? You must be outta your skull."

Yes, yes, everything Larry said was true. On top of that, the woman kicked me out. She kicked me out, *me*, the guy who loved her. And now she expected me to come running back the minute she beckoned. Had I lost my pride as well as my reason?

It was ten in the evening. "Peter Bent Brigham."

"Room one thirty-one, please."

"One moment, please." Click. "A *Main*, Mrs. Ford—" Then, for a tantalizing instant I heard Judy's voice: "Johnny . . . ?" Click/transfer—extension one thirty-one/we were disconn— bzzz . . . bzzzz . . . click.

"Judy?" bzzz . . . bzzzz . . .

"Johnny . . . ? Hello . . . hello . . ."

"Judy? You there?"

"Oh, *John*ny . . ."

"We're going through a lot of intrigue here, with the switchboard."

"I know . . ."

"Are you okay . . . ?" Pause. Then that sexy, voluptuous voice, Judy's voice, said, "I love you . . ." and the feeling flooded through me, a blend of joy, fear, and excitement. I couldn't help it. Deep in my heart I *knew* this was another manipulation, that Judy had engineered the whole episode, kicked me out and then placed herself in a position of such extremity that I'd *have* to come back to her, have to forgive her.

And I sensed that, if I did return to Judy, it would be on another level, the ante would be raised, the stakes would be higher, because now I saw there was no length to which Judy would not go, no barrier she wouldn't crash to enact the drama she knew her life had to be. And this very recklessness, to me, was irresistible. I had never encountered such daring; it fascinated and enticed me.

At the same time, in the rational part of my mind, I resented being manipulated. And I determined to fight it.

"I love you," I heard myself say (some fighter you are, schmuck).

"Oh, please do . . ." Judy whispered. "Please love me . . . please want to be with me . . ."

"Yes, baby . . ." (Don't be this easy, you must make her pay to get you back.)

"Are you going to come and get me, Johnny . . . ?"

"Yes, baby, I'll be there soon." (Not even the guts to hesitate.) "After I do a few things here."

"Why can't you come tonight? What are you doing down there?"

(You don't have to answer this. You don't have to allow her to quiz you.) "I have to do some *Draft Dodger* things, and . . . I have to set your record contract with my lawyer . . ."

"Well, I won't do it," Judy said.

"Why not?"

"Because."

"Because what?"

"Because you're mean." (Oh, she's so fuckin' endearing. Isn't she endearing? I could retch.)

"Baby . . ." (And yet it feels right to be in consonance with her. It feels wrong to be fighting with Judy . . . because the good part is so fabulously good . . . and I want to get that back, I want it more than anything.)

"Do you want Annie to bring you anything? You have her number?"

"Yes, I don't need anything but you, dear."

"I'll be up tomorrow night . . . that's a promise."

"Don't forget now . . ." Judy put sleepiness into her voice.

"No, I won't."

"Don't break your promise . . ."

"I won't . . ."

"Promise?"

"Promise."

"I love you . . ."

"I love you."

It was nearly eleven. I dialed Boston again. "Annie, hi. It's John."

"Yeah, I just called the hospital," said Annie. "They didn't take anything with them, you know, they just took Judy, so I'm going over tomorrow to bring her her glasses, and *Nicholas and Alex-andra*. You know what other book might be hip to take?"

"Oh, Annie, believe me, if she has *Nicholas and Alexandra*, that's plenty. You know where the glasses are?"

"Yeah, they're in one of those JAL flight bags. You know what else is in there? My mother gave me three pounds of that fresh-cut frozen turkey . . . boy, I'll bet it really stinks by now."

"You know what might perk her up, Annie? She has a hat on order at Lord & Taylor. It's all paid for, and if you could stop by . . . the sales slip is by the telephone somewhere . . ."

SUNDAY, DECEMBER 1

This afternoon I called Harold Arlen. I thought he might give me some clue . . .

"Harold, you've known Judy a lot longer than I have. Maybe you can give me some advice about this goddam self-destructive mechanism of hers."

"Mmmwell, that's a complicated affair," said Harold. "And I would tell you, between us, it's a medical affair. You can't do it. Nor I, nor anyone else. You can't really handle it or be con-structive."

I don't accept that, I thought. I'm going to get what Judy needs. "Do you know any doctor she's seen over the past five or six years?" I asked him. "I'd like to get her into therapy, if I could."

"No," said Harold, "I think they shy away from her, most of them, unless it's a complete stranger who doesn't know. What she needs is a strong guy, like Sid was in that respect, to get her work . . . and, yes, she needs a psychiatrist to get her over the hump."

"That's what I'm saying, Harold."

"But that doesn't mean it'll *last*, that's what's so sad and tragic." Harold sighed a deep, cantorial sigh. "I haven't helped," he said.

"You *have* helped, Harold," I told him, thinking about the eleven hundred dollars he'd paid the Leroy, "more than anyone else."

"I wish I knew what to suggest," he continued, "but most everyone knows you can do just so much . . . and I think you've done an awful lot.

"I'm trying."

"And don't lose heart," he went on, "and don't take it personally if something goes wrong." The way he said that struck a chill into me, raising the hair on the back of my neck. Nothing was going to go wrong, I wasn't going to *let* anything go wrong.

"Now, uh . . . I don't know anything else I can say that's . . . *dark*," he said. "It's disheartening. There's just nothing one can do but pray."

I put the phone down. Harold was wrong. There was a lot more one could do. One could protect oneself, for example, from falling down from fatigue. The way to do this, I imagined, would be to collect a coterie of five or six people, people Judy really liked, to take turns round the clock, keeping her occupied while I caught up on my sleep. Annie and Jenny could form the nucleus of this group, and could I ask Marvin, I wondered, to put in a couple of hours a day? Probably not.

The phone rang, and I picked it up. It was Harold.

"Guilt . . . guilt," he said, "reeking *guilt*. No, I feel so deeply about it . . . but, I'm *tot*ally experienced, and what I said is true as can be. I know it sounds crude . . . and unthinking—"

"Not at all, Harold," I said, as my heart went out to him over the line. The poor man had been brooding about it.

"What I would suggest," he said, "is to try to get the best agent there is, if they'll . . . if they'll take it on. You know."

"Well, she's *got* CMA, which is a pretty high-powered agency."

"Well, can't they get her some concerts?"

I explained to Harold that it wasn't a question of getting the work, it was a question of conquering Judy's anxiety about performing, her terror of having to constantly top herself, and how, at Lincoln Center, only her great love and respect for him had forced her onstage.

Harold was shocked to hear this. "It's almost . . . in*sane* to talk that way about her reaction to herself," he said. "It's unbelievable that she'd be a coward."

"Yeah, well, people are funny," I muttered inanely. Harold

gave a mournful chuckle. "Mmmwell, that's a nice . . . euphemism," he said.

What he means is that she's crazy, I realized, hanging up for the second time. Bonkers, bananas, round the bend, off the deep end, deranged, seriously disturbed, out of her mind, psycho, nuts, with impaired cognitive powers, loco, crackers, demented, unhinged, gaga, was what he'd meant. Well, I thought, we'll see.

MONDAY, DECEMBER 2

Armed with a double supply of Ritalin, I rode back into the Valley of Uncertainty on Eastern's five-thirty shuttle. I had asked the druggist for an extra thirty Valium tablets as well. I had the feeling I was gonna need them.

Marvin met me with a car at Logan Airport, and, on the ride into town, I boasted to him of what I'd accomplished before I left New York: in my lawyer's office, I'd completed the negotiation of Judy's recording contract with Bob Colby; in addition to approval of all material to be recorded, Judy would get a cash advance when she signed.

"And Begelman told me there wasn't a company in town that would touch her," I bragged. Marvin glanced at me from behind the wheel. "Just be careful, will you?" he said.

Yes, yes, I'll be careful, I thought impatiently. They couldn't *know*, these people who thought like Marvin and Larry, they didn't realize that when something like this comes along, something so immense, so much larger than the rest of your existence, when that happened you had to restructure your priorities; you had to move your mundane, ordinary ideas to the backseat and embrace the adventure with daring. You had to take chances.

Judy was not prepared when I walked into her room at Peter Bent Brigham. Annie hadn't delivered the "female things" she'd asked for, the nightie and the perfume and the lipstick, the tools with which Judy could make herself glamorous and seductive.

There she was, in her wrinkled white hospital gown, the kind that ties in the back. The gray streaks were growing into her hair again, and she looked bony, pallid, and frail.

"Hi . . ." she said, tentatively.

"Hello, Judy," I responded and gave her a reserved kiss on the cheek. Judy's fingers tightened about my arm. I could sense she was excited to see me, and why not? I represented escape from confinement and a resumption of the laughs and romance.

Still, I had finally convinced myself that, if we were coming together again, it would be on a new basis. I was going to make this clear to Judy: no more nonsense. And I meant to maintain my distance till we got that settled.

I managed to maintain my distance for about forty seconds. Judy was pulling me toward the bed. And, as at the Leroy, I was glancing nervously at the door. "Judy—"

"Listen," she said, "you were the one who was so, nn, con-*cern*ed about the bed . . ."

It was true. During our conversation from New York, to cheer Judy up, I'd asked her whether the bed she was in was big enough to accommodate us, and whether it went up and down, so that we could, too. I hadn't gambled on Judy's leaping on me the minute I walked through the door. But she needed to entice me now, needed to get me back in her corner.

"Come on, you big chicken," she whispered, and once again I jammed the back of a chair against the door, zipped down my pants, and hopped on Judy.

And then (this is too perfect) right in the midst of our re-union came a knock at the door.

"Judy?"

It was Annie, arriving with the nightgown and cosmetics. At the knock, I popped out of Judy like a cork and actually fell from the bed to the floor, my pants around my ankles. As I tried to struggle to my feet I could hear Annie pushing the door against the chair. She couldn't understand why the door wasn't opening.

"Hold on!" I screamed, as Judy began shrieking with delight. This was just the kind of situation Judy adored, we were in a Feydeau farce. Judy shook with uncontrollable giggles.

Annie, the sweet creature, didn't know what the hell was going on. Even our flushed faces and exaggerated eyeball-rolling gave her no clue. I mean, who would think they were inter-rupting a love affair at six-thirty in a hospital?

When Annie displayed the makeup case full of combs and co-lognes, Judy eyed her dolefully. "You're a little late," she said.

There was a wheelchair in the hall outside the room, and Judy wanted to show Annie how proficiently she'd learned to navigate in one of these, so we commandeered it. Judy hopped into the seat, and we began a tour of the ward.

We wheeled Judy into a semiprivate room, where two elderly ladies were playing after-dinner checkers. The women looked up in surprise as the chair rolled in.

"Hi," Judy said to them, "my name is Judy. Would you like to hear some Christmas carols?" The ladies weren't sure; they were a little nonplussed.

> "God rest ye merry gentlemen
> Let nothing ye dismay"

Judy sang.

> "Remember Christ, our Saviour
> Was born on Christmas day . . ."

She gestured to me and Annie to sing along. We joined her on the third line.

> "To save us all from Satan's pow'r
> When we had gone astray
>
> Oh, tidings of comfort and joy, comfort and joy
> Oh, tidings of cuh-hum-fort and joy."

Beside me I heard Annie slide up to the major third. The women were smiling with genuine pleasure now. Someone had come to entertain them. Judy, the choirmaster, raised her hands to conduct us. We had suddenly become a Chorale.

> "Hark, the herald angels sing
> Glory to . . . the newborn king—"

And when this one was finished, Judy pulled her wheelchair into a smart about-face and rolled herself out of the room. "Cheerio," she called back to the ladies, "Merry Christmas."

Propelling herself into two more rooms, Judy regaled the oc-

cupants with carols, spreading an early dose of Christmas spirit
through the ward.

But Room number four was a sobering experience. In this
room was a man in the last stages of terminal cancer. His body
had shriveled to a bony frame, and support systems were plug-
ging his nostrils and junctured into his arm. His sunken eyes
gazed at us cavernously as we barreled Judy gaily up to his bed.

We each registered his condition simultaneously. *"Uh* oh . . ."
I said, and, in a single motion, we swung Judy's chair quickly
around and zoomed back into the hall.

That put an end to the caroling. We put Judy back in her bed,
and Annie and I prepared to leave.

"Remember . . ." Judy said, as I kissed her good-bye, "we
have a date tomorrow . . ."

Judy's doctor was allowing her out for dinner tomorrow night,
and we were going to Anthony's Pier Four.

"I'm counting the hours," I told her. Indeed I was. Tomorrow
night Judy and I would have a little talk.

TUESDAY, DECEMBER 3

I set the apartment in order. I took cleaning downstairs, I
washed dishes, I bought food and liquor, I straightened up.
Annie came over to work on an orchestration for the London engagement.

With Judy in the hospital, it's easy to function efficiently, to
create a base, an anchor of calm and security. I needed an atmosphere like this to return to after being with Judy's quixotic
capriciousness. Yet the excitement of being with her is an excitement unparalleled.

I picked Judy up at seven. She'd taken care to look as attractive as she could for me, in her beige suit, her new black torero
hat from Lord & Taylor, and the gorgeous mink coat, the one
she got when she posed for a fur advertisement. This coat has a
self-belt I can do tricks with; I love to swing the belt over Judy's
head, catching her behind the waist and pulling her to me. Then
a light kiss on the eyes, a murmured endearment, a smart tug as

I knot the belt in front. Oh, is that romantic. I may not look like Ty Power, but I see no reason I can't act like him.

Anthony's restaurant is built right on the water, and from our table by the window we had a view of the river traffic, illuminated by the silver moon in this breathlessly clear night.

"I'll have a nn, *double* vodka martini . . ." Judy said to the waiter.

"You'll have a single vodka martini," I told her.

I was going to be stern tonight, an authority figure. Tonight was my night to lay down the law: no more childish behavior. No more tantrums. No more bullshit. We conduct this relationship like adults, understand? This is what I've planned to tell Judy tonight, but oh . . . how can I spoil this beautiful moment, with the tugs sliding silently by in the moonlight, with Judy on her best behavior, biting my finger suggestively, charming and funny and lovely. How could I mar this perfection with my "heavy furniture" speech? I simply didn't have the heart for it.

Or should I say the balls?

WEDNESDAY, DECEMBER 4

We brought Judy home from the hospital, Annie and I. Judy was embarrassed to pack her douche bag and tampons, her "feminine things," while I was in the room. A curious modesty, I thought, in front of her lover; but Judy was Victorian about some things.

Back at the Prudential, Judy wanted first a drink, and then a piano. "I think it's time we started nn . . . *sing*ing in this apartment."

Fine. Great idea. How could we *not* have a piano, Judy, John, and Annie, three people whose lives revolved around music? I dialed the Baldwin Piano Company. Disappointing; they would only rent pianos for performances in theaters and opera houses. At Steinway the rates were exorbitant, and, again, they rented solely concert-size grands, which they would deliver only to a theater. Wurlitzer would be happy to rent, except they had nothing presently available. However, they did mention a fellow named Ken Darrell, at a place called the Furniture Company of America. He might be able to help us. I tried calling, but Darrell was out. Try again later.

"I'm going over to Jenny's," I announced. Jenny had phoned and asked me to visit her; it was important, she'd told me.

"What about the piano?" Judy wanted to know.

"The guy's out. We'll have to wait till tomorrow." Judy put on her pouting expression. "I want a piano nn, to*night.*"

"Well," I shrugged, "lotsa luck." And I went out the door.

When I arrived at Jenny's apartment there was luggage in the hall. Jenny had a shopping bag ready for me.

"What's this?" I asked her. Jenny looked at me, and I could sense a heavy weariness in her. I knew she hadn't been well, recently.

"The doctor tells me I'm close to mononucleosis," Jenny said, "so I'm going down South, John, for a long time. I need a rest. I'm returning Judy's things."

I looked inside the bag. There were two or three books, a bracelet, a cotton sweater; nothing Judy required very urgently. "I don't get it, Jenny," I said, "did Judy lend you these things?"

"No," Jenny said, quietly, "she gave them to me. But you know Judy; someday she'll get in a snit and accuse me of running off with this stuff. I don't ever want to give her the opportunity to call me a thief. I'd rather not have the stuff." Jenny went to her closet and produced a mink coat. The coat was worn, its condition less than glistening; still, it was a handsome fur.

"This was the coat Judy was wearing before she did the Avedon sitting." Jenny was referring to the "What Becomes a Legend Most" photos. "Revillon didn't pay her for the session," Jenny informed me, "they gave her the coat instead. For tax reasons. So Judy made me a present of her old one." Jenny handed me the fur. "Take it back to her, please."

Silently, I folded the coat over my arm. I picked the shopping bag up. "Okay, Jenny," I said. I wanted to say something more, but nothing too great seemed to occur to me.

"It was fun," Jenny said, and she came to me and pressed a

kiss into my cheek. A feeling of sadness came over me. I thought of my plan to form a coterie for Judy, and then I knew what it was I wanted to say, I wanted to say oh Jenny, please, stay and help me, help me, we could make such a stunning, celestial force out of her, we could create such wonders with her, performances that will be written in flame and blaze in *Variety's* anniversary issues for eternity . . . please, Jenny, stay . . .

But all I said was Have a good trip.

I didn't tell Judy the reason, I just told her Jenny was cleaning out her house for the move South and was returning some stuff.

"Well, what am I supposed to do with two minks?" Judy asked me.

"Gee, Judes, *I* don't know," I kidded her, beckoning with my fingers. "It'd make a great lining for my new cape."

"Okay," Judy said, and she threw Annie a knowing glance.

"What?" I said. "You have other plans for that coat?" Annie started to giggle, and I saw Judy trying to suppress a smile. "What's going on here?" I said.

At that moment the buzzer rang from downstairs, and both the women burst into inexplicable laughter. Obviously, something was happening here.

"Okay," I said, resignedly, "whadja do, French my bed?"

"We got a piano!" said Judy, breaking up.

"You're kidding," I said, amazed. It was seven-thirty in the evening.

"Judy didn't want to tell you," Annie said.

"Why not?"

"She was afraid you'd be angry. You know, when you couldn't get one and all." Judy smiled at me tentatively.

"I thought it might compromise your nn, mascu*lin*ity."

"Don't be a jerk. I think it's terrific. How'd you do it?"

"Well, I just got on the phone with this fellah, Ken . . ." Of course she had. I knew exactly what had happened; she'd breathed her magic name into the phone, and this fellah Ken had said *Judy Garland,* holy Monopoly! I'll have it there in ten minutes, and by God, here it was, on its way up, and poor Judy had been afraid my delicate ego couldn't take it.

The doorbell rang, and Ken Darrell wheeled a Baldwin spinet into the apartment and started a party. We gave him a drink, and I sat down to play, and Judy sang a song, and Ken called up his girl friend, and by nine-thirty we were having a hell of a time. We sent out for Suds, that's what Ken drank, Suds, and Ken's girl friend got a little drunk and tearful about Judy: Judy, oh, Judy, she kept saying, you're so beautiful, I hope you get what you want, you deserve it, you've had such an unhappy time of it . . . she kept doing that kind of boring talk, but you couldn't get too angry at her, she was drunk, after all, and she was Ken's girl friend and Ken had accomplished the impossible, getting this beautiful piano up here at seven-thirty on a Wednesday night . . . and finally, about one in the morning, I managed to push everyone out the door, with much kissing and hugging and promises of eternal friendship and If you ever want anything call me and I never thought I'd get to meet Judy Garland and Thanks again and Don't forget now, if you ever and You have our number and Okay Annie, tomorrow about two, and finally, at last, the drifting voices vanished down the hall.

Judy came out of the bathroom in her nightgown. I was lying on the bed, propped up on a pillow against the wall, reading. She lowered her eyes and looked at me demurely from beneath her lashes.

"You sent for me, Professor?" I recognized my cue.

"Yes, Amanda, come in. And would you shut the door? I can hear that damn chapel bell clear across the campus." Obediently, Judy shut the bedroom door and came to the bed. I took her hands in my own.

"I'm a little concerned about your grades, Amanda," I said, paternally. "That's why I asked you to meet me here in my apartment at (I checked the clock on the night table) one forty-five in the morning."

Judy's eyes searched my face anxiously. "Have I been . . . doing badly, Professor?"

"I'd say there's room for a great deal of improvement, dear, especially in uh . . . biology. Why don't you sit down here, on the bed."

"Here?" Judy sat beside me.

"Very good, Amanda. You take direction well." Judy frowned at me. You weren't supposed to break character during these improvisations, but there were moments I couldn't resist. "Now, I had to fail you last semester, Mandy, because you obviously didn't understand Chapter Seven: Reproduction in Mammals."

"You always give Miss Roberts an A in biology . . ." Judy said.

"Miss Roberts," I said, adopting a puzzled expression. "Is she the one, ah . . . ?"

Judy held her hands in front of her chest, pantomiming a large bosom. "She's the one with . . . mmm . . ."

"Ah, yes. The big tits."

"You always give her an A."

"Yes, I do, Mandy, because Miss Roberts has under*stood* Chapter Seven. She knows all *about* Reproduction in Mammals. Now because I'm fond of you, Amanda, I'm going to give you a little private tutoring." I put my finger to her lips. "Now these . . . are your labia."

"Labia," Judy repeated the word like a child.

"Right. Now, when I press my labia to yours, Amanda, we'll experience a biological sensation: shall we try it?" I kissed her. A look of amazement crossed Judy's face, as if she'd just discovered the answer to a great riddle. "Oh, Pro*fes*sor . . ." she said.

"That's a good start, Mandy. Now this time, I want you to take your tongue and work it around in my mouth, like this . . ." I kissed Judy again, speaking to her through the demonstration. "Good . . . ungg, good . . . now, at the same time, I want you to take your hand, and touch me . . . here . . ."

And so on. Eventually, the Professor would give Amanda a B-plus, with instructions to show up again tomorrow night to try for an A.

Judy always cast herself in the same role: the innocent young girl seduced by a wily, older male who played on her naiveté. One night, however, Judy wanted to switch roles. She suggested *I* be the innocent, a well-built farm boy like Li'l Abner, and she would be Mae West, the seductress. Abner was auditioning for a spot in Mae's chorus of musclemen. The setting was Mae's boudoir, backstage.

ABNER

Miss Way-ust? They sent me in here . . . ah'm applyin'
for the opening . . .
(long pause)
. . . in your company?

MAE

Sit down, young man.
(looks him over; licks her lips)
What experience have you had?

ABNER

Way-ull . . . ah kin chop a cord a wood quicker'n you kin
say Jack Robinson. Ah kin hitch up a team in two seconds
flat. Ah kin clean an outhouse by the time you turn around.
Ah kin—

MAE

That's not what I had in mind. Abner, I'm sure you're
very good at . . . whatever you put your hand to . . .
(It was nearly impossible to keep a straight face when
Judy said something like this, but that was the rule: no
breaking up, and no lines out of character.)

MAE

Now what experience have you had in show business?

ABNER

Ah reckon not too much, ma'am . . . 'less you count bein'
a tree in the Yuma County Christmas Pageant.

MAE
(unbuttons his shirt)
Well, let's take a look at you, Abner. Are you in good
physical condition?

ABNER

Oh, ah'm in fahn shape, ma'am. Anythin' ah have to do,
ah kin do it. Jest whut would mah duties be in this here
show?

MAE

Well, first of all, you have to be able to strip in ten seconds.

ABNER

Strip?

MAE

There's a lot of quick changes in show biz. Think you can handle it?

ABNER

You mean now?

MAE

Here, I'll help you.
(slips off his shorts)
Hmm. Not bad. Not bad at all.

ABNER

That part's easy, Miss Way-ust. Whut else do ah have to do?

MAE

Can you get it up, Abner?

ABNER

Get whut up, Miss Way-ust?

MAE

This thing here.

ABNER

That? Whah shore, lemme jest call mah sheep—hey, *Ger-trude* . . .

MAE

Forget about Gertrude, Abner. What if we did something like . . . this . . .
And so on. After lovemaking, we'd resume these roles: MAE would be lying languorously in bed, bathing in the afterglow, and ABNER would call to her from the bathroom:

ABNER
So whut do ya think, Miss Way-ust? Do ah get the job?

MAE
Mmm. Can you do this every night?

ABNER
This? You mean whut we jest got through doin'?

MAE
Yes, can you show up an hour before show time and do just this?

ABNER
Y' mean thass all there is *to* it? All ah have to do is show up an hour before show time and fuck an ole bag lahk you? Whah shore, Miss Way-ust—

MAE
(*Screaming*)
Burt! Larry! Get this two-bit hick outta here! He called me an old bag! Give him the heave-ho! Rhubarb, rhubarb.

And, as I came out of the bathroom, I would pantomime being grabbed by each arm and propel myself—as if I were being rudely shoved by two bruisers—out the bedroom doorway, crying Hey, wait a minute, whut's goin' on?

And I would slam the front door loudly, as "Abner" got the old heave-ho.

THURSDAY, DECEMBER 5

It's coming together. I've been able to confirm three TV shots for Judy. Merv Griffin, Johnny Carson, and Dick Cavett. And she'll be singing *my* songs! On the "Tonight Show" Judy will sing "It's All for You" (our love song) and a Christmas ballad . . . "After the Holidays." For Merv she'll sing "Hate Myself." We have yet to determine what to sing for Dick Cavett.

In addition, these shows have agreed to supply orchestrations, and, as at Lincoln Center, to give them to Judy after the appearances. The musical director at Griffin is Mort Lindsey, a friend of Judy's and an excellent arranger. We decided to call him at his Long Island home.

"Mort? Hi, it's Judy . . . I'm doing the show on the nineteenth . . . and you're going to write me an orchestration . . ."

"Oh, terrific. What're you singing, 'Over the Rainbow'?"

"No, not this time . . . it's a tune of Johnny's . . . you'll meet Johnny, he's very talented . . ."

"What's the tune?"

"It's called 'I'd Like to Hate Myself in the Morning' . . . oh, it's a nn, *dreamy* tune . . ."

"Yeah, and I've got fourteen days to do the chart. You better put it in the mail *yes*terday."

So I put a lead sheet of "Hate Myself" in an envelope and mailed it to Mort special delivery. Later that afternoon the phone rang with more good news. This was our day for it.

It was Harold Davidson calling transatlantic to confirm Judy's opening December 30 at the Talk of the Town nightclub in London's Leicester Square.

"It's a four-week booking, luv, and Delfont's willing to go twenty-five hundred pounds a week."

Judy and I, sharing the phone as always, pressed our heads together tightly. The exchange rate on the pound was two-eighty, call it three, three times twenty-five, why it was something like seven thousand dollars a week! We turned to grin at each other like a pair of happy hyenas. And just last month Judy was making a hundred a night at Three. What an incredible life Judy led.

"I'm putting the contract in the mail tonight," Davidson told us, "and would you like me to book you rooms in the Ritz?"

The Ritz! I was thinking, wouldn't that be wonderful! And maybe, after the engagement was over, we'd go to Paris, and God, wouldn't that be unbelievable, wouldn't it be the trip of a lifetime to see Europe with Judy. I began nodding vigorously to Judy from my side of the receiver.

Judy told Davidson Yes, the Ritz would be satisfactory, and she thanked him, and put down the phone, looking to me for a reaction.

"Wow," I said. "I'm excited."

Judy looked down at her lap. She seemed to be pondering something. "This is all your fault, you know . . ." she said.

FRIDAY, DECEMBER 6

We went to see Barbra Streisand in *Funny Girl*. In the cab on the way over Judy told me a story: "David (Begelman) took me to see her in Las Vegas, when she was just starting out . . . I was curious, because I never heard so many people nn, com-*plain*ing . . . 'God, is she ugly' everybody was saying, 'My God, I never saw anyone so *ugly* . . .'

"And they said it with such nn, *force* . . . and they said it so often that I thought, this girl must *have* something . . . and we were sitting at the table, and mmm . . . David was very proud . . . the agency had just signed Bob Goulet . . . they had a choice of signing either Bob or Barbra, and David kept saying 'Wait'll you see this nn, *ugly, ugly* girl . . .'

"And Barbra came out . . . and after her first number I looked at David and I said 'Well, nn, you *blew* it . . .'"

The picture was great. Halfway through I squeezed Judy's hand, and, when I felt no answering pressure, I glanced at her. Judy was asleep.

"Judy, look, she's on a *tug*boat, you gotta get up for this." Judy's chin came rapidly off her chest. "I'm awake," she said. But the next time I looked at her, she was nodding off again.

Leaving the theater, I remembered something. "You fell asleep on Tony Curtis, too," I said.

"Yes, isn't that nn . . . pe*cul*iar . . ."

"And you didn't have that much to drink."

"No . . . God, no, I've had nn, *gal*lons more to drink and stayed up for days . . ."

On the ride back to the Prudential we discussed this somno-lence of Judy's, examining the possibilities. It always seemed to happen in the movies. But we'd ruled out all the possible causes: Judy wasn't drunk, she wasn't tired, she wasn't bored.

As I closed the apartment door behind us the reason finally burst out . . . burst out with the force of an admission suppressed. Judy went to sleep in the movies for the most basic reason in the world:

"Because . . . *I* want to be up there . . . *I* want to be the one who's . . . singing and acting . . ." Judy's words were halting.

"Oh, my baby . . ." was all I could say in sympathy.

"I mean . . . there's nothing so nn . . . *shame*ful about that, is there?" She was looking at me as though I might chastise her for this. Good God, I thought, Judy Garland ashamed of wanting to *perform?*

"Baby, baby, of course not, are you kidding? Christ, when I hear Sondheim on the radio I want to go up the *wall . . .*"

"Because I can do that . . . I really can . . ."

"Honey, you can do it better than anyone, better than all the Streisands and Curtises who ever lived . . . and you're going to: we're going to New York and you're gonna do three sensational TV shots, and then we're going to London, and you're gonna knock 'em *dead.* You really are. I promise you."

SATURDAY, DECEMBER 7

For dinner tonight, in a burst of domesticity, Judy cooked a casserole. Baked beans, sausages, and brussels sprouts.

"What, no sushi?" I inquired. Today was, after all, the anniversary of Pearl Harbor. Judy regarded me with a jaundiced eye. "I'm not fond of Japanese food," she said. "I like nn . . . *Chinese* food, like Hildegarde Sprague." (Not her real name, and you'll see why.)

"Is Hildy a Chinese food freak?"

"When Hildy married nn, Jimmy Baxter, she discovered he absolutely a*dored* Chinese food, they used to eat it *const*antly, they were either out in a restaurant or Jimmy was using the nn, *wok,* he was simply gaga about it, with you know, nothing but wooden nn, u*tensils . . .* apparently, in China, your lips are not supposed to touch metal when you dine . . .

"And after they'd been married about a . . . month . . . I had lunch with Hildy, and she was telling me how the nn, *bloom* was sort of . . . wearing off . . . he really wasn't the man she'd thought he was, and she wasn't sure it was going to work out

. . . and finally, I got up the nerve to ask her about their nn, *love* life, and Hildy said, Oh sure, he eats me every night, and I said, Well, isn't that worth nn, *some*thing . . . ? And Hildy said Yes, but with those fucking *chop*sticks?

"Hildy has one of life's . . . nn, *seriously* dirty mouths. We were cutting a V-disc at Metro one afternoon . . . practically everybody on the lot . . . and Loretta Young was there, with one of her little . . . *charity* canisters . . . she was collecting for the Homeless Belgian Orphans, or some such . . . in addition to being Miss Prim, Loretta is one of our great . . . nn, *do-gooders* . . . and every time someone cursed, or swore . . . you know, they'd flub a take and say Oh shit or something . . . well, every time she heard a 'damn' or a 'hell' here would come Loretta . . . teet teet teet with her little canister, and she'd say 'That'll be twenty-five cents for the Orphans, please, you said a naughty word.'

"Well, by the end of the afternoon, almost everybody had given Loretta a quarter or two for the orphans, except Hildy, who thought Loretta was nn, you know . . . the *worst* . . . and Hildy was up there, recording, and she fluffed it, she sang something like 'Speak low, when you speak lunch'—and she said 'God*dam*it!' and there was Loretta teet teet teet with the canister, 'I'm sorry, Hildy, you said a naughty word, that'll be twenty-five cents for the Orphans.' And Hildy gave her one of her long, Hildy looks and said 'Loretta, how much would it cost me to tell you to go fuck yourself?' "

I was putting the remains of the casserole into the fridge. "This was really very good, babe," I said. Judy bridled. "Well, *thank* you," she said with some acidity. "Nobody thinks I can do anything but . . . nn, *sing*. I raised three kids, you know."

We watched a movie (Joan Caulfield in *The Petty Girl*, with an Arlen score) and, about one-thirty, Judy swallowed one of Dr. Klinger's sedatives, and fell asleep beside me, her broken, Bugs Bunny tooth peeking endearingly from beneath her upper lip. I punched the pillow affectionately and closed my eyes.

Dimly, through my semiconsciousness, I heard a male voice: ". . . two hundred and twenty-six enemy casualties, while allied losses are estimated at sixty-two. Elsewhere on the Vietnam front—" The voice seemed to be inside my head now. It was the radio in the living room, turned up so loud I thought the walls might crumble and the kitchen dishes shatter.

I leaped out of bed and into the living room. On the floor, the radio was blaring at an incredible volume. I bent and tuned it to a reasonable level, then shuffled back to bed, eyes closed, trying to retain the filmy, elusive vestige of sleep.

Christ, I thought, how stupid. Judy had been warned about "unnecessary noise" by the Prudential management, after her neighbor downstairs, Mr. Wayne, had complained about the piano. Wayne was the man who called the cops when Judy banged her head against the wall. After this unpleasantness, we didn't want any more complaints.

The overhead light was beating harshly on my lids. I opened my eyes and saw Judy by the bed, poking around.

"Mmm whayya want, hon?"

"I know there's a . . . nn, *rad*io here somewhere . . ."

" 'S in the living room."

"No, not that one . . . the other one . . ."

Judy exited, leaving the light on. I got up, turned it off, and flopped back into bed. Seconds later, the light went on again. Judy was still looking for the radio.

"*Oh* . . ." she said, with a little too much surprise in her voice, "here it is . . ." Aha! The idea finally penetrated. Judy wanted *attention.*

"Honey," I said, pulling her down on the bed, "I'm sorry I can't come out and play with you." I rubbed my knuckles gently along her spine. "I love you babe, I really do . . . I'm just tired now . . . I wanna get a little sleep . . ."

I closed my eyes, drifting off once more, and we were in a huge rowboat, Judy and I; we each had an oar and we were rowing furiously toward the shore. But the harder we rowed the more we seemed becalmed. And then the rowboat and the oars shredded away because the overhead light was pummeling my lids and Judy's voice was knifing in from the living room.

"Sure, sure . . . it's fine when they're up . . . but forget it when they want to sleep." I snapped awake. "Well, what about *me*?" Judy continued. "What am *I* supposed to do?" I turned to the clock. It was four-ten. "Same old . . . *bull*shit . . ." Judy said, from the living room.

I found myself trembling. I'm going to have to confront this, I was thinking, I'm going to have to sit down and go through this with her, because otherwise I don't know how we can keep this thing going, and the reason I was trembling, the reason my limbs were shaking so, was because I didn't know if Judy realized how serious this was. Please Judy, I prayed to her silently, just let me get *a little sleep.*

"Anyone I ever had, they all had to get their fucking . . . sleep . . . they all had to sleep their whole, fucking—"

"Judy!" I barked, with as much force as I could muster. "Come in here." There was a pause. Then Judy's voice shot round the corner. "Don't you . . . order me around . . . too many people have . . . ordered me around all my life . . . if you want to see me . . . you come on in here . . ."

My lips tightened in fury. Goddamit to fucking hell, all *right.* Enough of this shit already. I rose and marched purposefully into the living room. Judy was standing in the middle of the floor. I sat in the black leather chair.

"Okay, Judy, let's have it. What's on your mind?" Judy's eyes darted cagily to the left, then to the right. "Well . . . what's on *your* mind?"

"Sleep," I said. "Sleep is on my mind."

"Well, go to sleep then."

"Kinda hard, Judy, when you make it impossible."

"*I* do? *I* make it impossible?"

"Come on, Judy."

"How do I make it impossible?"

"Well, for one thing—" I began, and then stopped. I was feeling the familiar, sucking pull of game-playing; I'd felt suddenly cast again in the role of the professor. And I wondered, then, did Judy really sport this frivolously with the people who meant something to her? Was Judy so dangerously disoriented that she allowed this role-playing to destroy the foundation of every important relationship?

"For one thing what?" Judy prompted me. I searched her face for a crinkle in the eyes, a giveaway grin at the corner of her mouth, some sign that said Yes, this is a game, we're doing another improv.

There was no such sign. Judy seemed devastatingly serious. Okay.

"For one thing, you turned on the light," I said.

"I had to find my slippers."

"And after you found them? Couldn't you have turned the light off?"

"I couldn't find them." I sighed, patiently.

"All right, Judy—what about the radio?"

"What about it?"

"You have a perfectly good radio out here."

"You came out and turned it off."

"I turned it *down,* Judy, because if that guy Wayne complains again, they're gonna *evict* you."

"It wasn't that loud."

"Yes, it was, Judy."

She was pacing the room, eyes roving, seeking to fasten on some object or idea by which she could evade this interrogation. "May I have a drink?" she said.

"All right, look, Judy . . ." I shifted uncomfortably in the chair. "We have to talk about this."

"About what?"

"About *this.* The whole thing. Because if we're not careful, this is gonna come between us, and I don't want that to happen. So let's talk about it."

Judy looked guardedly at a point just above my eyes. "I didn't do anything," she said.

"Yes, you did, Judy; you deliberately provoked me into coming out here and paying some attention to you . . . and you wanna know something? That's your pattern!" My God, I told myself, so *that's* how it works, of course, of course! "That's your pattern!" I shouted at Judy, thrilled by this discovery. "You deliberately provoke people!"

Judy looked at me strangely. "Why should I do that?"

"To test the measure of their love."

"You're full of shit."

"No, Judy, wait, listen to this—" I was excited. I had discovered an important mechanism, something essential in Judy's character, and I wanted to tell her about it. "I'll show you how it works: the whole thing is on a series of levels, like a game show.

First plateau, second plateau. The first level is the initial commitment, getting hooked, which isn't hard with you, Judy . . . you're so fucking beautiful . . . the minute I saw you I wanted you . . ."

"Did you? I hadn't had a bath in a week."

"Okay, so we start going together, which is the first level, which is saying 'I care for you and I want to make you happy,' right? Okay, now I get really involved, I talk to CMA, I talk to the IRS, new orchestrations, the whole shmeer, and by this time we're in love, it's 'I love you and will you marry me?' and we're up to the second level, total commitment."

In my excitement, I rose from the chair. "Okay, he loves me." I was caught up in my impression of Judy. "He's taking care of the taxes, the bookings, the charts—and he wants to marry me. He must really love me. But wait a minute . . ." I put a thoughtful finger to my lips. "Isn't there something else he can do to show me how *much* he loves me? What would the next level be? I know. My bad foot! I'm supposed to stay off it, no liquor, so I know what—I'll run around, I'll booze, I'll do everything bad for the foot—hey, Johnny, look, I'm dancing, I'm drinking—"

I switched back to the John character. "Judy! What are you doing? You know the doctor said no drinking! Get into bed! No, we're *not* going out, we're going to the *hospital*." I looked at Judy. "You see how it works?" I said.

"Not really," said Judy. She was watching me as if I were a spider.

"What you're saying is, Oh sure, it's easy to love me when I'm being funny and sexy and talented, but will you love me when I'm a pain in the ass?"

Judy's jaundiced stare told me she wasn't buying any of this, but I *knew* I was right. I could feel it. I kept going.

"Okay, what now? He passed that test, he stuck with me, so what can I hit him with now? Oh, look at that, what's he doing over there, sleeping? Great. I'll use that for the next level. Let's see if he'll give up his sleep for me. Now how will I do this? I know, I'll *hurt* myself. Oh, Johnny, help! I cut my head! I'm bleeding!"

"Wait a minute, buster," Judy interrupted harshly, "hold the phone. You think I cut my head on purpose? You think I enjoy getting my head busted?"

"I think you need to hear me say, darling, I'll take care of you, no matter *what* you do to yourself, no matter how badly you damage yourself. Okay, look, here's the fascinating part: well, he came through, he took care of me, and he lost a lotta sleep doing it. I know he's exhausted. So let's use that for the next level. I'll wake him up again, and this time, let's see if he'll get up for something mmm . . . trivial. Because, sure, anyone'll get up if you're *bleed*ing, but now let's see if he loves me enough to get up for . . . for just *nothing*. I'll go in there, flip the light on a few times, I'll turn the radio on real loud, and let's see what he does."

My thesis was finished. I took a deep breath. "And so here we are, Judy, and you've won. You got me up for nothing, just to talk to you, to pay some attention. Except Judy, it's like poker . . . you keep upping the ante, raising the stakes, but honey, soon I'm gonna run out of chips, and that'll be it. I won't have anything left for you to play with."

The leather of the chair was sticking to my thighs, but I barely noticed it. I was too proud of myself for being so perceptive, for synthesizing this analysis. Judy can only thank me, I was thinking, for being so perceptive and mature. I was right.

"Well, thanks a lot," she said. But her words were bitter. "Thanks," she repeated. "It's my fault . . . again. Everything is always . . . *my* fault. All my fucking . . . life. Always *my* fault." The voice that could do anything dropped to a tone of weary resignation. "Mmm . . . maybe you're right," she went on. "Mmm . . . maybe this is why I seem to have . . . *alien*ated everyone . . . my friends . . . my children . . ."

"Baby," I said.

"Well, it hasn't been all fun, you know . . ."

"Honey, look, I may be all wet . . . this is only a theory." You chickenshit, I thought, stick to your guns. Don't let her manipulate you. But what I said was "I only brought it up because it was coming between us."

"You mean otherwise . . . you wouldn't have told me?" Judy's tone implied that perhaps I'd been keeping something from her.

"It never would have occurred to me without this," I said. I was suddenly terribly thirsty. I went into the kitchen, opened the icebox, and took out a jar of Tropicana grapefruit juice. I drank the cold, tart liquid straight from the bottle. It felt wonderful. As I was screwing back the cap I heard a long, painful wail from the living room. It started low and built to an agonizing intensity. I dashed back into the room.

Judy was standing, legs apart, slightly bent, in a strange, stunted position, like a tree in a Japanese print. Her mouth was twisted into an ugly grimace.

"Well," she spat, "at least you've given me a way to . . . *get off* . . . !" She took a halting step forward. I moved toward her. "Judy—" But she fended off my approach with a stiff arm, like a football player.

"No!" she cried. "It's been too long . . . the lady's been on-stage . . . too long . . . and now it's time to get the fuck . . . off!"

She was nearly shouting. I had never heard Judy this way, upset and vehement, and castigating herself. I felt helpless before her force, as if I'd arrived at the scene of a freeway accident and could only wait with the others for the sound of the ambulance siren.

"It just . . . isn't worth the struggle anymore . . . it just isn't. When you find out that . . . everything you do to . . . nn, *please* people is only . . . driving them away from you . . ."

She was facing the window, staring out toward Lord & Taylor into the gathering dawn. A minute went by. When she finally spoke, her voice was subdued.

"I guess you're right. I guess I've been doing this all my life. Well, I won't do it anymore, I promise you. I won't try to give, and give, and *give* . . . what's the sense? I've lost my children . . . I've lost you . . ."

"You haven't lost me, darling."

"Yes, I have . . . I know I have . . . you just told me so . . ."

"I was just trying to show you—"

"How much I've driven you away from me."

"No, Judy, only how you *might*—"

"Unh huh. Unh huh. There it is. He's calling her 'Judy.' That's the sign, that's the sure sign." She swung round from the window to face me. "And do you know what people always tell me when they leave me? As their ass vanishes through the door? 'This is for your own good.'"

"I'm not *leav*ing you!"

"You will."

I began to shout. "There! You see! You're doing it! You're practically *will*ing it to happen!" I grabbed her by the soft meat of her arms, pressing her to me in a frenzy. "Judy, don't don't *don't* do this—stop while we still have a chance, don't drive me away!"

"I already *have*." On the word "have" Judy tore loose from me violently and stepped back. "Oh, what's the use . . . ?" Her words were cracked and rueful. "Look, you did your best . . . and you were honest with me . . . which is more than most people have been. And you did give me something . . . something I've been looking for a long time . . . a graceful exit."

What does that mean? I was thinking. What is *that*? "Now Judy . . ." I said. My voice must have carried a tinge of anxiety, for Judy shot me a contemptuous look. "Oh, don't worry . . . you won't be involved . . ."

The way she said that conjured fresh headlines in my mind (GARLAND DIES AS CONSORT DESERTS LOVE NEST). I tried to remember how many Seconals Judy had left, and was there a blade in the bathroom? And then for some reason I was sitting on the stool in the kitchen. I must have gone in for more juice. And I was crying, I couldn't help it. Judy stood in the kitchen doorway.

"Listen," she said, "I want you to go."

"Why?" I managed to blubber.

"Because . . . if I do the things you say I do . . . then I'm bad for you . . . I'm not good for you . . . I want you to go before I destroy you."

I tried to smile. "You're not destroying me . . . I'm pretty tough."

"No . . . I want you to go. Now."

I stared at her through a long, long moment. I couldn't believe it. "Go on," she reiterated. "Go pack a bag. Go on."

"No, Judy, I won't."

"You better. Do it now . . . save yourself . . ."

"I can't," I said wetly. "I love you. You're the only woman I ever really loved."

"Yes, I believe that. So save yourself. Get out."

"I can't . . ." I said miserably.

Judy's arm was raised, she was grasping the door molding at eye level. Now she put her forehead on the back of her hand. "I . . . I don't want to be responsible for . . . making you feel . . . like my children feel . . ."

"Judy . . ." It was so hard to speak, the emotion kept distorting my mouth. "Judy . . . I can h-*help* you . . ."

"No. It's too late."

"Only if you th-think so . . ."

"I think so."

Well, that shocked me. That was a stunner. Giving up, she was *giving up*. I'd never heard that from her before, no matter how scared or depressed.

"Well, if that's true . . . then it *is* too late."

"That's what I said."

So here was a turning point, I realized. Judy was declaring herself beaten, and we could all go home. I could cut my losses, Judy was saying, and get out now, if I wanted to. But some misguided and foolhardy heroism in me didn't want to.

"I don't accept that, Judy . . . I just don't," I said. She tried to say something, but I plowed on. "—and if nothing else, I want my chance . . . I want the chance to show you you're *wrong*. You *can* change."

"I can't," Judy moaned. "I'm too old."

"You're *not* too old."

"I'm forty-six," said Judy. "And with my life, that makes me about four hundred and twelve."

"It doesn't *matter*, you can *change*, I *know* you can, I've *seen* it, you're a resilient woman, you can bounce back—"

"No, darling, I've bounced back too often . . . the spring is shot . . ."

"Bullshit."

We were facing each other, like bull and matador, over bloody sand.

"I want my chance," I repeated, hoarsely. Judy moved slowly to the living room couch and sank into it wearily, closing her eyes. "All right," she sighed. "Let's go through it once more." She clasped her hands behind her neck and bent her forehead to the top of her thigh. "Let's try to stop the drinking, and the pills . . . and the missed concerts . . . and let's try and make me . . . well again. Is that what you're saying?"

Her voice sounded worn now, lacking in conviction, vitiated by those four hundred and twelve hard years. She seemed small, shriveled, and spent. A sudden, visceral fear in my gut asked me whether maybe she wasn't right about herself. Well. Too late now. I'd made my declaration, for better or for worse. I knelt beside her and put my hand in her lap.

"Yes," I said. "That's what I'm saying."

Minutes later I was trying, with the aid of a Valium, to seduce back the sleep I'd finally earned. But my head was jumpy with flash frames of the scene I'd just played with Judy, and the echoing, offscreen voices were sounding in my mind:

LARRY

John, you're young, you've got a career ahead of you . . . and she's washed up, she's had it . . . forget her.

JENNY

She's run through a lot of people, John . . . don't let her devour you . . .

I became aware of Judy's presence in the room. I turned and saw her approach and kneel by the bed. She placed her forearms on the blanket, near my feet.

"Hello, darling . . ." I said, reaching out my hand to her. From the foot of the bed, Judy looked at me tentatively. "Would you . . ." she began, tremulously, ". . . would you mind . . . hearing my prayers?"

I had never known Judy to pray before. "Of course, sweetheart," I said. Judy bowed her head. When she spoke it was against the sound of the seven A.M. traffic many stories below us. Boston was waking up.

"God bless Johnny . . ." Judy said softly, "and God bless m-me . . ." Her voice caught, broke very slightly on "me," and suddenly the sight and sound of this tender, pathetic supplicant turned my face away, and I was dampening the pillow with my emotion.

I don't remember the rest of Judy's prayer, for a song was forming in my mind, even through my involuntary spasm, pulled from me as if Judy had reached down my throat and into my guts and wrenched it out of me to lie naked, covered with after-birth, before her need.

"Thank you . . ." Judy said when she finished. She rose and returned to the living room . . . and I took my yellow legal pad from the floor and my green felt-tip pen from the night table, and I wrote down Judy's prayer:

"God bless Johnny . . . and God bless me," I wrote. Then I added:

> "And God help me find
> The love I hope can be
> And God, if you care
> What happens at all
> You won't let me slip
> You won't let me fall
>   So give me courage
>   Or whatever it takes
>   And please . . . let me make
>   Only tiny mistakes
>   And let him love me . . . and God, if you do . . .
>   I promise I'll never ask another thing . . . of you."

SUNDAY, DECEMBER 8

I awoke to discover our renegade pranksterism has finally backfired. A couple of nights ago, in the apartment, we were entertaining Marvin and Annie. I was at the piano and Judy was singing. It was about twelve-thirty A.M., but of course no one was giving a thought to the time.

And then the phone rang. It was Mr. Wayne again, one floor below us in 11J, disturbed by the noise. "Can't you people keep quiet?" he hissed irately into my ear.

"Whom do you wish to speak to, sir?" I asked him.

"Just tell that Garland woman to stop making such a racket. It's past midnight."

"We have no Miss Garland here, sir," I said. "What number are you calling?"

He hung up. Judy giggled gleefully. This was her favorite kind of situation. She began dancing a violent clog on the uncarpeted floor. I ran to the keyboard and started playing "After the Ball Was Over" in a heavy waltz beat: *"After the ball was over After the break of oom chick chick oom chick chick—"*

This went on for a while and finally Wayne sent the police. "Oh, gentlemen, come in, sit down, have a beer—" Judy said to the two arriving officers, who were young and awestricken, and no match for Judy.

"I must apologize for Mister Wayne," she said to them. "He must be some kind of nn, *nut.* As you can see, we're not engaged in any, nn, raucous *party*ing . . . we have a few friends in and we're sitting here quietly, enjoying a drink. Are you ready for a beer?"

The rookies declined. They were embarrassed. "We're sorry about this, Miss Gahland," said one of them, the taller one, apologetically, "we have to investigate every cahll."

"Well, of *course* you do," Judy said. "But I think it's nn, *shame*ful that he's pulled you out of your nice warm squad car for this." She caught the short one staring at the piano. "Oh, would you like me to sing you a song?" She crossed to him and squatted shamelessly by his chair. Marvin and Annie were gazing in rapt admiration, holding their breath at this high-wire act of Judy's, but I had to look away. I was having trouble keeping a straight face. I slipped onto the piano bench.

"I bet I know what you want to hear . . ." Judy said to the shorter rookie. She slid her eyes in my direction, and I began the introduction to "Over the Rainbow." By the time Judy finished her rendition, those two cops would have put Boston under martial law for her. They left, caps in hand, as Judy ran to the phone book.

"Okay, let's *get* him," she said gleefully, and I knew instantly that keeping Mr. Wayne awake had become the evening's entertainment.

Judy located his number and dialed and handed me the

phone. "Mr. Wayne," I said when he answered, "my name is Davis, police department, complaint investigation. I understand you have a complaint?"

"Well, I thought you people were sending someone over," he replied.

"What is the nature of your complaint, Mr. Wayne?"

"Well, I already told one of your people—"

"If you don't mind, Mr. Wayne, we'll need it again, for the files."

"The woman hasn't put rugs down, that's all. I can hear her every footstep."

"And how long have you been a resident of the building, Mr. Wayne?"

"About six years."

"And what is your occupation?"

And was he married, and was he a registered voter, and had he served in the military, and was there a history in his family of chronic paranoia—until finally he got wise and hung up on me.

Judy leaped into phase two of operation Wayne. "I'm going down there," she announced. "Who's coming with me?" Nobody budged. "Okay, you chickens," Judy said. "I'll go myself." And she went out the door. Marvin looked after her with concern.

"Leave her," I said. "She'll be okay."

But after twenty minutes had passed, Marvin could stand it no longer. So the three of us, Marvin, Annie, and I, went down to the eleventh floor, where we found Judy attempting to kick in Mr. Wayne's door.

"I tried to reason with him . . ." she puffed, between kicks. "I asked him to (kick) come to lunch so we could talk it over like (kick) civilized human beings . . . let's have it out, I said (kick) but not him . . . not this one . . . he just keeps (kick) yelling at me—"

Wayne, cringing with terror, had double-locked himself inside. He would not open the door. "Please, Miss Garland," he was crying, "I have to get up at seven . . . this goes on night after night, please let me get some *sleep*—"

And then we heard him on the phone, shrieking to the police: "I need protection, she's violent! You've got to send somebody immediately, she's trying to break down my door!"

I made a waving motion to Judy, Annie, and Marvin, backing them off down the hall a few feet. I had an idea. I knocked firmly on the door.

"Mistar Wayne," I bellowed in my best Irish brogue, "this is Inspector Muldoon. May Oy see you far a moment?"

There was a pause. Then Wayne's voice came guardedly from behind his door. "What do you want?"

"May Oy see you far a moment?" I repeated. Down the hall, my three friends were cupping their mouths in their hands.

"Oy must wahrn you, Mistar Wayne"—I said, when he gave no response—"that if these complaints continue, Miss Gahland is going to sue you for harassment, and you could very easily find yourself involved in a nasty court battle which might result in your being fined fifteen thousand dollars plus legal fees!"

I saw Judy digging her nails into her wrist in an effort to restrain a burst of laughter. Tiny whimpers were audible now behind the door. We had turned poor Mr. Wayne into a gibbering wreck.

"Come on," I said to my partners, starting toward the elevator. "He's had it."

MONDAY, DECEMBER 9

But I was wrong. It was we who'd had it. In the morning Donald Sisk, the Prudential manager, called to say that Miss Garland would have to move out. Mr. Wayne's latest complaint had been corrosive in its intensity and, added to the other noise complaints, Sisk said, the building simply could no longer tolerate this behavior. The Prudential would return her security deposit, he continued, but Miss Garland would have to be out by December fifteenth.

Judy took it badly. Once again she was being rejected, shunted aside, cast out. She was ready to do an hour on it, but I headed her off at the pass.

"Oh, fuck it, Judy. We're going to New York anyway, and then to London. What do we need Boston for? We'll find a place in Manhattan. I've already got several leads from that lah-de-dah Pat Palmer who makes me dress up like Bernie Baruch." By

being forceful and optimistic—and, above all, funny—I managed to jolly Judy into viewing her eviction as a blessing in disguise. We'd start a new page in New York, a fresh chapter in
London.

Packing, of course, was gonna be a job. I called a high school
girl over to help. I'd found her card days ago on the bulletin
board in the Star Supermarket downstairs. She sews and repairs
clothes. God knows Judy's wardrobe could stand revitalizing.
Her name was Bunny Carnazzo, she was sixteen, and she arrived
about two-thirty.

"Okay, Bunny, let's sort all this stuff into three piles: stuff to
be packed, stuff to throw out, and stuff that has to be fixed."

Judy's neck craned anxiously out of the bedroom. "Wh . . .
what are you throwing out?"

"Don't worry, honey, nothing we need."

"This dress needs a button, Mister Meyer. Shall I fix it?"

"Yes, please, Bunny. And any buttons you find missing, see if
you can replace them."

We borrowed an ironing board from next door, and Bunny
opened her sewing kit and set to work industriously in the living
room, replacing buttons and raising hems. The three cases were
spread open on the living room floor; Judy's two red ones, my
brown one, and a red Valpak—plus the red makeup case and
hatbox. Judy had enough luggage to move Napoleon's troops.
Getting this baggage together was going to be a major exercise
in logistics.

In classifying the dresses, shoes, papers, photos of Kennedy,
and half-squeezed tubes of eyelash glue, I soon found myself
becoming impatient with anything that wasn't absolutely essential.

"You're not throwing out that jacket, are you?"

"Judes, we've been looking for the skirt for three weeks, it's in
ratty shape, and you know you'll never wear it."

"We'll find it."

"Judy, we've got enough clothes here to last till they find
Amelia Earhart."

"Just like the furniture," Judy burst out at me. "I'll never see it
again. And my *jewelry.* Where's my jewelry?"

"I spoke to Hertz. They haven't found it. I guess it's lost." My tone must have been too cavalier, for Judy bridled. "Sure, why should you care? It's not your jewelry. And what about my furniture?"

"You read the notice, Judy. Can you pay the storage charges?"

"No. It'll all be auctioned off. All my lovely things. Everything in my house." Judy's huge brown eyes grew misty. "All my pictures . . . my piano . . . I have a Vlaminck . . . and a painting George Gershwin did. Lem Ayers designed my living room . . . we used it in *A Star Is Born* . . . all that stuff is mine . . . Johnny, we've got to call them . . ."

"First thing tomorrow, Judes," I said without looking up. I was busy stuffing sixteen pairs of shoes into the bottom of the Valpak.

"Why do we have to wait?"

"'Cause we're *pack*ing now, Judes. One thing at a time, okay?"

"Oh, God . . ." Judy shook her head miserably. "Why does it always happen like this?"

"Look, Judy—" I said firmly. I was suddenly sick of her complaining. "—you can't fret about what's past. You lost your jewelry. Okay, it's regrettable, but it's done. You can't pay your storage charges. Okay, it's not the end of the world. Soon you'll be able to have anything you want, whatever you need. But you can't waste time crying about what's done. You've got to go on."

"Right. Fine. Never mind. Accept it. Go on. Well, I *can't* go on." Judy's voice rose in volume. "Everything I ever had is going down the drain—no, never mind shutting the door, she may as well hear it too."

"All right, that's *enough* of this," I said, angrily slamming the bedroom door. I didn't want Bunny Carnazzo broadcasting our catfights to her sophomore class. "Tomorrow we'll call the furniture company and see what we can do. Meanwhile, we're packing to go to New York. So why don't you get inside there and help Bunny sort the clothes. Jesus Christ, enough is enough. I'm doing everything I can, stop yelling at me."

Sullenly, silently, Judy went into the living room to help Bunny. I took a deep breath and tried to swallow back the emotion that threatened to drain me of whatever will, whatever power, whatever strength I still possessed. We had to get to New York, and I was the one who was going to get us there.

TUESDAY, DECEMBER 10

So I got on the phone to take care of business.

1. The Bellaire Storage Company, in addition to requiring twelve hundred dollars in back storage costs, will not release any furniture without Sid's signature. So that's that.

2. CMA has sent the AGVA contracts for the London booking. Now we must arrange transportation.

Thomas Cook tells me there are no ships sailing for either Liverpool or Southampton that arrive near the end of December. We'd thought it would be marvelously romantic to pack a steamer trunk, throw a champagne party in our stateroom, and churn out of New York Harbor on the Normandie, breaking up the captain's table every night and madcapping ourselves across the ocean.

But it is not to be. We'll fly.

"Thank you," I said to the travel agent and hung up. The phone was becoming sticky in my hand. It was noon, and time for a shower.

While I was lathering up, the doorbell rang. I heard Judy go to answer it. Two more policemen had come to the apartment. The doctors from Peter Bent Brigham, unable to reach Judy by phone, had sent the cops to investigate.

"Mahnin', ma'am, sorry to trouble you, we have a cahll to investigate the death of a Miss Judy Gahland."

"That's me," Judy said.

"You're Miss Gahland?"

"I have been for the past nn, *four* hundred and twelve years." The young officer frowned. "May we see some identification, ma'am?"

"Now hold the phone, gentlemen . . ."

"Just a fahmality, ma'am. You see, this is Doctor Ames Curtis of the Peter Bent Brigham Hospital. He wouldn't send us out if he didn't think there might be cahz for alahm. He wahned us Miss Gahland might be in serious trouble."

Judy examined both officers, up and down. "Well, look," she said finally, "shall we flip for it?"

Departure time was drawing near. I closed out my checking account at the Shawmut National Bank. I went to Lord & Taylor and bought Judy a new floppy hat, purple this time, as a morale booster for the trip. It was always good to have some extra fillip, a gewgaw or an item of clothing to give our exit snap. And Judy wanted to dress up for our triumphal return to New York City.

I called Arleen's Bridal Service for a limousine. We're going to throw all Judy's baggage in the trunk and make the trip by car; this'll be easier than shipping the stuff and flying, which Judy hates anyway.

Much is being left behind for lack of room. Our shiny new Jordan Marsh kitchenware, for instance. "Annie," I said, "they're yours. Wear them in good health."

Annie looked up from her music copying. She was rushing to finish the orchestrations in time for England. "Hey, can I drive with you guys to New York?" she asked Judy.

"Oh, Annie, no . . ." Judy said, then dropped her voice to a whisper. "We're going to nn, *screw* in the backseat . . ."

"And Annie, the furniture," I said. "Some of it is leased, some of it is Ben Freeman's . . . can you take care of it? Here are the phone numbers."

And where will we stay in New York? Certainly not with my folks on Park Avenue. Not with this mess of baggage; Herbert would go in*sane*. The "Merv Griffin Show" has offered to arrange accommodations for the two or three days before the taping, so at three this afternoon, I called the producer, Bob Shanks.

"We're coming in a week early, Bob," I announced, and heard a stunned pause on the other end of the line. "If you could get us hotel space," I went on, "we'd really be grateful. Judy prefers the Carlyle, if you can swing it."

Recovering his equanimity, Bob said he'd see what he could do. But at four-thirty he called back. "John, the Carlyle is booked up, and so is the Plaza. I'm going to try the St. Regis now."

"Okay, look, Bob—we're leaving at six. If you don't get the St. Regis, leave a message for us with the night manager. We'll pick it up when we get there."

The buzzer rang, heralding the arrival of our driver, Joe Bazarian. Joe was a stolid, unflappable guy in his early forties who looked as if he might have driven Greyhound buses cross-country before he settled in Boston. Together, we began hauling cartons and cases downstairs, where Joe had parked a white 1968 Cadillac limousine.

We made *thirty* trips. I counted. Thirty trips, loading the trunk, the backseat, the front seat with suitcases, with the Valpak, with hatboxes—the artifacts, the detritus of Judy's life.

And this is only part of it, I kept thinking, riding the elevator up and down, there's more of Judy's life at the Bellaire Storage Company in Beverly Hills, and more still at the St. Moritz Hotel on Central Park South, and where will this trail end? Maybe Judy was doomed, like the Flying Dutchman, to circle the globe, leaving pieces of herself wherever she lighted, like some jittery, incandescent firefly.

We didn't look back as Joe pulled out of the Prudential driveway. We were thinking of the items we'd left behind, the calls we'd forgotten to make, and we let Boston slip away without saying good-bye.

It was the last time Judy was to see it.

"What time you think we'll get there, Joe?" Joe kept his eyes on the road. "We should be able to make it in about four hours," he said.

"Nn, can we find some . . . *mar*velous place to stop for dinner?" Judy wanted to know. She was thinking about her liquor supply. I'd fixed her a quart container of vodka and cranberry juice, which she was sipping through a pair of straws, but it was unreasonable to expect it to last all the way to New York.

We made a rest stop at a Holiday Inn on the thruway. Some function was in progress in the dining room, and a lady recognized Judy. "Oh my goodness, pinch me!" this lady cried. "I must be dreaming!" So Judy pinched her and signed an autograph, and we climbed back in the car.

"Guess what?" I said. "While you were in the loo, I made us reservations at Stonehenge."

Judy was elated at the mere sound of the name. "You mean in *England*?" I told her Stonehenge was a restaurant in Ridgefield, Connecticut, with one of the best kitchens on the East Coast.

"Mmm, maybe . . . Johnny *Green* is the chef there . . ." Judy giggled. She was referring to one of M-G-M's most prominent musical directors.

"He was a great nn, gour*met,* you know. He liked to give din-

Judy in pants suit—as she looked when we met. This was the outfit Judy appropriated from the set of *Valley of the Dolls*. (Photofest)

"I'd Like to Hate Myself in the Morning"—the song that brought us together. She sang it on *The Merv Griffin Show* and in London. (Author's collection)

My father and mother. They weren't really what you'd call bucolic.

Marjorie Meyer, my mother, tried not to act star struck, but asked Judy for makeup tips, loaned her a pair of earrings.

Herb Meyer, my father, viewed Judy as a disruption in his kitchen. She left the butter out. (Author's collection)

In the Meyer living room, clowning with my Maltese Cross. Marjorie took these, embarrassed to be acting like a tourist. But I'm glad she did. (Author's collection)

Same sitting. Looks like I'm supposed to
be doing something—but what? Dancing?
(Author's collection)

Mary McCarty, my employer, ran the nightclub Three. She paid Judy $100.00 to sing there. The enclosed CD is of our rehearsal for this appearance. (Photofest)

Harold Arlen, composer of "Over the Rainbow," paid Judy's hospital bill. A fastidious dresser, painfully shy. (Photofest)

Judy with Sid Luft, husband #3. "He was a gangster" was Judy's description. I accosted him in the dentist's chair. (Photofest)

Judy with David Begelman, her agent and onetime lover. A smooth operator, he stole thousands from Judy and Sid, but she dropped charges, unwisely. He later committed suicide. (Photofest)

Judy with Kay Thompson, her mentor, Liza's godmother. She was also the mother of the flatulent dog. (Photofest)

Judy with Dean Martin and Frank Sinatra. Martin: "Willya look at the legs on the girl singer?" Sinatra: "Yeah, and they go all the way up to her ass." (Photofest)

Mickey Rooney, Judy's co-star in over a dozen early films. He insisted she become partners with him in a chain of musical comedy schools. (Photofest)

Judy and John, signing autographs. Judy was (almost) always gracious to her fans. However, I once heard her bark, "Not now!"

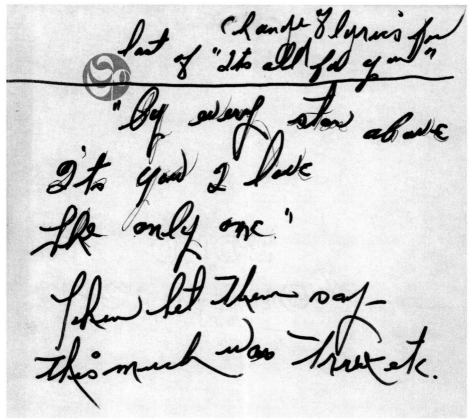

Judy's handwriting. She rewrote my lyric to "It's All for You"—and improved it! (Author's collection)

Program, Talk of the Town nightclub. Union rules forbade the taping of this show, so I did it myself under the table. (Author's collection)

Judy with Mark Herron, husband #4. This was how you looked after spending a month with Judy. (Author's collection)

Tom Green, Judy's beau before me. He dropped off a shocking packet of info to the Park Avenue flat. Marjorie said he looked like a "Yalie." (Photofest)

Judy with Mickey Deans, the guy who replaced me. Supplied Judy with pills; under his supervision, she OD'd and died. We nearly had a fistfight in London. (Photofest)

John Meyer, the author. I'm still here. Still composing. (Scott Wynn)

ner parties to show off his . . . cooking. And he was rather a nn, *fuss*budget too, everything had to be just so when you visited . . . you know, the ashtrays got emptied the moment you nn, dropped an *ash* . . . and he made a bass in a pastry shell, and he made a soufflé, and he served some rare nn, *nec*tar . . . and he was just, you know, nn, *preen*ing himself with all the compliments. There were just the six of us, Vincente and me, and Howard Dietz, who was wooing some girl at the time, and . . . toward the end of the meal, Howard became . . . ill. He grew paler and paler until he finally had to . . . *rush* from the table, and we heard the most nn, *sick*ening noises coming from the bathroom . . . and then Howard reappeared, looking nn, totally *green* . . . and Johnny, with great concern (Howard was head of publicity), Johnny asked him if he was, you know, o*kay* . . . and Howard said 'Don't worry, Johnny—the white wine came up with the fish.' "

It got me excited when Judy told stories; she was so wonderful at it. "Tell me about David Rose," I said. "You never talk about him or Vincente."

Judy raised her eyebrows in a helpless expression. "There's not really a lot to say about him. I was, nn, *very* young . . . I didn't see much of him because he was nn, in the *ar*my . . . and when he came home all he did was play with his nn, *trains*. He *loved* electric trains." Judy paused, thinking about it.

"Vincente was very fastidious," she went on. "He'd come home from the studio about six, he'd have one nn, fast mar*tini*, dinner, and then—wropp! Right into bed. To sleep, I mean. And he snored . . . oh, he snored dreadfully. I remember one night (hee hee) he'd bought me this rather . . . *hand*some . . . black onyx ring. And one night his snoring just . . . an*noy*ed me so . . . I took the ring"—Judy made a fist—"and gave him a *smack!*"— Judy brought her fist down—"right on the bridge of his nose, and he went 'Wraaagghhh!' "—Judy clutched her face—"And I quickly, you know, grabbed some blood and smeared it on the night table . . . and I said, 'Darling, you must have turned in your sleep . . .' We had to send for the doctor. The next day he went to the studio with his nose in a . . . *sling!*"

Judy took a sip through her straws. It was a long ride, but, as the darkness descended and Joe turned on his beams, we began to mellow out, throwing lines, drinking, necking a little, relaxing into the dim, plush interior of the limousine. We were intimately squeezed together by the cases and hatbox beside us on the backseat, and Judy was making a game out of pulling my earlobes. She was trying to get them to touch my shoulders. By nine o'clock we'd left the unpleasant aspects of our departure behind us.

At Stonehenge, we insisted Joe join us for dinner, though he tried to demur. Nonsense, we said, and plopped him down with us at a table by the fireplace. We ordered wine, and duck, and steak, and suddenly we were having an uproarious time.

After dinner we went exploring and discovered a piano upstairs, in a private salon. "Sit down, Joe," said Judy, "we're going to rehearse my nn, *tele*vision songs . . ."

And we sang and played "Hate Myself" and "It's All for You" and "After the Holidays" for Joe, our audience of one. Then we ran through them again. As we began this second rendition, I noticed we were being observed from the doorway by the staff; several waiters, a couple of busboys, and a stern-looking woman with brown hair who announced herself as Mrs. Stockli, the wife of the owner/chef, who politely told us we had to stop.

"But it's only eleven-*thirty* . . ." Judy protested.

"We have to close, I'm sorry," said the woman, with a slight accent.

"Oh, Mrs. Stockli," said Judy, preparing to attack obliquely, "the food was absolutely nn . . . mag*nifi*cent, and we thought we could show our appreciation with a few songs . . ."

Unh unh, I thought, beckoning to Joe, Judy's gonna have a job on her hands with this one. There was a Teutonic stolidity about Mrs. Stockli that would brook no argument. I could tell she wasn't going to succumb to Judy's honeyed blandishments, no matter how charmingly delivered.

I took Joe downstairs, and the two of us stepped outside the front door and stood on the flagstone steps, drinking in the cool atmosphere, watching our breath make puffs of steam in the chill.

Judy pushed the door open and beckoned to me. "You go talk to her," she said.

"What's the story?"

"That dried-up old bitch won't let us stay the night. I know they have rooms. See what *you* can do with her."

I shook my head. "Sorry, Judes. Whatever you got yourself into, this is your battle." I'd decided I wasn't taking on any more of Judy's windmills than were absolutely necessary—and staying the night at Stonehenge definitely didn't qualify.

"Oh, you *shit*," Judy said to me.

"Listen, Judy, the hell with you," I responded. "If I wanted to, I could get into sixty fights a day over you and your stupid whims. Druggists, hotel clerks, maître d's—there's no end to it. Now I'm sorry, but I'm not gonna go yell at Mrs. Stockli just to make you happy." I started toward the car. "Come on," I said.

Petulantly, Judy got into the car, and we set off once more. But she refused to let go of the incident. I was disloyal, a traitor. "Just like everybody . . ." she said, spitefully. "When the going gets rough, you're not there for me . . ." She moved to the corner of the seat, as far away from me as she could get.

We rode along in sullen silence, Judy staring morosely out the window. I closed my eyes, wondering whether I could catch a little nap, but the sound track in my head was too loud and too frantic. I opened my eyes. Judy had turned her back to me, and her body attitude was one of rejection. I put a hand on her shoulder but she shrugged it off crankily.

"Hey, hey, hey, all right now, let's be friends." I leaned against Judy's back, circling her stomach from behind with my arm. "Come on Judes, you know I'd do anything for you . . . within reason. I just can't keep getting my head blown off time after time." I nuzzled the back of her neck with my nose. "Hey, you know what I'm going to do when we get to the St. Regis? I'm gonna call room service and have them send up a gallon of baby oil, two little Nubian children with fans, and an aardvark with a three-foot tongue . . ."

And then I caught myself wondering, Hey, why should I be the one to make up?

Part Three

❊ ❊ ❊

The Return to New York

WEDNESDAY, DECEMBER 11

I was still wondering when we hit New York, about quarter to two in the morning. Bob Shanks was supposed to have booked us rooms or left a message at the St. Regis with the night manager. Well, they never heard of us at the St. Regis. There was no room and no message. And Mr. Carey, the night manager, wasn't there.

"Look," I told the desk clerk, "we've got to get rooms tonight; I've got Judy Garland out there in the back of a car." The clerk was as accommodating as he could be. He dialed the Pierre, the Regency, and the Warwick. None of them could take us. "There's four conventions in town, Mr. Meyer," he said to me.

Damn it, I thought irritably. Shanks was supposed to have taken care of these arrangements. Frustrated and angry, I climbed back into the car. "Take us to Fifty-third and Seventh, Joe," I said. I figured the Americana might have room.

Judy and I approached the desk together, Judy carrying her new purple hat in her hands. "I'm Mr. Meyer," I said to this clerk, "and I need a double room, if you have one."

The clerk thumbed through his reservation file. "Mr. J. Meyer, sir?" he inquired, looking up. "Yes," I said. I was surprised.

"I believe Mr. Shanks from Channel Five called us earlier?" the clerk continued.

"Yes, yes—" I said, getting excited. So Shanks had come through after all! But why hadn't he left a message at the St. Regis? The clerk was looking at Judy, and suddenly a flash of recognition crossed his face. While I was signing the register I saw him disappear into an office behind the desk. He reappeared a moment later with an older, graying man who took in our appearance with an impassive glance. This man murmured something to our clerk and retreated back into the office.

The clerk turned to me with an almost apologetic smile. "Mr. Meyer," he said, "I've just been informed we'll require a deposit from you, in cash."

"May I ask why?" I said, in an injured tone.

"Hotel policy."

Judy had been listening to this. Now she grabbed my arm and

whispered urgently into my ear. "Don't you see—? They have me *blackballed.*"

No, I couldn't believe this; Judy was making it up, it was another of her provocative games. Impatiently, I shook her hand off my arm. I needed to get this endless day of traveling and uncertainty over with.

"All right," I told the clerk, taking out my checkbook. "How much is that again?"

The clerk looked terribly chagrined. "I'm sorry, sir, we cannot accept a personal check."

"*What?!*" The edge in my voice nearly shaved his head. "You mean to tell me—"

"Hotel regulations, sir," said this unfortunate minion. Several people were interested in this now, their attention caught by my raised voice. They had begun to recognize Judy and were hovering around the scene.

"Darling—" Judy was talking to me again. "If you had a million in cash on you, you still wouldn't be able to get a room here."

"*Every* hotel takes checks," I protested.

"They have me blackballed," Judy reiterated, "don't you under*stand?*" She began tugging my arm. "Come on," she said, raising her voice five or six decibels, "this is nothing but a big cathouse anyway, a whorehouse. A cathouse and a whorehouse. Who needs it?"

Judy waved her purple hat in an expansive, screw you gesture, and the eight or ten onlookers suddenly gave our exit a cheer. "Tell 'em, Judy!" and "God bless you!" came from this impromptu fan club as we made our way down the steps and back into the car.

"It's Sid, that prick," Judy was saying to me. "He's got me all tied up. He's ruined my credit in this town. He's got all my money, that no-good bastard, he's tied up all my projects . . . *Laurette,* what a marvelous film that would be . . . but that sonofabitch, after all the money I made for him . . ."

"Take us uptown, Joe." I leaned through the glass partition into the front seat. "Eighty-fourth and Park." Herbert and Marjorie would have to take us in. They couldn't refuse their firstborn in a moment of extremity, could they? Could they?

Judy squirmed her way up into the partition beside me. "You know, Joe . . ." she sighed, ". . . if I died tomorrow, nobody would miss me." Joe glanced at her. "That's no way to talk, Judy," he said. "What about your kids?" Judy seemed to ponder this a moment. "What would you do, Joe . . . in my shoes?"

"Judy," said Joe, "with all your talent . . . you could have the world at your feet . . . people love you."

"Oh, Joe . . ." said Judy, tearfully, and she reached over and grabbed his right hand. "Thank you . . . thank you so much . . ."

We arrived at Park Avenue, and Joe and I made another thirty trips upstairs. When the last carton and case had been lifted from the elevator, and the Meyer foyer was crammed to overflowing, Joe extended his hand.

"Joe"—I stopped him—"it's four in the morning. Why don't you stay over? There's lots of room."

Joe shook his head. "I gotta get back."

"Jesus, Joe, all the way to Boston? Tonight?"

"Yeah. I gotta get back." Judy went to Joe and threw her arms around him and kissed him. "Thank you . . ." she said. I slipped a fifty-dollar bill into his hand. "Thanks for everything," I said. "You were absolutely sensational."

"Keep up the good work," Joe told me as he stepped into the elevator. "Take care of her."

I'll do what I can, I thought.

Poor Bob Shanks. We descended on him like a pair of angry hornets. I called him first, about one-thirty in the afternoon. I told him of our nightmare experience; of how no word had been left at the St. Regis; of how we'd been humiliated at the Americana; and of how, finally, we'd ended up at my family's place.

Bob was sorry, he said, especially about the Americana's behavior. He couldn't understand why they should insist on a cash deposit. "You know, frankly," he told me, "they all are a little reluctant, to tell you the truth. We were having trouble."

"Well, whether they are or not," I said, "that's your responsibility."

"Well, no it isn't, John, now wait wait wait wait wait. I think we'd better get squared away quickly on this. We'd love to have her on and everything, but I *cannot* pick up all of her bills for ten days. We're a scale show, she has to come on like Harry Belafonte or anybody else. I just cannot get in one of those situations—"

"But you *made* the reservations—" I said.

"Well, John, what can I do? I called the way I always do, we get very good service as a rule, and they screwed it up, I apologize for that. We had about three hours' notice, and we did our best. I'm not the manager of the St. Regis. I'm *stunned* at the Americana. I mean, people walk in off the street and they're not required to pay a cash deposit."

"Yes, but from Judy's viewpoint it's—"

"I understand that, but I think one must examine one's . . . track record. I mean a tourist can walk in and not be asked for a cash deposit."

"All right, can you do anything about it now?" I said. There was no point in keeping Bob on the defensive without achieving some positive result. Like a room somewhere.

Bob sighed. "I cannot authorize more than two nights, John, in a hotel, and the room only, really, which I was going to do next week, when I thought you were coming in. Even at the jeopardy of blowing the date, which I would be sick about . . ."

"Look, she's not asking for ten days."

"I mean I was shocked yesterday. I want to do everything I can to make it nice and right."

"I'll call you back."

It was Judy, however, who called back. Once again, the conversation began with Bob's apology. He said he'd gone down the whole list of hotels, the St. Regis, the Regency, the Plaza. Judy was not mollified.

"I think it would've been nice, actually . . ." Judy said to him, "I mean, this is just a . . . *tip* . . . from me . . . if you'd have let me know in some way, or left a note—"

"We *did*," Shanks insisted. "I left it with a Mr. Carey at the St. Regis—"

"Well, he wasn't there," said Judy, with an air of finality. Shanks grew defensive. "He *said* he would take care of it, and that was the plan you and I had agreed on, and we followed it through."

"Well then, where's the room?" Judy said.

"Well, they didn't have any room, but uh . . ."

"Well, why didn't you call me back in Boston and tell me that?"

"Well, you know, we did speak about that—"

"You told me there was no room at the Carlyle—"

"That's where we started, right. Then we tried the St. Regis, and then we talked again—"

"No, you didn't talk to me," Judy said.

"Well, yes, I spoke to John, and he said All right, we're leaving, so you and I agreed that I would leave word—"

"No, you and I didn't," said Judy. She was deliberately nit-picking and caviling to make things difficult for Bob. "I didn't know anything except that I was going to be at the St. Regis."

"Well, no," said Bob, "because that was clear before the last time we talked."

"What seems to be the problem?" Judy asked him, now that she'd berated him into a corner.

"I don't know," he said. "All the hotels are booked. We tried the Plaza, they accepted the reservation, as did the St. Regis, and then five minutes later they would call us back and say they'd made a mistake, they didn't have any rooms, and . . . I don't *know* what the problem is. I asked, and they said there're conventions in town and they're booked. And we tried *every*-thing . . . we have a tie-in, a connection with the Hilton and we couldn't even do *that*. The town is booked. Then, we *did* finally get the Americana thing, I called Carey back at the St. Regis and I said 'Miss Garland will be arriving there, will you please leave word for her that the reservation is at the Americana' and he said 'I'll take care of it,' which he has in the past . . ."

"I know Mr. Carey," said Judy, "because I used to live at the St. Regis; however, he was off. Because we drove in from Boston, we went to a great deal of trouble, and . . . and I was really looking forward to working with James Mason and also, you know, meeting you and nn, *doing* a good show . . . but so far it's a bit dis*cour*aging, and it's kind of . . . *old hat*." Judy leaned on the words.

"You know," she continued, "I don't know what this whole *problem* seems to be, picking up *all* my bi—I don't want anyone to pick up any bills. I have enough money to pay my bills. I'd like some *salary*." Judy paused. "I mean, just scale," she emphasized.

"Oh, of course, of course," Shanks said.

"That's all. And it's usually the policy of any, of any show, to . . . if anyone comes from another town, to pay their hotel expenses just *for that amount of time*. Now that's the usual way."

"Yes," said Bob.

"And I don't *know* any other, you know, 'cause I'm not . . . a *producer*." Judy italicized the word scornfully. "And uh . . . but I simply would've liked to be on the show," she added.

"Well, me too," said Shanks, "and I'm awfully sorry if it's—"

"Where's Mr. Griffin?" Judy said.

"—blown," Shanks finished. "He's—"

"Whaddya mean, 'blown'?" Judy interrupted loudly. "Who blew it?" Her tone was deadly.

"Well, no, I say I hope it's not," said Shanks. "And I would be very sorry if it is—"

"Well, I think that's entirely up to you . . ." said Judy. "Entirely."

"Well, I am quite, you know, I really, it's out of my hands, almost . . ." Bob fluttered. "There's nothing I can do."

"What do you *mean* there's nothing you can do?" Judy expostulated. "Then who *can?*"

"There are *certain* things I can do, and beyond that, I . . . I can't . . ."

"Well, what are the 'certain things'?" Judy wanted to know. She was going fishing now, after having initiated this game of brinkmanship. Something in Judy led her to provoke these crises. She had done the same sort of number on the set of *Valley of the Dolls*, Jenny told me. As for me, hunched over my tape recorder, I could only monitor this conversation in amazement. Would Judy really blow the "Merv Griffin Show"?

"Well," Shanks began, "I thought you would be coming in next week, and I, in my mind, was quite willing to, you know, let you have two or three nights in a hotel, which we don't ordinarily do, we aren't equipped to do *that*, but you are an exceptional—"

"Mmm, yes," Judy agreed. "That's very nice of you."

"It's not much, I grant you," Shanks said, "but we are a scale show, and that's the reality I have to live with. I did not make the budget."

"You know, you're funny," Judy said, pityingly. "You are." She might have been addressing a bird with a broken wing. Aww.

"I don't mean to be," said Bob.

"No, and I'm not saying it in a mean way, it's just that I've heard this kind of . . . people who are put in the middle, as you obviously are, always sort of say nn, you *know*, there are certain things that are my responsibility, and there are certain things I just can't take care of, and . . . people like myself are always left out in left field wondering what in the hell . . . *hap*pened."

"Now wait a minute, Judy," Shanks remonstrated, "you know, we set a date for the nineteenth, we figured you'd be in the eighteenth or so and everything was fine. At three o'clock yesterday I get a call you're coming in. I was quite willing to, I had no idea it would be that difficult to book a room . . . we started running into problems immediately with that . . . and the arrangements got confused, and I feel *very* bad about it, I don't treat people this way, and especially you—"

"Oh, that's all right," Judy said, "I'm used to it."

"Well, no," said Shanks, "and I'd . . . I'd like to break that habit if that is the truth, the case, I'd like you to go away saying well, by God, it didn't happen with them, you know, and they do appreciate me and care . . . and that's the truth of it, Judy."

"Thank you," said Judy.

"Now, beyond that, I do have a limited budget, you know, we're not a Dean Martin show"—Shanks was referring to a glitzy West Coast variety show that had lots of money to spend —"and so I was really looking forward to your coming in next week—" What Shanks meant was that he was unprepared to deal with Judy and her requirements before the eighteenth.

"Well, nn, my *good*ness!" Judy cooed, "I came in early because I wanted to get something . . . lovely to wear . . . and I wanted to look fine because James Mason . . . and I got *so* ex-

cited, and I . . . and Mort Lindsey . . . and I haven't been on
. . . Mervyn's show before . . ."

"Ever," said Shanks.

"And uh . . . I was really very . . . thrilled about it. But uh
. . . the only thing is that uh . . . I guess it just didn't work
out."

Again there was silence at Bob's end of the line. He hadn't really accepted it when Judy said she was canceling before. He
had no idea of the kind of power game he was involved in here.

"Well . . . I'm very sorry to hear that," he said, finally.

"Well, it wasn't my fault . . ." said Judy. "I've been here." I
was gazing at the revolving tape spools and shaking my head in
admiration at Judy's sheer balls. Where, Judy? I asked her mentally, *where* have you been?

Shanks was trying to recover now. "Well, I really think we're
both blameless . . ." he hazarded. "The only thing that's gone
wrong, really, is that uh . . . a hotel clerk didn't uh . . ."

"I tell you what," Judy cut him off, "maybe it would help nn,
me . . . as a woman . . . if we would just forget this. And uh, I
would like to talk to Mort Lindsey because he's gone to a great
deal of trouble about the music, and . . . I would just like to
talk to him." She thought about this a moment. "I would also
like to *get* the music," she continued, "because I went to a great
deal of trouble, we both, we *both* did, we both be*liev*ed in . . .
you know, doing the show, 'n we were, I was looking forward to
it par*tic*ularly . . . and also, I'd love *you* to send me a great big
bouquet of white 'n pink roses with a little note just saying,
Sorry it didn't work out . . . and that'll make everything fine."

Unbe*liev*able balls, I was thinking. First she cancels the appearance, then she wants to take the music with her, and, as a
capper, she wants him to send her flowers for this!

On his end, Shanks was trying hard to assimilate this.

"You think it can't work out?" he said now, tentatively.

"I don't, I don't know *how* . . ." Verbally, Judy threw her
hands in the air. "You're the one who seems to think it can't . . .
I . . . you know, it seems that I'm just such a nn, hopeless *prob*-
lem . . . mmm, that always makes me laugh . . ."

"Not at all, not at all," Bob mumbled, lamely. This was his
moment to rise to the occasion, but he was totally floored by

Judy's blitzkrieg, her deadly escalation of the stakes. No hotel?
she was saying. Okay, no show.

What Bob should have said was, *Darling, I'm so sorry, it's all
my fault, I apologize, here are some roses, and I'll find you a
room by this afternoon*—and dealt with the details later. But he
didn't. All he said was Not at all, not at all.

"Yah, well, nn, about any extra ex*penses*," Judy said, reopen-
ing negotiations, "I have oth—"

"Unhappy as it sounds," Bob said, "I have to say, though,
that between now and the nineteenth I just can't—"

"Well, between now and the nineteenth," Judy said acidly,
"I've got two other shows to do, dear."

"But I can . . ." Shanks paused, trying to pick his mind up off
the floor.

"I don't know whether you heard what I said," Judy primed
him.

"Yes, I did," said Bob.

"So you see, all of the nn, *thing* wasn't up to you, and you
weren't nn, re*spon*sible"—Judy colored the word with the con-
tempt she reserved for those "heavy furniture" people who refused to accept the obvious—"and you wouldn't have had to pay
all of that nn, *cash* 'n everything . . . but the only thing is . . . I
would like to speak to my friend Mort and uh . . . I . . . as a
matter of fact, I did drive in from Boston, I did pack, we did
have a verbal agreement on the phone, and I would like to go
away with uh . . . with some kind of grace, and I think you
should grant me that . . . I mean that's the least you can
do . . ."

Shanks, trying to salvage something from the wreckage she
was making of his afternoon, said, "You know, I can, I can, if
you . . . would want to honor and keep the date, I would love
to . . . pay for your hotel for two nights . . ."

But Judy had moved beyond that now. "I don't think it's necessary," she said.

"I'm quite anxious to do that."

"Mmm, well, I don't know whether I am or not." Judy gave a
little laugh. "At this point, unfortunately. You know, people's enthusiasm has a way of getting . . . *quashed* by a feeling of uh
. . . re*jec*tion and . . . and—"

"Well, if you—" Shanks tried to say, but Judy rolled viciously over his words.

"—and if you don't care enough—"

Shanks said something here, but Judy was not to be deterred. "Look, wait a minute, hold it buddy," she spat through the wire. "If you don't care enough, if you *don't care enough*"—Shanks was trying to form a sentence but Judy wouldn't let him—"IF YOU DON'T CARE ENOUGH," she barked, "let the lady *off the hook*."

"Well, I'm trying—" Bob said.

"But in a nice way," Judy finished.

"Let us do that to each other, yes," said Shanks, obviously shaken.

"Yes," said Judy, "but I'm . . . you're not a lady."

"No, I'm not," Bob corroborated.

"You're a gentleman. I hope."

"That's correct. And I try to behave like one."

"Well . . . mmm, why *shouldn't* you?" Judy asked him.

"Well, there's no reason why . . ." Bob said, and stopped. He had forsaken all initiative, he was unmanned, flustered, and wanted nothing so much as to get off the phone and away from Judy's castigations. A long moment passed in silence.

"You seem to have some . . . deep-seated *anger* . . ." Judy said to him, trying to get him to say . . . who knows what? "I don't know what your—"

"No," said Bob. "I'm disappointed that I would have to point it out."

"Point it out? Point what out?"

"Nothing," said Bob, almost inaudibly. He was practically under the rug.

"That you're a gentleman?"

"There's no anger," Bob said wearily, "and there's no problem. I have told you what I can realistically do, I'm deeply disappointed that that's not satisfying to you. There were problems last night that were beyond both your and my control, there were third parties, and I, I cannot—nor should either one of us —be held to blame for that, and I apologize for that, as I would to any lady being inconvenienced that way . . . and I'm trying

to do all that I can to make it comfortable for you to come on
. . . and beyond that, I just can't do anything, that's all."

"I understand," said Judy, very Gracious Lady now. She
wanted to wrap this up.

"I uh . . . I'm *very* sorry," Bob repeated.

"That's perfectly all right," Judy said, as though she were forgiving a salesgirl at Tiffany's for printing an incorrect zip code.

"I can't think of anybody I'd rather do it for, if I could."

"Well, thank you," Judy reiterated, "and I *do* understand. And,
meantime"—she continued in a brisker tone (she didn't need to
hear any more of Shanks and his inept apologies and excuses; if
he couldn't handle her tantrums and shitfits, then the hell with
him)—"may I get back to realism again? I would like to talk to
Mort. Is Mort anywhere in the building?"

"He probably is, yes," said Shanks, and you can hear the relief
in his voice, "if you can hold on, I can probably switch it down."

"Okay, fine," said Judy.

"Let me make sure he's down there, first—"

"—right—"

"—before I switch you." Shanks was handling Judy now very
gingerly. "I'll put you on hold for a moment—"

"—thank you."

"—see if he's there—"

"—Right, okay." Judy's tone was saying Come on, already.
There was a pause, and then Mort Lindsey's voice said, "Judy?"

"Hi . . ." said Judy. "I'm sorry things didn't work out."

"Huh?" said Mort.

"Things didn't work out," Judy repeated.

"Well, what's happening?" Mort asked, trying to get some
purchase on the situation.

"Well, *I* dunno . . ." Judy sighed wearily, as if she'd just been
building the pyramids. "I came into town last night, and it seems
that Mr. Shanks is very up*set* and so forth . . . I don't know
what's happening, and uh . . . all I did, want to work with you
and want to work with James Mason, I thought it could be a
nice show, but . . ."

"Well, when is the date? You're supposed to be on the nineteenth?"

"Yah, but . . ." Judy let her voice trail off.

"Well, what's happening up there?" Mort asked her.

"What's happening where? I'm in New York," Judy said quickly. "I don't know. I really don't. Except it's embarrassing . . . I'd love to hear the orchestration . . ."

"Well, it's about halfway through now," said Mort, "you know, I'm still, 'cause I have a little time . . ."

"Well," Judy said, "I've got to . . . I can't come there, honey . . ."

"Yeah," said Mort, having no idea what he was saying "yeah" to. Come where? he must have thought. What is all this about?

"Uh . . . maybe *you* can call him and find out what's going on . . ." said Judy, the little manipulator. She knew what she was doing. Mort would call Merv, and Merv would talk to Shanks, and then we'd see about things.

"Look," said Mort, right on cue, "lemme call you back."

"Okay," said Judy, in the tone of a forlorn little girl who's been trying and trying and *trying* to do the grocery shopping correctly.

"I'll talk to him," Mort said. "Where can I reach you?"

"Have you got a pencil?" said Judy.

Forty-five minutes later an emissary from the "Dick Cavett Show" arrived. Len Friedlander.

"What would you like to do on the show?" he asked Judy.

"Well . . ." Judy said, "I could nn, *tell* some stories . . ."

"Tell the Sprague story," I said to her, mischievously.

Judy demurred. "Oh, Johnny . . . it's too . . . *naughty.*"

"Okay, tell about Peter A. Follo."

So Judy told the Peter A. Follo story, and a story about Harry Rapf, who had been one of Louis B. Mayer's assistants. Len marked these names on a pad.

"Now is there anything you want to sing?" he asked. Judy looked at me. "Oh, I don't know if I can really . . . *sing* anything . . ." She turned to Len. "You know, Johnny just wrote me a . . . *new* song . . ."

Friedlander perked up. "Really?" he said, and a different expression came to his eyes. I realized he had no idea I was a songwriter. No one did. No one was quite certain just where I fit in. Was I Judy's piano player or boyfriend or manager or writer or what?

"Yeh-heh-ess . . ." Judy laughed. "One night I said to Johnny, 'Do you mind if I say my prayers in front of you?' . . . and he said, 'No, of course not' . . . he was half asleep . . ."

I had to avert my eyes in embarrassment at Judy's graphic depiction of our intimacy—which, of course, was why she was telling this story, always the *provocateuse*, always looking to start trouble.

". . . so I knelt down," Judy was saying, "and I said, 'God bless Johnny, and God bless me' . . . and Johnny hopped out of bed, he grabbed a piece of paper and wrote some words and quickly nn, *ran* into the living room . . . in his shorts . . ." She was watching, hoping to get a rise out of me, but I was assiduously studying the nap in the carpet.

". . . and he started playing changes . . . he wrote it so fast I was still praying when he got back . . ."

"Fantastic," said Friedlander. "Could we hear it?"

"It's the most nn . . . *moving* song . . ." said Judy, and she turned to me with a sweet little smile that was at the same time a challenge.

Okay, sweetheart, I thought, as I went to the piano. I may have written it, but you've got to sing it. I'll call your bluff.

THURSDAY, DECEMBER 12

Annie's back, thank heavens. I can use the assistance, God knows, what with preparing for three TV shows and getting ready to leave for London.

Annie came in today to deal with the trauma of taking Judy to the dentist. Judy has an unsightly, chipped tooth turning brown in the middle of her uppers; she's let it go for years now, because she's absolutely terrified to go to the dentist. But this has to be done. Normally, I would accompany Judy on a mission like this, but today I have a conflicting appointment with David Grossberg, my lawyer, to set the final details of Judy's recording contract with Bob Colby. So faithful Annie is taking the responsibility for seeing that Judy gets to West Fifty-seventh Street in time for her appointment with Dr. Pact. Is that a great name for a dentist, Dr. *Pact?*

Annie had a hell of a time. Judy tried stalling and procrastinating ("where's my nn, *pan*ty hose?"), tried diversionary tactics ("nn, let's have a drink at the Plaza"), but Annie was firm and managed to bring Judy into the building five minutes early. In the lobby, Judy spotted Sid Luft. Annie refused to believe Judy. She thought it was another of Judy's delaying ploys.

"Don't be silly," Annie said. "What would Sid be doing here?"

"Look," Judy insisted, "I was married to the man for quite a long time and I know what he nn, *looks* like . . . hey you, hey fella . . ."

It was Sid all right. "Hi, Toots, what're you doing here?"

Judy explained she was going to the dentist.

"Oh yeah? Lemme see—" Sid grabbed Judy's jaw and pinched it open. He peered inside her mouth. He was going to the dentist, too, a different man on another floor. It was one of those buildings that specialize in dentists' offices. Sid was having root canal work done.

"Take care of yourself, Toots," Sid said as he stepped off the elevator. Judy let the door close after him. "Prick," she said.

Half an hour later I showed up in Dr. Pact's office. Judy was dancing with excitement. "Sid's here!" she cried. "He's on the tenth floor, having nn, *root* canal. Get down there, Johnny."

I wasn't so sure. "And just what am I supposed to do when I get there?" Judy made two little fists of frustration. "Mmm, you can nn, ac*cost* him." I thought it over. "Okay," I said finally. "I'll accost the *shit* out of him."

I went down to the tenth floor and walked in the dentist's door, through his waiting room, and right to the back of the chair in which Sid was being treated.

"Yes?" the dentist said to me inquiringly, looking up from Sid's mouth. I ignored him and moved to the left of the chair. Sid's head was clamped into a nearly horizontal position, but his eyes slid over and saw me. The draining tube in his mouth made a sucking noise.

"Hi, Sid," I said, breezily. "My name is John Meyer and I'd like to talk to you about Judy. I need to ask your advice about a few things. Could we meet for a drink?"

"Sure, Jah . . ." said Sid. He sounded like he'd had a shot of novocaine. He didn't seem to question the strange circumstance of our meeting. Obviously, this was a man accustomed to strange circumstances. He didn't even bother to remove the draining tube.

"How's the Oak Room?" I asked him.

"Naa . . . I duh li' i' . . ." It was tough for Sid to speak against the novocaine and the tube, but he managed. "Hoo 'oithy. 'Ake i' hunh kinco bah . . . hunh kin co bah . . ."

"The King Cole Bar? In the St. Regis?"

"Eth." I looked at my watch. It was now three forty-five. "About six-thirty?"

The man in the chair tried to nod, but the dentist was holding his face firmly. I could see his teeth were really in horrible shape. If ever a guy needed dental work, it was Sid.

"Eth," he said again, and I left the office, abandoning Sid and his mouth to whatever the dentist had in store for them.

Judy was in the chair when I got back upstairs, so I left Annie some money for Dr. Pact. We needed to keep his goodwill, he was the only dentist in the country Judy would trust because he knew how to cope with irrational fear. He was a pediatrician of the mouth. Perfect for Judy.

"And Annie, tell Judy I'm meeting Sid at six-thirty in the King Cole Bar."

"Oh, wow! She'll love it."

"Yes, but it means I won't be able to check us into the Hilton. Can you handle it?"

"I think so. Is there anything special I have to know?"

"No, just tell them Merv Griffin has arranged accommodations for Judy. It's all set."

"What time will you be there?"

"Soon as I'm through with Sid. Probably around eight."

Sid arrived precisely at six-thirty. I'd been afraid he wouldn't make it, that he'd stand me up, figuring I wanted something from him. Which I did. I wanted several things, access to the furniture, for instance. Or the orchestrations. If I could somehow get Sid to fork over those orchestrations, we'd really be in business. But I knew I would have to be cagey to get them.

Sid's face was still full of novocaine. He must have been in real agony, he ordered tea. He had the look of a boozer, the flesh was puffy beneath his eyes, hanging loosely from his chin and his cheeks. He looked like a miserable basset hound. His eyes were wet, but with a smiling shrewdness in them that had nothing to do with mirth.

I opened by knocking Judy, to disarm him. "Christ, Sid, I don't know how you took it all those years. This broad is a complete wack, I can't do a goddam thing with her. Whatever you say to her, she does the opposite. I don't know, how did you handle her?" Sid smiled his mirthless smile, showing his tobacco-stained teeth.

"Well, the only thing you can do with Judy . . . you can't handle Judy. You can just give her her head and try to steer her a little . . ."

"Yeah, but how?"

"Well, John, you see, a lotta the time Judy doesn't know what's to her own best interest. What's best for Judy Garland. I'll give you a for instance. She had this pair of cocksuckers right by the balls. Fields and Begelman. She had 'em right by the short hairs. We were gonna sock 'em with a suit for two and a half million . . ."

"Yah, I heard."

"And we woulda got it."

"What makes you so sure?"

"What makes me sure?" Sid grinned at me again, reached into his breast pocket, and produced a Xeroxed copy of a judge's writ. I scanned it rapidly. It was densely typed, and I can't remember the wording, but—in effect—the document subpoenaed Fields and Begelman into court to face charges of withholding salaries to Judy in the amount of thousands of dollars.

"When Freddie and David see that," Sid continued, "they'll shit. And they'll settle, because they don't want the whole court thing, and because they know I'm right." He sat back in his chair. "I'm going ahead without her, anyhow. A lotta that money is mine. Group Five laid out a lotta cash for Judy. And I was Group Five." He took a sip of tea. "The worst thing Judy coulda done was drop this suit. She cut her own throat. If she'd stuck with me she coulda had it good, she coulda hadda lotta cash, she never woulda hadda work again. But now . . ." Sid shook his massive head.

"This'll probably take a coupla years," I said, inadvertently mimicking his speech pattern.

"Sooner than you think, sooner than you think. I'm pushing it through real fast." A look of irritation crossed his face. "I just wish that fucker Wong would leave me alone. You wanna know something? I can't take a job over a hundred a week because that little fucker'll attach my salary."

I'd heard Sid say this to Judy on the phone in Boston. I murmured something sympathetic, and then I asked Sid about the orchestrations. He smiled indulgently.

"Now what is she gonna do with that music?" he asked me rhetorically, apparently, since he didn't wait for an answer. "Does she think she can work? The minute she gets any loot that fucker Wong'll be right there with his hand out. That music is better off with me. I can take care of it."

"There's a guy named Marelli in Boston who says he can get it," I said. Sid narrowed his eyes, and in that menacing instant I saw why Judy had called him a gangster. "Oh no, he can't. You better believe it."

The way Sid looked, I believed it. I was suddenly eager for our drink to be over with. I stuck my hand in the air, signaling for the check. Then I remembered something else. "Yeah, and also, Sid, Judy's concerned about her furniture." Sid's expression did not change.

"Yeah, well, you tell her she can come and get it. She's welcome to it, all she has to do is pay the storage costs for the last year and a half."

I felt him closing himself to me. Maybe the novocaine was wearing off, or maybe he just didn't like me, but whatever the reason, it was time to go. I put some money on the table, shook hands with Sid, and left.

It was chilly outside, and I headed for the Hilton with a brisk step. As I reached Sixth Avenue I realized what I should have done: I should have offered Sid a cut of Judy's money, the money Wong was going to let her keep when she started working. I should have offered it to him in exchange for the orchestrations.

Shit. It was too late to catch him. I wondered if we had his New York number.

Merv had arranged a two-room suite at the Hilton. He'd sent flowers, and even given her two hundred and fifty dollars in cash. The note said "Just some mad money."

It looked like Judy's tactic had paid off. When Mort asked Merv what was going on about Judy (as Judy had so expertly primed him to do), Merv's reaction was Whaddya *mean?* He had then called Bob Shanks, whose unpleasant duty it had been to inform Merv the date was blown. Blown!? Merv had flown into a rage. You idiot, how could you treat Judy Garland like that, are you crazy? For two lousy nights in a hotel? He had called Judy personally to patch things up, apologized at length, and finished by telling her he'd arranged a suite at the Hilton and was even having a piano moved in.

So Judy was purring now. She was so enthusiastic about her victory that she'd ordered seven bottles of liquor sent up from room service. Liquor, however, was not part of Merv's treat. He might have been crazy, but he wasn't stupid: the hotel was under strict instructions that Judy's bar tab was her own responsibility.

I stared at the bill from room service, practically asphyxiating from the lump of outrage rising in my gorge. "Judy, this is a bill for *a hundred and sixty dollars!* Are you out of your fuckin' *mind?*" Judy knew we were low on cash.

"But Johnny . . . aren't we having Bob Colby up here? Don't we need something to offer him . . . ?"

I was moving from the living room to the pantry, counting the bottles. "I don't fuckin' be*lieve* this," I cried. There was Canadian Club, Hiram Walker, Smirnoff, two brands of Scotch (J&B and Dewar's), and a fifth of Courvoisier brandy. Judy had spent a hundred and sixty dollars for booze we could have bought across the street for maybe seventy bucks.

Judy was eyeing me coldly. "Here we go again," she said to me. "Judy the idiot. I don't know why she can't do anything right. Oh, she can sing a little. But I'll be goddamned if she can move into a hotel room. Unh unh. Not her. You can't leave her alone for a minute."

I felt the edge of Judy's sarcasm curdling my saliva. What was I going to do with this woman?

FRIDAY, DECEMBER 13

We taped the "Dick Cavett Show" today. I say "we" because I had to play piano for Judy when she sang a medley of Peter A. Follo songs, starting with "You Lousy Jippy Jippy Jap" and finishing with "Uncle Sam Is Going to Build an Army."

Though Rex Reed was later to call this show "an unmitigated disaster," Judy was very entertaining, telling the Harry Rapf story ("Mr. Mayer, this is the best piece of pie I ever had in my whole mouth") and sparring energetically with Lee Marvin.

And then Cavett asked her to sing. Bobby Rosengarten's band played an introduction (the orchestration had been written and copied in *twenty-four hours!*) and Judy sang "Prayer," the song I'd composed after our wracking scene in Boston.

She did not sing it well. For openers, the song was only a week old, and she barely knew it. Secondly, her voice was in ragged shape. So, in addition to cracking vocally, halfway through her rendition, Judy lost track of the melodic line and had to finish on an uncertain, upward surge.

It was agonizing for me, standing off camera, thirty feet away. She had introduced the song as having been composed by "a marvelous songwriter by the name of Johnny Meyers." In the wings, I sighed. After two months of sleeping with me she still didn't know there was no S on the end of my name.

Squirming in discomfort, I listened as Judy made hash out of the first tune I'd ever had performed on network television. At the same time, here was Judy singing to millions about the most intimate and personal thing that had passed between us:

> " . . . And let him love me . . .
> And God . . . if you do . . .
> I promise I'll never ask another thing . . .
> Of you . . ."

We went back to the Hilton to catch the show that evening. As Judy stared at the screen, watching Dick Cavett cross and uncross his legs and fiddle with the arm of his chair, she said, "My God, he's nervous . . . why do I make everyone so . . . nn, un*com*fortable?"

"Because, Judes," I said, "no one knows whether you're going to sing 'Over the Rainbow' or open your veins."

Judy giggled. "Sometimes I do both . . . at the same time."

SATURDAY, DECEMBER 14

About two this morning, Judy finally allowed herself to be hungry. She hadn't eaten all day, surviving solely on Ritalin. When Judy performed, I couldn't limit her Ritalin dosage; her emotional dependency was acute.

Now she felt like some chili. "Let's see if we can get the nn, *bell*boy to fetch us some from Clarke's . . ."

So we got the bellboy up, and I gave him a twenty-dollar bill and sent him off for chili-to-go—and would you stop in at Smiler's and pick up a quart of cranberry juice, please?

But by the time he got back, at three-twenty A.M., the chili was cold. "Could you bring us one of those nn, *heat*ing things?" Judy asked him. "One of those serving ovens," I explained, "with the Sterno?"

No, said the bellboy, they were all locked away now. Room service stopped at three. As he departed, I set my mouth for tepid chili. What the hell.

Judy didn't think so. She was hungry, and she wanted to eat what *she* wanted to eat, not what the world told her she *could* eat. Judy hung on to an idea with the tenacity of a Gila monster. She just didn't want to go to bed, she was looking for a little action someplace—where could we start some trouble?

"I know," she said. "Let's go to Arthur and visit Mickey."

"Who's Mickey?"

"Oh, he's nn, marvelous. He manages Arthur. He beat up a CMA agent once, on the street."

Great, I thought, just the kind of guy I'm dying to meet.

So we called Arthur. Sure, Mickey said, come on over. I'll

send the car. And fifteen minutes later we were in a Cadillac limousine driven by a nice blond woman who dropped us off at East Fifty-fourth Street.

Mickey greeted us effusively and led us through the dance room into the rear enclave of the now-darkened club. In the late sixties, Arthur—which was Sybil Burton's brainchild—was the first dance club with any cachet (the Peppermint Lounge was merely tacky), and people like Jackie Kennedy could be seen doing the Hully-Gully and the Twist inside its mirrored walls.

Mickey indicated a round corner table, and, as we sat down, I got my first good look at the man with whom Judy was destined to end her life, the man who became her fifth and final husband.

He was not unattractive, I have to admit. He had a sharp, straight nose, and longish, unkempt hair. The word that came to my mind was "raffish." Mickey and I were to have a short but intense skirmish in London, and even now, within seconds of our meeting, I felt a jockeying for position with him. From the first Who-can-break-whose-fingers handshake. As it turned out, my instinct was correct.

There was roughly twenty minutes of Whatcha been doin' and some Jackie stories and a Boston story and then Mickey said, Hey, why don't we go to my place for breakfast? We can stop and pick up some eggs.

"Do you have any . . . nn, *vod*ka?" Judy was being careful.

"Sure, gallons," said Mickey. "Mattie—" he called to the bartender, who was putting the bar to bed, "grab a bottle of Smirnoff. John . . ." he turned to me, "what're you drinking?"

"I'll have some wine," I said, "anything you have at the bar." From the cooler, I saw Mattie produce a bottle of wine. From the shape of its neck I could see it was a Bordeaux.

The blond woman drove us to the nearest Smiler's, and the three of us went shopping. We grabbed a cart and began loading all kinds of junk into it: eggs, bacon, English muffins, peanut butter, tapioca pudding. As we approached the cashier Judy said, "I want a ride."

So I picked Judy up and put her in the cart (why was this not as amusing as it used to be?). I hoped the eggs wouldn't break.

As Judy was wheeled through the cashier's lane, I threw the

obligatory lines almost by rote, as if I were on automatic pilot.
Yes, we're going to sauté her and serve her on English muffins. I
just wasn't in the mood for it.

Mickey shared an apartment on East Eighty-eighth Street.
Three and a half rooms with a workable kitchen. Mickey's room-
mates were surprised and delighted to see Judy, and she made a
big deal of her entrance.

I grabbed the shopping bags and took them into the kitchen. I
unpacked the eggs and tossed some butter into a skillet. I didn't
want to be a spoilsport, but I couldn't join in the alleged hilarity
going on in the living room. I bit open the package of bacon.

Mickey appeared in the kitchen doorway. "Here," he said, and
tossed me that bottle of Bordeaux. My heart leaped as I saw the
label. It was a '61 Margaux, an exceptional wine, even in its
frosty condition. I uncorked it, wondering whether we'd be here
long enough for it to warm and show its breeding.

Judy called to me from the living room. "Johnny . . . come in
here and meet Charlie . . ."

Mickey's friend, Charlie Cochran, was a singer/pianist who
knew a lot of arcane Cole Porter tunes. So I turned the eggs
over to Mickey and joined Charlie at the piano, where we took
turns outdoing each other in obscurities.

"Do you know 'Rap Tap on Wood'?"

"Oh, sure. Do you know 'It's Bad for Me'?"

We were side by side on the piano bench singing Cole Porter
till Judy chased Charlie away. She accused him of coming on to
me. Mickey had stretched out on the couch in his T-shirt and
Jockey shorts. Suddenly there was a very uncomfortable atmosphere in the apartment.

Judy sang some songs from *Easter Parade,* and the evening
blurred into morning, cold and gray. We left about eight o'clock.
Mickey stood in his doorway, seeing us to the elevator.

"Give me a call," he said.

Gratefully, I crawled into bed at the Hilton. When I awoke, it
was nightfall again, six P.M. I looked to my left. In her twin bed,
Judy was fast asleep. I should have got it on film. I don't think a
picture exists of Judy sleeping.

I showered, dressed, and taped a note to the bathroom mirror with the Park Avenue phone number. I was going to run uptown and bring back some clothes, since my suitcase was there.

Uptown, Herbert fed me, and Marjorie asked how things were going. I told them of the latest adventures and crises; the Cavett show, the Bob Shanks contretemps, the hotel mix-up. My parents listened halfheartedly.

"You look a little haggard," Marjorie said.

"Par for the course," I explained, throwing some shirts, slacks, and a jacket into my suitcase. The phone rang, and it was for me. Linda, a friend of long standing, was inviting me to a party.

"Great!" I exclaimed. "May I bring someone?"

"Sure," said Linda. "Who?"

I told her.

"Well, of course—how marvelous! I'd be thrilled!"

I cabbed back to the Hilton with anticipation, eager to place before Judy the plum of a fun party, a party I knew would be filled with bright people, a party with a piano, a party to show off at.

As I got out of the taxi on Fifty-third Street I brushed snow from my coat and welcomed the warmth of the lobby. The weather had turned nasty, cold, and blowy. The snow was coming down slowly and evenly, one of those soft, steady snowfalls that would last for hours. I was glad to get inside.

Judy was still sleeping. I sat on the bed beside her and gently shook her shoulder. "Baby . . ." I murmured into her ear. I felt Judy struggle up through her sleep. She wrapped her arms about my neck. "Don't ever leave me, Johnny . . ." she whispered. "Don't ever . . ."

"No, baby . . ." I said, luxuriating in the warm intimacy of her sleepiness. And then I said, "Honey, how'd you like to go to a party?"

Judy was snuggling into my shoulder. "Mmm . . . party . . ." she said. I waited for her eyes to open, for the charge of excitement to shoot through her, as it always did when there was something up. I waited for her to ask me Where, Whose party, Who'll be there? I must have held her for a minute and a half before I realized she was asleep again.

"Hey, Judy, listen—I've got a party for us. It'll be fun." I watched Judy's lips part slowly, but she didn't say anything. A thin string of saliva bridged her upper and lower lips, at the corner of her mouth. She's doped up, I told myself. Probably with Seconal. I rubbed my knuckles firmly into the back of her neck. Judy gave a small groan of annoyance.

"How many Seconal did you take, Judy?"

"Mmm . . . couple."

Shit, I thought disgustedly, this'll throw off all my timing. I'd plotted our sleep schedule carefully, to allow for the rigorous week of TV appearances that would begin on Monday. If I let Judy sleep now, on Saturday night, she'd be up all day Sunday, all Sunday night, a nervous wreck by Monday. And I'd be a wreck with her. The only thing to do was to get her up.

I brought her ear to my mouth. "Where's the Ritalin, honey?"

"Mmm . . . pillbox."

I rummaged through Judy's purse and found the pillbox. It was empty. I left the bed and roamed the suite, looking for just a few grams of Ritalin. Nothing. I could not find one solitary tablet, not in the bathroom, not on the night table, not on the dresser, not on top of the TV set—and not on the floor, I discovered, brought finally to my knees to peer under both beds, praying to spot a couple of the tiny, slate gray specks on the carpet.

We were out of Ritalin. I glanced at the telephone. It would be impossible to track down one of Judy's doctors at ten o'clock on a Saturday night.

And then I remembered: two blocks from the Hilton was the Park Sheraton Hotel, with a pharmacy that kept Judy's prescription on file. I was sure I could fast-talk them out of twenty pills.

I shrugged into my coat. As I left, Judy was sleeping like a contented koala, breathing regularly. And all is turmoil about her, I thought.

The block between Sixth and Seventh avenues is the longest in the city. I cursed my way through the half-frozen puddles, my hands jammed deep into my pockets, my neck pulled into my collar. I watched my breath make little puffs of steam between the snowflakes.

Fortunately, I had no trouble at the Park Sheraton. They gave me the prescription. As I stood in line at the cashier, waiting to pay, I grabbed a pack of pocket Kleenex from the counter and tore it open. My nose had started to run.

Back at Judy's bedside, I slipped her four tablets. Did you ever try giving pills to a sleeping woman? It's not easy. You have to hold her head upright with one hand, and tilt the glass to her lips with the other, and pinch her Adam's apple, and wipe the excess water from her chin, and push a wastepaper basket against her chest when she starts to retch.

Eventually I got the pills down Judy's esophagus and retired to the adjoining room to read the Sunday *Times*, which I'd bought at the Hilton newsstand. I figured the pills would take effect in half an hour or so and we could meet Linda at the party.

I picked up tomorrow's Arts & Leisure section.

Thirty minutes later I finished the theater news and was about to start on the Book Review when I glanced at Judy, lying in the next room, still motionless, still drugged. I crossed into the bedroom and once more shook her by the shoulder.

"Come on, Judy, let's go, rise and shine."

Judy was still in a stupor. Nothing made any sense to the dull and vacant pupils she turned on me. "Judy, come *on*," I said, a little more urgently, "we're going to a party."

"Mmm . . . you go . . ." she said, her lids closing again. I felt a sudden surge of resentment. Okay, fuck it, I thought angrily, stay here, sleep all week, throw all the work and planning down the toilet, I don't care. I'm going to this party with or without you. Enough of this shit.

All right, I told myself, softening somewhat, I'd give Judy another quarter hour, and if she didn't show signs of animation by then, I'd leave and meet Linda alone.

I went back to the living room couch and opened the Book Review. Some trout fisherman in Ketchum, Idaho, had been an intimate of Hemingway's and his reminiscences were critiqued on the front page. Ernest had been a great outdoorsman, knew how to cast his trout line, never killed an animal unnecessarily, yeah yeah yeah, the usual Hemingway bullshit.

But halfway down the page the review quoted a remark the guy had heard from the famous author. It was in relation to the fine, true experience of shooting zebras or some such, but Hemingway had said, Remember, once you have the memory of an experience, no one can take it away from you.

I looked at Judy, asleep just twenty feet away from me. Something made me rise, and—marking my place in the article with my finger—walk slowly to her bedside. I stood there, gazing down at her recumbent, quietly breathing form, and suddenly the tragedy of it welled into my throat with a choking gush, and I found myself fighting to blink back simultaneous terror and pity.

I swallowed rapidly, twice, three times. Yes, I thought, Hemingway is right, once you have the memory of something it's yours forever, and my mind, as if spun into reverse by the press of a projector button, was instantly reviewing the hundreds of fine and hideous things Judy and I had been through together; the food fight at Larry's, Mr. Lee's hat, the hospital fuck, playing poker, carrying her over the Fenway threshold, dancing at the Shelton Towers . . . and the songs, oh, Christ, the wonderful singing, the way she'd lasered into me with her voice, the way she'd made something vital out of dead words and music, yes, it seemed to me my songs had been dead before I brought them to her, and she'd borne them, given them birth, given them life from the womb of her mouth, and nobody could take that from me, no one could erase my memories, even this one now, remembering it as it happened, fixing in my mind forever the image of my own tears, dropping helplessly on the blanket, nobody could ever take that from me, no, nobody . . . ever . . .

And I knew then, through this clanging, irreversible feeling, that hope was over . . . that Judy and I could never make it together.

I fell on the bed and pressed my face into the hollow of her side, just above the hip, and shook with a barrage of great, wracking sobs I'd never known I was capable of before Judy.

This woke her. At least to the point of semiconsciousness. "Wh . . . what is it . . . why are you crying . . . ?"

"Oh, Judy . . ." It was difficult to speak with my nose full of tears and a mouth contorted with anguish. "You just do it to yourself, every time . . . and there's no way to fight it . . . it's inside you, it's inside you, and I can't help you . . . it's inside you . . ."

She was beneath comprehension. "Wh . . . what's inside me?"

"You just make it impossible . . . for anyone to help you . . . because you won't let them . . . something inside you defeats you . . . and destroys you . . ."

I was blabbering like an infant, feeling the moisture running from my nostrils down over my upper lip. I kept shaking my head and blubbering. I stumbled to my feet and jerked a length of toilet paper from the roll in the bathroom, enough to blow my nose on.

"Johnny . . ." Judy said, "don't you love me?"

"Of *course* I love you!" I threw myself violently back upon her. "That's why I'm crying, you jerk, because I love you and I can't help you . . . *no*body can . . . it's inside you, and you're the only one who can do something about it . . . but you won't . . . you can't . . ."

I sat on Judy's bed and breathed in as many deep gulps of air as I could, sniffing back the phlegm. I had to stop this sobbing. I felt completely drained. I sat there for perhaps a minute, watching Judy's eyes slip from incomprehension to rationality and back again. She lay, inert, on the pillow. I could see she'd be asleep again soon.

"All right, look . . ." I said weakly; even to speak was an effort. "I'm gonna go to this party . . . I'll give you a call later . . ."

I got up, went into the living room, and put on my coat. As I left the suite, Judy was lying on her right side, facing the window. The eye I could see was open, but I knew it would close again within a few seconds.

As the door clicked shut behind me, I wondered whether Judy realized what had just happened.

SUNDAY, DECEMBER 15

I lurched out into the snow and pulled open the door of a cab. "Sixty-sixth and Second . . ." I told the driver, giving Linda's address. I couldn't stop crying.

Linda opened her door to find me trembling in her hallway.

"My God—" she said, "what happened to you? Do you want a drink?"

"Cuppa tea—" I blurted wetly and crawled onto her couch. "Listen, I . . . I can't make this party . . . but I need to talk to you . . ."

And for the next two hours I told Linda the story: how I'd met and fallen in love with perhaps the greatest entertainer of our generation; how I'd seized the chance to help her; how I was beginning to get her back on her feet with TV shots and a club booking and a recording contract; and how, finally, it was going to be impossible.

Linda listened sympathetically, plying me with tea. From time to time her eyes widened in amazement, and several times she shook her head in incredulity.

Somewhere around three in the morning I began to shiver uncontrollably. Linda brought me a blanket. "Do you want to stay here?"

"No, no, I'll be okay . . ." My teeth had begun to chatter. "I guess I'll go home. Th-thanks for listening to all this . . ."

I couldn't stop shaking.

When I got to Park Avenue I lay down in bed, and I swear I made the mattress vibrate with my ague. I closed my eyes to sleep, but the scene in the Hilton kept screening itself in my head, and my body felt so hot I had to kick off the blanket, and then the next moment I'd be shivering with cold again.

Finally, I managed to sleep a few fitful hours, and when I awoke I felt as rotten as I'd ever felt in my life. I wanted to go to the toilet, but for some reason I couldn't get out of bed. My legs refused to obey my brain. I was simply too weak.

My sister Priscilla was asleep in the adjoining bedroom, the very bed in which I'd made love to Judy for the first time. Through the open bathroom door I could see her snoring form.

"Priscilla . . ." I tried to cry, but no sound came from my throat. "Priscilla—" I tried once more, and a feeling of panic seized me. I couldn't speak. I couldn't speak and I couldn't walk, what the hell was wrong with me?

By my bed was a stack of books. I took the top book from the pile (I remember it was *Portnoy's Complaint*) and, mustering all my strength, I heaved it into the bathroom, where it hit the tiled floor with a loud slap.

I grabbed the next book and slung it, too, into the bathroom. I had to wake Priscilla. She had to get me up and dressed and down to the Hilton, because—whatever my relationship with Judy—she still had to rehearse my songs for the Johnny Carson taping on Tuesday.

I pitched another three books into the bathroom before Priscilla finally stirred and woke up and came to my bedside. She squinted at me sleepily. "You don't look too good," she said.

I pantomimed writing. Priscilla brought me a pad and a pencil. "Got to get to Hilton," I scrawled.

Priscilla left the room and returned, moments later, with a thermometer. Impatiently, I stuck it in my rear (our family would never trust an oral thermometer).

"You can't go to the Hilton," Priscilla told me. "You've got a temperature of a hundred two and a half." And then she said something else to me, but I can't tell you what it was because I had begun to drift in and out of consciousness.

MONDAY, DECEMBER 16

What I had was the flu. The Hong Kong flu, they called it that year, and it was the most debilitating illness I ever had: one of those chilling, shivery fevers that sucks you into its vortex, whirling your brain around, squeezing the fluids out of you as you lie helpless, and boiling your eyes in their sockets until it aches even to read.

I spent the day in a near delirium, thrashing about in sweaty misery, barely knowing where I was or who was with me . . .

The notes in my datebook tell me that Tommy Newsome, the "Tonight Show" orchestrator, came over to check the charts on "It's All for You" and "After the Holidays," but if he did, he must have been turned away at the door. I remember nothing.

I have a note that reads, "Sent P.A.M. (Priscilla) to Hilton for tape recorder." I must have asked my sister to do this, but I have no memory of it. Priscilla tells me she went down there, but Judy wouldn't let her in and was abusive about it, too. I wanted my recorder back so I could tape the "Tonight Show."

TUESDAY, DECEMBER 17

Judy called, of course. A lot.

"Well, just how sick is he?" she wanted to know. "I need him."

"Judy," Priscilla said, "he's got a fever of a hundred and four."

"That's nothing," was Judy's response. "I've gone onstage with a hundred and *six*. I have to tape the Carson show today . . . where is he? I need him!"

Judy continued to bombard the house with calls. Later on, she had Annie call. "Judy needs the lyric change on 'It's All for You,'" Annie would tell Priscilla, and Priscilla would come to my bedside, and I'd write the lyrics weakly on the pad, unable to exert enough pressure on the pencil to make a fully legible mark. Priscilla would deliver the change to Annie, who, in turn, relayed it to Judy.

The calls began to come so frequently that I had to move into Priscilla's bed, which was near an extension phone. By this time I was able to make myself audible, if only in a whisper. I still could not produce a tone.

On a late call, about midnight, Annie said, "Judy told me she's pregnant."

Pregnant? I thought. "That's impossible," I gasped, hoarsely.

"I know," said Annie. "I said to her, 'Are you sure?' and she said, 'Other people have babies, nobody ever says to them Are you sure? But here I'm having a baby, and everyone's asking me Are you sure, are you sure?'"

"Totally impossible. Judy told me her tubes were tied off."

"That's what I said to her, 'I thought you were tied off,' and she said, 'Yes, but at Peter Bent Brigham the tubes melted.'"

"She's fulla shit . . ." I croaked into the phone. Poor Annie, I thought, not yet twenty and having to deal with a crazy lady all by herself. As if she'd read my thought Annie said, "Are you ever coming down here?"

"Soon as I can walk, Annie . . . can you keep things under control?"

"I'm trying . . ." Annie lowered her voice, as you so often had to around Judy. "We're a little depressed right now," she told me.

"Oh Christ, what's wrong?"

"We called Reubens . . . we wanted them to deliver the Judy Garland sandwich—you know, the one they named after her. And they've discontinued it."

I don't believe this, I thought. First she's pregnant, and now she's depressed because Reubens has canceled her sandwich. Amazingly, I could see how these two disparate facts carried the same emotional weight with Judy.

"Okay, Annie, here's what you do," I rasped. "Tell her Colonel Sanders is naming a wing after her. The Kentucky Fried Judy Garland Memorial Chicken Wing."

"Okay," said Annie, "I'll talk to you."

Two minutes later the phone rang again. It was Annie. "Judy says you didn't say 'good night,'" Annie said to me harshly and abruptly hung up.

Hey, I thought, that's not something Annie would do. Judy forced her to do that, I know she did. And what did that mean? Why was Judy being nasty? I knew all too well. She didn't care that I was sick. In Judy's mind this was another defection, another betrayal. When I need him he isn't there for me, that's what Judy was telling herself. That fink, he's just like all the others. When you need 'em, they disappear.

WEDNESDAY, DECEMBER 18

"You're not gonna believe this," Annie said to me.

"What?" I murmured. I was beginning to get my voice back.

"We called room service for hamburgers, and Judy told me to get her some mashed potatoes . . . so they only have french fries, right? So I'm arguing with this woman on room service, and I'm pleading with her, trying to get her to send us mashed potatoes, and she's giving me a real rough time . . . so I finally said, 'Judy, all they have is french fries' and Judy got real mad and said 'You tell her it's for JUDY GARLAND, and she *must have mashed potatoes* before she sings!'"

I started coughing into the phone. "Hysterical," I said. "Did Colby come over? Did he bring the check?"

"She made him go down to the bank and cash it," Annie said. "She wouldn't sign the contract till he brought her the cash."

Naturally, I thought. Judy has no bank account here. But we had the money! Terrific! We needed that money to get to England.

"How'd you like the 'Tonight Show'?" Annie asked. Judy's Johnny Carson appearance had aired last night. It had been woeful.

"What was all that crap about sugarplums?" I said.

"I know. Christmas bullshit, I guess. Did you like the chart on 'It's All for You'?"

"It was okay. The guitarist missed a change a coupla bars from the end."

"I know. And she blew your name again. She put an S on the end."

"She blew the name of the *nightclub*, for chrissake. It's not the Town and Country, it's the Talk of the Town."

"I know. They fixed it at the end of the show, though. How'd you like the way she did 'After the Holidays'?"

"It was—" I stopped in midsentence. It was hard to answer that. Judy, with less than half a voice, had simply croaked her way through the number, sounding pathetic. However, in a peculiar way, this worked; the croaking underscored the pathos of the lyric, making it even more dramatic. But you couldn't call it good singing.

"What can I say?" I said to Annie. "It worked. Here, put her on, I'll tell her something nice, now that I can halfway talk."

"Um . . . she's in the john," Annie said, and there was an unfamiliar, strained note in her voice. Something's going on down there, I thought, and Annie can't tell me about it.

"And hey, what was that number last night, Annie, with the sudden hang-up?" I said.

Once again, Annie dropped her voice to a whisper. "Judy made me do it," she told me. "She's mad at you."

"Right. I had the nerve to get sick." I wasn't going to get into the way I felt about Judy's attitude. "Are you rehearsing 'Hate Myself'?"

"Yeah, but we're having trouble with that new lyric, the Arthur Treacher one—"

"Forget it," I said. "Do it the old way. Don't throw anything new at her now."

THURSDAY, DECEMBER 19

Today, at three, Judy taped "I'd Like to Hate Myself in the Morning" for the "Merv Griffin Show." Though I wasn't really recovered enough to leave the house, I cabbed shakily down to the Hilton. I wanted to hear all about it.

In her suite, Judy was looking febrile, bouncing all over the room (high on Ritalin, I could tell; Annie told me later she'd had fourteen pills in twenty hours). She was prancing about in a white mink coat the Griffin show had rented for her. The coat was gorgeous, and, naturally, Judy didn't want to give it back.

"I think they'd nn, *adore* this coat in London . . ." she said to Annie.

"How'd the taping go?" I said. I wasn't interested in helping Judy rip off Merv Griffin's mink coat.

"We didn't do the 'Arthur Treacher' lyric," Annie said.

"Just as well," I said, sinking gratefully to the couch. I was feeling very fragile. This is a mistake, I thought, I shouldn't be doing this. I should go home. I'm sick.

"They got the nn, *cue cards* all mixed up . . ." Judy said to me, "and I had to . . . start again . . ."

"And Arthur Treacher—" Annie began.

"Mmm! Arthur was . . . divine!" Judy chimed in. "And guess who came to visit me backstage?"

"Max Schmeling," I said.

"Margaret Hamilton!"

"Oh, terrific," I said, with as much energy as I could muster. "C'mere and give me a kiss." I tried to rise from my seat.

"No," said Judy, backing away from me.

"How come?" I asked her. Judy turned to Annie. "You tell him," she said. Annie could not meet my eye.

" 'Cause Judy's engaged," she said.

The following item appeared in Earl Wilson's column in the New York *Post* a few days later:

JUDY'S MARRYING AGAIN . . .

Judy Garland happily announced at Arthur this morning that she'll be getting married Dec. 30 in London to good-looking Mickey Deans, former bandleader and pianist who's general manager of the club and advisor to Arthur International.

"They look very serious about it to me," said Merv Griffin, at whose Christmas party for his staff they made the announcement. Judy referred to Deans, who's about 35, as "my fiancé." Judy added, "I finally got the right man to ask me. I've been waiting for a long time."

They hope to be married in London about the time Judy opens there at The Town & Country. Judy and her fiancé told us that her children hadn't been informed of her decision. "Nobody knows about it but my attorney, and he just looked surprised," Judy said.

When we told Judy we hoped she'd be very happy, she said, "It's about time." Deans said he's very proprietary about Judy, and that she asked him whether she could dance with Merv Griffin. He said, "Sure, he's a friend." They said the marriage talk started as a joke and wound up seriously, Deans saying, "I'm not kidding" and Judy saying, "I'm not, either." It all began with Judy coming into the club, and Deans, as general manager, becoming friendly with a lady customer.

FRIDAY, DECEMBER 20

Shit, I thought. You leave this woman alone for five days and look what happens. Marrying Mickey, how was this possible? He was so crazy. At least that was how he'd appeared in his apartment, as he lay around in his underwear.

And what about all our plans, our trip to England, our drive through the Château country, what about *that?* How could she betray me this way?

I should have questioned her immediately about this, but I was too shocked to say anything, and in my weakened condition I wasn't up to the confrontation. Later I kept urging myself, Pick up the phone, for chrissake, and confront her; ask her what the hell is going on? But I was too humiliated by the implication: if Judy could switch lovers so effortlessly, what did that mean in terms of our relationship? It meant it was weightless, flimsy, meaningless, and that hurt worst of all. I felt like a cuckolded husband.

SATURDAY, DECEMBER 21

And it kept gnawing at me. That bitch. After all I did for her. After all my planning, all my effort, all my faith that together we could restore Judy to her rightful eminence; now the idea seemed ludicrous, no more than a naive fantasy. She had never believed in it anyway, never truly shared this dream with me, because here she was running off with someone else.

You're jealous, I told myself, it's as simple as that. But jealous not of Judy's romantic defection (though that hurt too, of course) but, more poignantly, I was devastated by being supplanted in my position of power, in my ambition to rebuild Judy. That was the part that just killed me.

SUNDAY, DECEMBER 22

I went to the Hilton this afternoon, weak as I was, to see what I could do about things. It was a nearly impossible thing for me to do. My impulse was to simply stay home under the covers and nurse my wounded pride. But I forced myself to go down there.

I found Annie sleeping on the living room couch, and Judy sitting up in bed, staring glassily at the TV screen, conducting the Boston Pops orchestra along with Arthur Fiedler. The bedroom had begun to reek of that unhealthy, cloying aroma I'd smelled too often before: it was Judy's fetid blend of stale makeup, Ma Griffe, and booze.

I can't stand televised music. I switched the channel on the

TV set and found *Quo Vadis,* one of the all-time dumb movies.
Gladiators and tyrants. I sat down on the twin bed beside Judy's
and, as I watched Peter Ustinov's impression of Nero, I could
feel Judy looking at me. Her eyes had regained a measure of
comprehension.

"Mmm . . . how do you feel?" she asked me.

"I'm okay," I said. "How about you?"

It was the wrong answer. The real answer was, I feel betrayed, I feel humiliated, I feel miserable. What are you doing?
Why are you behaving like this?

But there was a pride in me I could not overcome. If Judy
wanted to choose someone else, I would not grovel before her. I
saw instantly now that I had no stomach for the confrontation
I'd come down for.

"How about you?" I'd said. Judy gave me an uncertain smile.

"Well, you know . . . I have these, nn . . . morning
flashes . . ."

I became aware of Annie, standing in the doorway. "Yeah, I
heard," I said, dubiously. "So you're still pregnant?"

"Sure I'm still pregnant," Judy said. "You think it goes away
overnight?"

Annie shifted her considerable bulk in the doorway. "You
mean you're going to have John's baby . . . and marry Mickey?"
she said. I knew Annie was on my side. I could have kissed her
for saying that.

"Oh, Mickey loves children," Judy responded. Annie and I
both stared at her for a long moment, and then Judy began
shaking her head from side to side, as if to clear it.

"Look, I don't know if I'm marrying *any*body . . ." she said.
"I'm going to take my baby . . . and go to London . . . and then
I'll go to Switzerland. I'll name him Elby."

"Elby?" said Annie.

"Yes," Judy said, "L. B. Meyer."

For once, I thought, she got my name right. No S on the end.

"And Mickey will be its father," Annie pursued. Judy looked
down at her bedsheet. "Yes," she said. There was a pause. And
then Judy said, "Johnny doesn't want to marry me."

I felt my throat tighten, and I tried to swallow. "Annie," I
said, "excuse us for a minute, would you?" All at once I could
feel my pulse, trying to knock its way out of my wrist, for in

Judy's tone I'd heard a hint of ruefulness, a hint that perhaps, if I tried, I could recapture her. She was inviting me to try. I rose from the bed.

"Judy," I said, "I'll take you down to City Hall right *now*."

I still can't believe I said that to Judy, because deep down, she was *right*. I *didn't* want to marry her; my epiphany by her bedside the other night had convinced me of that, and yet . . . and yet I couldn't imagine being without her, living without the excitement she brought me, the feeling of strength and talent and invincibility . . .

"Come *on*," I whispered urgently, "I'll take you down there right now."

Judy started from her bed, and for a moment I thought she was going to do it, she was going to come with me, and in that moment I knew a sinking, a dropping, a falling in my heart and stomach such as I had never experienced, as if I had suddenly seen my signature on my own execution order. In that moment I felt as if I was plunging into a bottomless abyss, a sinking, dizzying, headfirst tumble, but at the same time I wanted it, I WANTED IT, GODDAMIT—

Judy abruptly sat down at her dressing table. "I can't," she said, "I've promised Mickey."

"Oh, *fuck* Mickey," I barked.

"And you've got to get out of here . . ." Judy continued. "Out of the bedroom, I mean . . . Mickey's coming over . . ."

I let out a deep sigh, a sigh that was a mixture of disgust and relief, and walked into the living room, where Annie tried not to look at me. She had heard it all, of course.

"Did you manage to get the 'Hate Myself' chart from Mort?" I said to her, eager to change the subject. Without turning to me, Annie nodded.

"Is she gonna take it with her to London?"

"She better," Annie replied. "She only has ten tunes."

MONDAY, DECEMBER 23

Judy was delivering her messages through Annie now.

"Hi. Judy says could you come down and show Mickey the tag on 'Hate Myself'? And do you have the new opening?"

Yes, I had been working on a new opening number for the London engagement, but, I thought, Judy has a lotta fucking nerve asking me for it now. Oh, I knew what she was doing: she was pretending we could compartmentalize our relationship; just because we'd stopped being lovers didn't mean she no longer wanted to sing my songs.

And what was this "show Mickey" shit? I wouldn't show Mickey the hair on my ass. They could both go screw themselves, I thought, and then, like the miserable, pusillanimous jerk I was, I sloshed down there in the snow and did exactly what she asked me to. I sat at the piano and showed Mickey, who played a little (not as well as I did, I noted with satisfaction), the arrangement on "Hate Myself."

"Oh, Johnny . . ." Judy said after this, "play Mickey your song about the 'woman's pride.'"

So okay, I let Judy put me through my paces like a trained dog and played my song about the woman's pride, and watched Mickey smiling with false bonhomie and admiration, looking around the room, trying to avoid his discomfort.

And in this way I abetted Judy's perfect manipulation: she was rubbing Mickey's nose in my talent, even as she was making me sit up and do tricks before Mickey, the new man in her life.

And we were both too weak to do anything about it.

TUESDAY, DECEMBER 24

After yesterday I have no desire to see Judy again. Not with another man in the position I once enjoyed. It's simply too painful.

On the phone, Annie told me a small, oblong box had been delivered from Tiffany's. When Judy opened the box she found a string of elegant pearls. The accompanying card was signed by Tony Bennett, and it said, "Have yourself a merry little Christmas."

As for me, it was the worst Christmas I ever had; sick, depleted, agonizingly disappointed. I could not stop crying inside.

WEDNESDAY, DECEMBER 25

Christmas Day I stayed home, moping about the house. I have no notes on this day, and I don't remember it at all. I was retreating, obviously, unwilling to face the situation, unwilling to admit the defeat of my ambitions, of my whole life's purpose, it seemed.

Judy and her new entourage leave Friday for England.

THURSDAY, DECEMBER 26

The new opening goes like this:

> "I'm back in business
> I'm here as usual at the same old stand
> And let me just announce that it's simply grand
> Back in business again
>
> I'm back in business
> I closed for alterations and hid myself
> But now the goods are comin' down off the shelf
> Back in business again.
>
>> Fresh air . . . fresh start
>> New hope . . . new heart
>>> A new dream behind my eyes
>>> (Vop!) Let's sell some new merchandise!
>
> I'm back in business
> I think tonight I'm gonna do fifty shows
> I'll hang a sign out sayin' 'we never close'
> Back in business, and how!
> I'm back in business now!"

I was supposed to bring a tape of this number downtown to the hotel, but when I got there, Stan Freeman was at the piano, putting one of *his* songs on tape. The song was called "I Belong to London," and it was going to function, Judy informed me, as her opening. Wasn't Stan simply *brilliant?* He came up with this wonderful song *overnight.*

All I could do was gape at her. As Judy was telling me this, I
felt a numbness sweep over me; I was trying to avoid the pain
of yet another humiliation. I stood silently by the couch as Stan
played the number once more. I felt as if I'd been hung in a
freezer case.

After Stan left, Judy asked me to play "I Belong to London."
She could have asked Mickey, he was right there. But she asked
me.

And I am ashamed to tell you I played it.

Then, while I was still at the keyboard, she wanted to sing a
few songs. "Oh, Johnny . . . let's sing 'Who' . . ." she said. "This
is the song, you know, that has an impossible nn, *fini*sh. It's so
abrupt, 'Who? who? No one but you'—Vonk! and it's gone—"

And we sang "The Darktown Strutters' Ball" ("To*morr*ow
night"??!!) and "It's a New World" (from *A Star Is Born*)
and during these we had a reprise of *Mickey's* discomfort.
Mickey sure didn't like the rapport Judy and I obviously had as
singer and accompanist.

Judy made a lotta points this afternoon.

FRIDAY, DECEMBER 27

Departure day. I came to the hotel to help with the final details.
I told myself it was to make sure the "Hate Myself" chart was
packed, but the truth is, I was simply unwilling to let go of
Judy. I found I couldn't be in the same town with her without
wanting to be near her, no matter what the price turned out to
be in humiliation. I was beginning to feel I was trapped in an
epic soap opera. I know it sounds absurdly lovesick, but I am
telling you this is the effect Judy had on people. I wasn't the
only one who experienced this emotional disorientation with her;
it happened to many others. Judy chewed you up and spat you
out. It was like having a love affair with a Cuisinart.

Today we had Bobby Cole, who'd conducted for Judy during
her last Palace engagement. Today he was at the piano, showing
Mickey a sheet of music that looked like a road map to Darien,
Connecticut. It was the bolero arrangement of "What Now, My

Love?" that Judy had done at the Palace. Judy was desperately trying to put together enough orchestrations to make up a show.

Bobby was explaining the piano-conductor sheet to Mickey. "It goes back to bar seventy-two here," Bobby said, pointing with his finger, and Mickey was trying (as I had) to look like he knew what he was doing. He was nodding and saying "unh huh" a lot. "Right. No problem."

They better have a real hip conductor, I thought, at the Talk of the Town.

Charlie Cochran ran in with a new hat for Judy. A new hat seemed to be the talisman of departure.

Poor Annie was stretched out feverishly on the couch. She was really sick with the flu. Bobby Cole came over and sat down by her feet.

"Hey, man," he said to Annie, "what're you doing later?"

I left about six. There was nothing more to do. "Have a good trip," I said to Judy. "Have a great opening."

Judy moved to kiss my cheek, in the traditional show-biz manner, but I thought, Unh unh, and kind of pulled away, on the pretense of shaking hands with Mickey. Mickey and I were involved in a charade of our own, pretending we could tolerate each other.

"Take care of her," I said to Mickey, in false camaraderie.

And Mickey nodded confidently.

SUNDAY, DECEMBER 29

Judy's troubles began the minute she stepped off the plane. A UPI release today featured a picture of Judy being served a writ by a private detective at Heathrow Airport.

"The writ is aimed at preventing the singer from appearing at a London cabaret," said the release. "It named her as a defendant in a suit challenging her scheduled opening tomorrow at the cabaret, the Talk of the Town." The writ had been issued, the item stated, by "two theater agents who contend Miss Garland is under exclusive contract to them and cannot appear without their consent."

From my bed of pain, I smiled gleefully. Fine, I thought. Let's see how Mr. Fix-it handles this one.

THURSDAY, JANUARY 2, 1969

The "Merv Griffin Show" aired tonight, and I gathered my family around the big RCA console in my father's bedroom to watch.

For the past week I'd been convalescing quietly at home, alternately kicking and congratulating myself. True, I'd blown the most romantic, stimulating adventure I'd ever known; on the other hand, I'd been prudent enough to save myself from immolation in Judy's cauldron of despair. At least I was still alive.

It was hard to know how to feel; the disappointment of losing Judy was acute. However, I could now get back to my own life. Larry is telling me there's important interest in *The Draft Dodger*. If I pursue that interest with vigor and intelligence, I can probably arrange a Broadway production.

Meanwhile, here was Judy, singing "Hate Myself" on the TV screen. She started off like a house afire, ripping into the song with great energy. "I'd like to hate myself in the morning," she sang firmly, "and raise a little hell . . . tonight . . ."

The voice sounded different than it had before, as if it had gained body, as if there were more of it; Judy was singing something *up*, something dynamic and happy—she sounded good!

But then, at bar fifteen, she lost her place: "Cut loose and pull out the stops out" she sang, incorrectly, "Who cares if they c—wait, we've got the cue cards all mixed up . . ." Judy said, as a bewildered band played on behind her.

"We've got to make them much bigger . . . or . . . start from the beginning, Arthur . . . don't you believe?" she said, turning to Arthur Treacher, Merv's sidekick.

And Arthur Treacher said, "I believe anything you say, ducky." And Judy said, "Darling . . ." and Mort started the introductory eight bars again, but Judy didn't wait for the introduction, she jumped right in with "I'd like to hate myself in the morning . . ." which threw the band momentarily, but Mort brought them expertly back into synch, and Judy was off and running, and when she began the second chorus her rhythmic high spirits were so infectious that the audience began clapping along with her, we were in the midst of a typically brilliant Garland rendition, one she finished in a blaze of energy, giving a marvelous growl on the final line:

> "—But what a dandy time
> *I'll have* (that was the growl)
> Toniiiiiiiight!!!!"

"*Beautiful!*" Merv yelled, rising from his chair, and the audience gave Judy an ovation that went on for a minute and a half.

"That's great!" Merv said to her. "See, you tackled a brand-new song."

I turned to look at my mother, who was frowning at the screen in concentration. She had just heard the major variety entertainer of our time deliver a terrifically effective rendition of her son's song on a program that would be broadcast across the length and breadth of the United States, its territorial possessions and Canada.

Marjorie turned to me with a questioning look. "Is that dress a Dior?" she said.

WEDNESDAY, JANUARY 8

Variety came out today, with a review of Judy's opening:

> Those looking to Judy Garland for an impeccable, stopwatch-timed, disciplined nightspot act clearly don't know what the gal is all about. The act has too many errors to satisfy the purists.
>
> But those who are not abashed by genuine nostalgia and who can recognize and rise to the peculiar alchemy that makes a woman a personality as well as a performer will have a very good time at her five week London cabaret debut. And there's a profitable SRO crowd every night to prove it. Those who are sniffy are mainly so in the cloak-

rooms and on the way home. The majority are embraced by
Miss Garland's warmth, ebullience, and affable way of
bringing enthusiasts into the act.

At the show caught she made her entry 45 minutes late.
Not exactly professional behavior, and she paid for it by
facing an at first sticky audience. They applauded Burt
Rhodes and the orch. playing an overture of Garland hits
(first time any Talk Of The Town topper has received such
a come-on bouquet) but then tended to sit on their mitts.

But by the time she had sung "I Belong To London" for
starters, "Judgment Day" and "The Man That Got Away,"
all was forgiven. "Just In Time" came just in time and lit the
act, as, at the star's invitation, 50 or so fans invaded the
stage, sat on it, and made it a party.

Miss Garland doesn't bother much about new songs.
They're for the new little telly-birds. She plies her trade
with a small batch of old trusties which she can sing side-
ways, backwards, and upside-down, and, when in the mood,
is quite likely to do so.

Clad in a silverish trouser suit she looks pretty chipper.
The torso's fined down and the happy smile's still there. The
voice tends to rasp and croak too often but it's still vibrant
and a peppy belter. She also moves, not particularly gracefully, but with the deft verve and energy of a pro.

Her songs are interspersed with overlong, but quite funny
gagging in which she chats up folk in the ringside seats and
which she appears largely to ad-lib. After "You Made Me
Love You," "For Me And My Gal," "The Trolley Song," and
"Rockabye Baby," Miss Garland wound her 45-minutes act
with the obligatory "Over The Rainbow."

With this number loyalty is strained. The plaintive, wistful notes of "Rainbow" no longer climb to the ceiling and
hang shimmering from the chandeliers. The hush that for
years has misted the stoniest eye is missing. The dream is
over. In fact, she seems darn relieved to have the audience
help her out with the w.k. ditty.

Yet, make no mistake, the Garland magic, warmth, and
heart are as irresistible as ever.

Nagging question is how long can Judy Garland keep it

up? How long does she want to? Audience affection and goodwill are there, but there can be a limit to how long folks will watch a well loved champ gamble with her talent.

Meanwhile, Judy Garland's alive and well, living in London and doing very nicely for Bernard Delfont at "Talk Of The Town," where she's admirably backed by Burt Rhodes and the resident orch, having brought no special musicians with her.

Rich.

I put the paper down. So Mickey had managed to pull it out of the fire and get her on. Well, good for him, I thought, in a sudden burst of empathy. He must have gone through hell, with the lawyers and the injunctions, and going to court and all that shit, and all the time trying to keep Judy on the same planet; he must have gone through the tortures of the damned. He was probably trying to catch a nap somewhere right now.

I picked up the review and read it again, this time with a more critical eye. I didn't like its faintly superior tone. Who was this "Rich" guy, anyway, who couldn't even get the song titles right? "Judgment Day" indeed. The name of the song is "Get Happy," Rich, okay? And who the hell are you to tell us "the dream is over"? We'll let you know when the dream is over, buddy, okay?

And, most important to me, where's "Hate Myself"? You don't mention it, Rich. Could it be that Judy decided to cut it, out of spite? It would be just like her.

It bothered the hell out of me.

FRIDAY, JANUARY 10

Bob Colby's going to England. He's arranged a recording session at a London studio on the fourth of February. Judy will record "After the Holidays," "It's All for You," and "Hate Myself." Do I want to come?

Well, of course I want to come. The only problem is money, goddamit. I'd run through all my BMI money, and there wasn't time to take a piano job.

WEDNESDAY, JANUARY 15

Variety was on the newsstands again, with more disastrous bulletins:

> Judy Garland, who recently arrived for a local nitery date, has been hit by a third writ during her brief stay here. Latest legal paper stems from the government's Income Tax department which claims $1,216 on Miss Garland's alleged 1964–65 profits "as a film actress."
>
> First writ, secured by a couple of agents, failed to prevent her appearance at Talk Of The Town nitery. The second writ was obtained by Harrods, the London store. It sought payment for an alleged debt dating from 1964.

Also, Judy and Mickey's marriage plans had been temporarily blocked. Apparently, British law required a fifteen-day residence period. I wondered whether these two weeks would give Mickey second thoughts about the idea of a wedding.

That sometimes happened.

FRIDAY, JANUARY 17

A piece of good luck! Bob Hall, who had escorted my mother to the Arlen benefit at Lincoln Center (and had heard Judy excoriate poor Irv Squires at Clarke's later), happens to work for Japan Airlines; he told Marjorie he can get me a round-trip ticket to London for three hundred dollars, which is unbelievably cheap.

Of course I said I'd take it. If Judy's recording my songs, there's no way I'm not gonna be there. No matter what I have to do to arrange the fare.

The flight is this coming Tuesday, at ten in the evening. Bob says he's even arranged a photographer for the JAL magazine to snap my picture as I board.

Part Four

❋ ❋ ❋

London

WEDNESDAY, JANUARY 22

I should have been elated, I suppose. Here I was, arriving in a glamorous world capital to supervise the recording of my songs by Judy Garland.

But it didn't feel like that. It felt like I was arriving in a strange town, unattached and aimless, uncertain of my reception, and forced to watch my pennies.

As I dragged my sixty pounds of luggage through Heathrow Airport (saving tips) my one comfort was that Bob had arranged the JAL limousine to take me to my destination.

But what *was* my destination? Judy and Mickey were staying at the Ritz—on money that I'd arranged. Ironically, I was not in a position now to afford such luxury.

I stepped outside the terminal to the *kerb* (I was in England now) looking for the limo. People eddied past me, catching cabs, being met. They all had a place to go; they lived here, or they were on business trips with expense accounts, letters of credit, Eurocards.

There was no sign of a car or a driver.

I parked my stuff by a row of phone booths and fell in line at the money exchange counter, keeping an eye on my bags, twenty feet away. What if my clothes were stolen? Wow, I thought, the ideas your mood inspires. Last time I was here I wouldn't have had that thought, I ruminated; ten years ago, not yet out of college and eager to rough it, eager to see Europe the Hemingway. Sure, fine at twenty, but not so appealing at thirty. At twenty, I'd survived nine months in this town, playing piano in a coffee house in the Haymarket, and smuggling pornography in from France. I'd roomed in a bed-sitter, a peculiar, English accommodation; one room and a hot plate, and the heater took a sixpence. Miserable. Please, I prayed, not again.

"How much, sir?"

I changed two twenty-dollar traveler's checks, which left me a hundred and eighty dollars, American. One hundred and eighty dollars to last me till February fourth, the date of the recording session. One hundred and eighty dollars to live for two weeks.

Schmuck, why did you come so early? I asked myself. You must
be mad.

"Fourteen, seven and nine, sir, there you are." God, how British they were here. Fourteen pounds, seven shillings and nine-
pence, yes. And a tankard of stout please, there's a good chap.

I scanned the terminal. Still nothing. No courteous chauffeur
in cap and jodhpurs, no Bentley quietly humming outside. Just
the unfamiliar English faces, and the time change, and ten-thirty
in the morning, and beyond, the half-bright, gritty haze . . . and
Judy.

And Mickey.

I stepped into a booth and called the Ritz. Phone calls had
gone up tuppence since 1958.

"Ritz Hotel, good morning."

"Charles Cochran, please." Something told me to ask for
Charlie; he would be an ally, he'd tell me what condition things
were in. You never knew with Judy, and the *Variety* clippings
had been disturbing.

I listened, envisioning the staid clerk (clark?) in his striped
morning coat thumbing through his directory. Behind him
would be a row of sedate mahogany boxes, neatly stuffed with
keys and mail. I could hear the cushioned hum of discreet lobby
activity as I waited, but it was taking too long, and then, somehow, suddenly I knew—

"Sir, we haven't a Mr. Cochran registered." I felt a dryness in
my larynx. "He's with Miss Garland," I hazarded.

"Would you like me to ring Miss Garland's room, sir?"

"No, no, that's all right—" I told him quickly. Judy had probably just gone to bed. And anyway, I had our meeting all mapped
out: it was to be a special ringside surprise at the club. Besides,
no one should arrive anywhere before three in the afternoon—it
simply isn't civilized.

It was this frame of mind that prompted me to ask, "Have you
a single?"

"For how long, sir?"

"For tonight."

"Just for tonight, sir?" The inflection was polite but quizzical.
"Yes, sir, there is a single room available."

"At what price, please?"

"The room is twelve pounds, sir."

"Good," I said decisively, "I'll take it."

I must be an idiot, I thought as I hung up. Twelve pounds, that was thirty-four bucks for God's sake—roughly a sixth of my total assets. For one night in a hotel. I was about to call the Ritz back when it occurred to me I'd better find cheaper lodgings before canceling.

In my wallet, I found the name of a friend of a friend, Howie Schuman. Maybe he could put me up. Free would be even better than cheap. I had the name of people he was living with, but, after drawing a blank from both the directory and information, I gave up on him.

My bags were sitting outside the door, waiting for me to get located. I opened the book, found the number of an Englishman I hadn't seen in ten years. He was still at the same address—111 Park Street. He even answered the phone.

"Dennis, it's John Meyer."

"Who?"

"John Meyer . . . you know, from the States?"

"Well, for heaven's *sake*. When did you arrive?"

"About an hour ago. How *are* you?"

"Not so well, actually. I've come down with this damn Chinese thing."

"I know, I just got over it."

"And I'm snuffling about the place like some kind of . . . I don't know what. Bill has been an absolute Florence Nightingale to me."

"Unh huh, unh huh. Listen, uh . . . I don't suppose you feel like company? Are you up?"

"Oh, heavens yes, I've been up since nine. Well, Johnny, it's up to you. If you don't mind running the risk of the Chinese disease . . ."

He doesn't sound too thrilled, I was thinking . . . but I need him. To put me up, or suggest someplace that isn't the Ritz, or . . . and then it struck me: I just needed someone to talk to.

"I'll take my chances, Dennis. Look, I'm at the airport now . . . how about noon?"

"Fine. Come ahead then."

I gave the terminal a last, hopeful glance. Something had

definitely gone wrong with my Bentley. Briefly I entertained the fantasy of cabbing it in (let's hit this town with a bang!) but I let prudence prevail, hoisted my bags to the top of a BOAC bus (seven shillings sixpence) and rode in to Victoria Station.

It's fun to ride on the top of a bus, and you can only do it in London, and January isn't cold there. The ride into town cheered me somehow, watching the shops go by from my elevated vantage point. W. H. Smith, Tobacconist. A pub, the Anchor & Crown (We feature Watney's Ale). I could feel the basic decency of the English rising from the street, from their neatly kept storefronts. Noel Coward's "London Pride" began running through my head.

Opposite me was a Fullow Amurrican from Houston who worked for IBM, and he told me a wonderful story: a friend of his, a computer programmer, was fired unjustly for someone else's mistake. So the day he left IBM, he programmed his whole row of computers for the last time; on the anniversary of his departure, he instructed them to erase their entire memory banks.

Somehow, hearing this story made me feel better.

Dennis looked flu-ridden, but he hadn't changed. He had a fresh job, as a play agent, and some new show albums. He was properly thrilled to hear of my Judy experience.

"She was on the telly, you know," he said and stopped.

"Yes?"

"She . . . didn't do well, I'm afraid, Johnny. It was from the Palladium, and they played her entire overture. She must have insisted on it, or maybe she was late, but the poor camera hadn't a bloody thing to do . . . it just kept switching back and forth between the musicians and the stage . . . and then, when she finally came out, well, Johnny . . . I don't know if she was drunk or not, but a lot of people thought so . . ."

I smiled tightly. I never figured out how to behave when people I liked said bad things about Judy. I still haven't. I decided to change the subject.

"Dennis," I said, "I need a place to stay."

"You do." Dennis clasped his hands below his chin. "Well, I always send people up the street to Basil's in Tredenham Court.

It's run by a pair of fussy old queens, but if that doesn't bother you it's very clean, it's reasonable, and if you're up by nine they'll give you breakfast. Basil loves to cook. Best of all, it's right nearby."

Dennis lived close to Piccadilly, and he was proud of that. "Well," he beamed, "it's West *One*, isn't it?"

The room Basil showed me was smaller and more cramped than the one I'd had ten years ago. It was a bed-sitter, yes, just the one room with the ubiquitous gas heater that ate sixpences, on the top floor of a five-story walk-up. The bath was down the hall, the mattress sagged, and the dusty maroon carpet was patchy with wear. The room was so tiny it could barely accommodate its two pieces of furniture, a bruised maroon armchair and an armoire with a faulty door catch.

Nevertheless, bed and breakfast for seven pounds ten (twenty dollars) a week was a bargain. I went back to Victoria Station, wrenched my bags from the locker, and dragged them up the five flights of stairs, cursing under my breath at their weight. I opened my suitcase across the arms of the maroon chair, and put my jackets in the armoire to hang out the wrinkles.

I decided I needed a bath, to wash away the flight. Above the tub was a water heater; you could see the pilot light igniting the boiler, just like a stove. Neat storefronts, yes, I thought, but the plumbing sucks.

After my bath, my body felt as if it had been weighted with lead; the day had enervated me, physically and emotionally. At three in the afternoon I found myself climbing into my saggy single bed . . . and closing my eyes.

When I awoke it was dark. The traffic outside sounded wet and rainy. Good old London, I thought . . . soon the weather will be seeping into my marrow.

I put a sixpence in the heater. Christ, it got cold. I shivered into my clothes, wondering sourly if I'd ever get back on a sensible time schedule.

I went round the corner and had "breakfast" in a cafeteria. Orange juice, tea, and a chicken sandwich—three shillings. The bread was dry. American cheap food is better than English cheap food, I thought, glumly. It was seven-fifteen in the evening, and I was eating breakfast. Everything was disorienting me; the town, the time change, and—worst of all—being alone and friendless. Colby and Hector would be arriving Sunday. At least then I'd have someone to talk to.

I stepped into a phone booth and called the Talk of the Town. I wanted to reserve a ringside table. I needed it for my surprise. But all they had available were balcony seats. Shit.

I hung up and dialed the Ritz. Mickey answered the phone. "Well, hello John Meyer. When did you get in?"

"This afternoon," I lied. I don't know why I said that, it just seemed to sound better. "Listen, Mickey, don't tell Judy I'm here, I want to surprise her by showing up in the audience tonight."

"Yaaah . . ." Mickey drawled. I could hear him cradling the phone against his shoulder, squinting, lighting a cigarette.

"But I just called and they don't have anything ringside. Can you fix me up? It'll be a big kick for Judy."

"Sure, John. Tell you what, meet me backstage around half an hour before the show, and I'll fix you up."

"Great. Thanks, Mickey, I'll see you there about ten-thirty." Show time was eleven.

"See you there," said Mickey.

"Remember, don't tell Judy."

The next four hours passed funereally slowly. I remember clearly the bus ride down Piccadilly, past Selfridges, to Leicester Square. In the Square I remember the minute and detailed examination of every shop and movie marquee (Richard Burton and Mary Ure in *Where Eagles Dare* at the Odeon) and the lengthy scrutiny, shoulders hunched against the drizzle, of at least ten restaurant menus (fish and chips, five and six). I remember my final decision: a slim, gray hamburger at a Wimpy Bar. It was no better than the chicken sandwich.

Promptly at ten-thirty I was at the stage door of the Talk of the Town, carrying one of the masks Jenny and I had bought Halloween night on our ride back from New Jersey. It was the "Gawgette" drag mask, the one with thick red lips and horrid blond hair. My plan was to plant myself at ringside and, when Judy made her entrance, to put on the mask and start cheering. I knew this would break her up.

The stage doorman was a tall, massive fellow in a gray cardigan sweater. I wondered if they were called "Pop" in England, too.

"Help you, sir?"

"I'm waiting for Mr. Deans. I'm a friend of his."

" 'E's not 'ere, sir."

"I know, I'm meeting him at ten-thirty." The custodian of the door gave a short laugh and turned to a man in a tuxedo who was leaning against the wall, pulling up his sock. " 'Allo, George," he called to this man, " 'Ere's a gentleman meeting Mr. Deans at ten-thirty."

The man in the tuxedo did not look up from his sock. "Is he, then?" he said. The towering doorman stared down at me benignly. "You'll be lucky if 'e's 'ere by midnight," he told me.

"Really?" I said.

"Aye, they don't show up, the pair of 'em, till twelve, twelve-thirty, sometimes one o'clock."

"Well, Mr. Deans *told* me . . ." I said, lamely. The doorman shrugged, and I could hear fox-trot music coming from the stage. They were playing "Dancing in the Dark," and I remembered Judy telling me about Arthur Schwartz's wife consoling him when his show bombed: "But Arthur," she'd said, "you've had so *many* flops."

I decided to lean against the wall and make myself inconspicuous. The giant doorman lumbered into the little green cubicle that served as his office and sat in an armchair that was a twin to the one in my bed-sitter. The band switched seamlessly from "Dancing in the Dark" to "Cheek to Cheek." Then, as if we'd been talking all along, the doorman spoke to me from his chair.

"And don't think the musicians are happy about it," he said. I looked at him with interest. "Oh, no, my friend, no indeed," he continued. "They've got their homes, they've got their families. Sometimes they don't get out of 'ere till two-thirty in the morning." I thought he was going to spit on the floor, but he didn't.

"Up till all hours," he grumbled, on behalf of his friends the musicians. He was glad, I think, to have a fresh ear to complain to.

The dance music stopped, there was a mild scattering of applause from the front, and several men in tuxedos pushed through the black drape that separated this area from the stage.

I leaned against the wall, my hands behind me, hiding the mask. I was getting the distinct impression that Judy's frivolous friends were not going to be welcomed with cheers around here.

Facing me, on the opposite wall, was a time clock (did everyone have to punch in?) and it said eleven-twenty. I pulled my shirt cuffs down, below the sleeves of my jacket, shifting from foot to foot. Waiting has always been hard for me.

At eleven fifty-five the club manager appeared, gave me a disapproving glance, and informed the doorman that no one was allowed to wait backstage. My new friend had to ask me, apologetically, to leave.

"Why don't you go round to the front?" he said. "I'll tell Mr. Deans when he comes in."

As the stage door shut behind me, I was cursing Mickey for hanging me up this way. Of course Judy was so unpredictable that who knows what had happened. If she'd fallen and cut her head on another table that would certainly fuck up Mickey's appointment book.

She better damn well show up bleeding, I thought, shoving the mask under my coat. The drizzle had turned to a light rain and I had to shield my surprise.

In the club lobby were some gigantic blowups of Judy's face: two immense head shots, and beneath the photo was written the phrase, "Evenings At Eleven," which now was making everyone smile.

A solicitous captain approached me. "Table, sir?"

"Uh, I'm waiting for Mr. Deans, I'm a friend of his and Miss Garland's. They told me backstage to wait here."

The captain frowned and crossed to the maître d', who was checking his reservation list at a tilted lectern against the wall. They huddled together a moment, and I saw the maître d' glance in my direction. They were obviously trying to figure me out.

So I went over. "Is there a question?" I asked, ingratiatingly.

I received a neutral smile from the maître d'. "May I ask your name, sir?" he said to me.

"My name is John Meyer, I'm a songwriter, and a personal friend of Miss Garland's. Mr. Deans asked me to meet him backstage, but they told me not to wait backstage, and suggested I come out here."

The maître d's practiced eye swept the reservation list, looking for my name. It wasn't there, naturally. I felt my ears begin to itch with embarrassment. The maître d' raised his eyes from the list. "Mr. Deans has said nothing to us about—"

"No, he wouldn't have," I interrupted, my gorge rising in frustration, "this is a *surprise* for Miss Garland."

"Yes, but you see, Mr. Meyer, many people come in here claiming to be friends of Mr. Deans and Miss Garland—"

His putting Mickey's name before Judy's somehow infuriated me. "Look, I understand your position," I began, as levelly as I could, and was about to deliver a speech of indignation when I saw his eyes flick down to the mask in my hand.

Oh, shit, I thought, and suddenly the wind went out of me. It just wasn't possible to erupt in righteous anger while brandishing a mask that looked like Charles Laughton in drag.

I was out on the street again, trudging through the rain to huddle miserably inside the backstage alley doorway like a matted stray cat. Above my head, the naked yellow bulb was haloed in the moisture. I tilted my head back, opened my mouth, and drank a few drops of rain. I caught myself singing Gershwin, the verse to "A Foggy Day":

> "I was a stranger in the city
> Out of town were the people I knew
> I had that feeling of self-pity . . ."

Why am I waiting in the rain like a schmuck? I asked myself. Let's get a cuppa coffee and come back in half an hour. No, I thought, I don't want to miss them. So I stayed in the doorway, getting damper and older.

Taxicabs pulled into the alley and discharged sets of people, and each time I saw the rich, orange gleam of the taxi lamp turning the corner, anticipation rose in my chest, and then, when it wasn't Judy, I could feel the anticipation curdle. When the

third cab had putted away, I became disgusted. Fuck it, I'm
going home, I thought. It was twelve-twenty. Who needs this?
My lovely new cape, the one with Judy's mink lining, was beginning to droop sadly. I decided I'd give them five more minutes.

They arrived at twenty to one. In a Rolls-Royce Silver Cloud
with a chauffeur. The driver came round and opened the stage
door first; then he opened the door of the Rolls, and I was
amazed to see a vicious-looking German shepherd leap from the
car and into the backstage area. A flash of black and gray fur.
Judy followed, and lastly, Mickey.

I'd backed away down the alley, so Judy wouldn't see me.
Now I yanked open the stage door and was met with a frightening vision; the shepherd was up on his hind legs, his front paws
on Judy's upraised forearm. She was shouting something like,
"Get down, get down—" and it looked like she was being at-
tacked.

I shut the door. There were people in there to deal with that.
I didn't need to ruin my surprise and get rabies at the same
time. I counted to twenty and then stepped once more inside the
stage door. My friend the doorman greeted me with a nod of his
head. "They just got in."

"Yeah," I said, "I saw them. Are they in the dressing room?"

"Dressing room? She's onstage."

"Onstage?" I whispered, incredulously.

"Miss Garland goes di*reck*ly onstage from her car. You can
probably catch Mr. Deans out front."

I dashed around to the front of the house, thinking, thanks,
Mickey. He wasn't by the reservation desk, and the captain had
to be sent for him. Finally, I saw him coming toward me, a
harried-looking figure in a white sweater and a tweed jacket. His
hair was all over his head. He had the Judy look—exhausted. I
wasn't surprised.

We shook hands. "Well, hello John Meyer," he said again. He
led me to the left side of the house. Leaning against the wall
was a tall Briton with a mustache. "John, meet John," Mickey
said. "This is John Traherne, Judy's physician."

"Nice to meet you," I mumbled, automatically. My eyes were
on the stage. Judy was into her third number and wrapping
them up. She looked trim, she was moving smartly, and the

crowd was responding. They had waited nearly two hours for her, but now it didn't matter. She was here, and she was great.

> "The man . . .
> That got . . .
> Away . . .

I felt the familiar thickness in my throat. I was always moved by Judy's singing, yes, but this time there was more to it than that. I had finally made contact. After a month of being lost and unmoored, I was back with Judy again.

Dr. Traherne was perceptibly touched. He leaned over to me. "Where can you go from there?" he said.

Now Judy was talking to the audience, gaining breathing time. I smiled in the darkness. I adored hearing Judy talk. She was so funny.

"I'm going through a terrible nn, *trauma* . . ." she said, "because I have to do a . . . *new song* . . . and they haven't taught me anything, mmm, new . . . since *Cavalcade*." The audience laughed. They remembered *Cavalcade*.

"When Clive Brooks was a *girl*," Judy finished. Again I smiled to myself. Judy had put an S on his name too. She suffered from Plural-itis. Now she put a hand to her eyes, shielding her face from the glare of the follow spot, and peered out into the orchestra.

"In fact . . ." she went on, "I do believe the nn, com*pos*er of this song is here tonight . . ."

Jesus, I thought suddenly, she's talking about *me*.

"Johnny?" Judy was calling to me from beneath her hand. "Mmm . . . are you out there . . . ?"

The spotlight was sweeping the tables, and everybody was looking around. I felt the old wildness stir within me.

"Over here!" I yelled, and began moving down the narrow aisle between the tables. As I approached, I could see that Judy was much thinner, her face looked drawn, but her energy was up, and she looked so alive.

"Ladies and gentlemen—John Meyer!" Judy said, and the room broke into applause, but I barely heard it; I was trying to figure out a graceful way to negotiate the four-foot rise to the stage.

There was no graceful way; I hopped up with as much agility as I possessed, and found myself face-to-face with Judy.

"How aah ya?" she said to me. It was exactly the phrase, uttered in exactly the same comedy accent, as she'd used the first time we met.

"I'm terrific," I lied and embraced her, which was a mistake. Immediately, Judy put her palm on my chest and pushed me back, and I got the message instantly: Don't get familiar with me, Johnny—we're not lovers anymore. Oh, Judy, I thought, don't be like that.

Judy had forced me back a step. "Would you like to sing your song?" she asked me.

"I'd much rather you sang my song," I responded. Judy pretended to sulk. "Well, okay . . . if you're going to be a big nn, *chicken . . .*"

"I'll sit on your stool, though—" I said, and moved upstage to the piano, where there was a bar stool. Burt Rhodes, the conductor, gave the downbeat, and the band broke into Mort Lindsey's eight-bar introduction to "Hate Myself." I spun around as if I'd just sat on a hot stove.

"Too fast, too *fast*—" I yelled at Burt Rhodes.

The conductor nodded in agreement and shrugged. "That's the way she wants it," he said. I listened, unbelievingly, as Judy raced through my song like an express train.

"I'd-like-to-hatemyselfinthemorning," she sang,
"Andraise alilhell toniiight . . ."

It was *awful.* The tempo we'd set together had been so *perfect;* hip, swingy, just right for the song's flippant attitude. This tempo threw the whole number away, leaving no space for the point of the words or the bounce of the tune. It was like $33\frac{1}{3}$ being played at 78 rpm.

Judy charged into the second chorus (the first chorus had taken maybe fifty-five seconds) and beckoned to me: "Come on out here, you big chicken!" she called.

So I hit the floor and began dancing downstage, in time to my own accelerated music. Judy was dancing, too, approaching me now to the same beat. As she neared me, I saw a thread had come loose from the sleeve of her white sequin top, and I grabbed it and started pulling, trying to snap it off cleanly, but the whole damn sleeve began to unravel.

The audience watched in astonishment as I danced away from Judy, laughing now, unreeling, foot by foot, a glittering fishing line of white sequins. I was giggling like a fiend. The crowd was really turned on, the women in the house were giving short, high-pitched shrieks, and some of the men were clapping in tempo.

> "I-just-might-hatemyselfinthemorning . . .
> But-whatadandytimei'llhave toniiight!!"

Judy's voice was strong and open, there were thirty pieces behind it, and, fast or not, the song was terrific. Judy and I gave each other a big hug through the cheering, and I bounced off the stage on springs, making my way back up the aisle. People smiled and said nice things to me as I passed, and I grinned and said Thank you, thank you.

Dr. Traherne was at the top of the stair ramp, clutching his drink. "Well, well, well," he said, "I've been wondering where that song came from."

Mickey materialized from the lobby. "Come on," he said, "let's go back." As we passed the maître d' he nearly genuflected before me. "Mr. Meyer, you must forgive me"—he began—"there are so many who are not legitimate. They all claim to be friends of—"

"I understand," I said to him with splendid noblesse, "don't worry about it."

"I am sending Michael back with your coat," he said.

Michael led us through a kitchen teeming with activity, past the musicians' greenroom, and into the backstage area. I began to realize what an extensive operation the Talk of the Town nightclub was, with a stage that could rise and descend, a fountain that sprayed real water, and several revolves. In addition to orchestra seating, there was a balcony level. It was more like Las Vegas than New York, I observed. A cross between Caesar's Palace and the Radio City Music Hall.

Traherne had disappeared somewhere. Mickey and I watched

the rest of Judy's performance from the wings, standing beside the light board. That fierce-looking German shepherd was prowling the area like a sentry. He came up and took a sniff of my hand.

"Down, Rags," Mickey said to the dog. He looked at me and smiled. "He'll tear you apart," he said.

Marvelous, I thought. Just what I came three thousand miles for, to be torn apart by a Nazi version of Lassie.

Onstage, Judy was saying something I hadn't heard before: "I'd like to dedicate this next song . . . to a very nn, *spec*ial man . . ."

Oh, of course. The next song was "For Once in My Life," a song of love and commitment. She was going to dedicate it to Mickey. Wonderful. I thought I was going to retch. How nauseating. Judy stuttered on for another minute about this very special man who had come into her life and how much he meant to her. They were engaged . . . as soon as the law allowed they were going to be married . . . finally, after all these years, she had found true love.

I was trying not to gag on my disgust. But I knew how I could make points here. I touched Mickey's arm." "She should bring you onstage for this," I said.

Mickey didn't blink. "You suggest it," he murmured.

After the performance, Mickey and I found ourselves alone in the sitting room adjoining Judy's dressing room, and I had the chance to stroke him again. It was no good, I'd decided, not to act like a friend to Mickey, no matter how I really felt. We all needed Mickey if we were going to get Judy into the recording studio. I, more than anyone, knew the value of making sure Judy was in the hands of a capable lieutenant, and that was Mickey's job now.

I watched Mickey mix a Rusty Nail at the makeshift bar. Yuccchh, I thought, as he poured Scotch and then Drambuie into a glass. Involuntarily, I shivered. Rags, the Nazi shepherd, lying by the banquette, stirred watchfully. Better not make any sudden moves, I thought.

Mickey took his drink to a chair facing mine and sat down

with a sigh of weariness. He gestured with his hand around the room. "I hadda have this wallpaper changed," he said.

I hadn't noticed the walls, but now I looked. The wallpaper was that red-flocked stuff you see in a Tad's Steaks. Or a New Orleans bordello. I wonder what he changed it *from*, I thought.

"Colby tells me you're doing a terrific job," I said, quietly, conscious that Judy and her dresser were in the next room. People are always buzzing about me behind my back, Judy had told me. Now I was one of the buzzers.

"Mmm," Mickey accepted my statement calmly. "You gotta let her know who's boss, that's all. Once we got that straightened out . . ." Mickey let his sentence trail off. His energy was obviously spent. This was the first chance I'd had to see Mickey in the light, and I looked him over carefully now. He was rumpled, unshaven, and tired. He looked the way you look when you've been with Judy.

"Oh, we had our fights, all right." Mickey shook his head slowly. "She's murder with this sleep business."

"Oh yeah?" I said, innocently. Tell me about it, I thought.

"I mean . . . opening and shutting the goddam drawers. Sending the fuckin' dog in to lick my face . . . having people call up."

No kidding, I thought, Judy did *that?* Gee, that doesn't sound like our girl, does it?

"I finally told her, 'Look, you pull this shit with your other guys, don't pull it with me.' That snapped her around. Believe me, that snapped her around fast." Mickey sank lower into the armchair and stared dully at the wall from beneath half-closed eyelids.

He had the whole thing under control.

We left the club around four A.M. The rain had stopped, leaving the air cool and humid. The English climate is supposed to do wonders for your skin, I was thinking, as we filed onto the street. The Rolls was waiting for us, humming in its silent, perfectly tooled, British manner.

"Come on back to the hotel and have a drink," Mickey offered, nicely. The chauffeur pulled out the jump seat for me, and, thinking we were being joined by Dr. Traherne or someone, I sat in the slightly cramped position of a jump seat rider.

Judy climbed into the backseat, then Mickey, and finally, Rags. The dog pawed his way up between his master and mistress and took a regal position in the middle of the backseat.

Well, I thought, at least now I know where I stand: above Traherne (he hadn't been invited back for a drink) but below the Nazi dog. I was beginning to hate this animal.

The Rolls purred smoothly through the streets of London. Halfway home, Mickey gave a shrug of annoyance. "We gotta get rid of this car," he said. "It's costing us a fuckin' fortune."

We pulled up at the Ritz, ancient, elegant, and ornate. Upstairs, the walls were a strange, institutional green, the mantels were marble, and the bathrooms were the size of a dining car. On the tile wall above the tub spigots were two bells; one to summon the valet, one to bring the chambermaid.

Judy and Mickey had a suite; living room, bedroom, and bath, plus a large dressing room. By the fireplace was a rolling trolley which I saw contained the remains of two meals. Dinner, I thought.

"Colby is so excited about the recording session," I said, as we entered the suite. I saw Judy throw Mickey a quick look, a look I didn't like at all. The look said, Deal with this, will you?

"Yeah, listen, John, that reminds me"—Mickey said—"we bought out Judy's recording contract. We're with Roulette now."

That look from Judy had thrown me, and now this statement from Mickey momentarily stunned me. A new record company? Would they want my songs? Then, retroactively, I heard the name "Roulette" and realized Mickey had to be kidding. Roulette was a Mafia-backed, now-defunct record company.

"Ha ha," I laughed faintly, trying to recover my equilibrium. This is Mickey's *shtick*, I thought, he's a tease. He likes to put you on.

"Seriously, John, we may have a schedule conflict."

"Yeh-heh-ess . . ." This was Judy, smiling a deprecatory smile. "I might have to nn, do a commercial in New York . . ."

"With Mickey Rooney," Mickey added. "CMA called a couple of days ago." He put out a hand to stop my objections. "We haven't signed anything yet."

"But Mickey," I said, as calmly as I could, "does it have to be the same *day?*"

"Look, we haven't signed anything yet. Let's wait and see what happens."

I didn't know what to say. I should have said, Look, god-damit, Judy accepted money for this, musicians have been hired, a studio's been booked, and she's fucking well going to do the session, and never mind commercials in New York.

But I didn't have the guts for this. Besides, if there was going to be an argument, it would strengthen my position to have Colby and Hector here as allies. Also, I rationalized, nothing was definite yet.

But I could sense it. They were gonna fink out.

Judy moved to the piano. "Oh Johnny . . . play something . . ." I knew she was only trying to take my mind off the bomb she'd just dropped. I sat unhappily at the keyboard, and, as I began to play "A Nightingale Sang in Berkeley Square," I noticed Mickey leave the room.

"Play 'It's All for You,' Johnny . . ." Judy cajoled me, after I'd finished "Nightingale."

As I shifted into the key of A Flat for "It's All for You," I couldn't help recalling the way dawn had looked, breaking over Manhattan through the window of the Shelton Towers. Was it only three months ago? It felt like years.

> ". . . With every move I make,
>   Breath I take,
>   Rule I break . . ."

Judy was singing, when we heard the loud clinking of dishes. I turned my head, still playing, and saw Mickey knocking a steel plate cover against the leg of the dinner trolley.

"Whaddya mean, 'not when she's on'?" he barked. "We gotta serve some food here." He picked up a serving spoon and dropped it loudly on a plate. He banged a fork against the gravy boat.

"I mean, we're not in business for our health, we wanna sell some booze here, know what I mean?" Mickey was doing his impression of the waiters at the Talk of the Town, "*Sure* we gotta serve now. What? Over the what?" he continued, at top volume. "I don't give a shit, 'Over the Rainbow,' over my *ass*, we're here to make some bread, y' know what I mean?"

Judy began laughing, and her laughter was sincere, I believe. Mine, of course, was not. It didn't matter. Mickey's *shtick* had accomplished its purpose.

We never did finish singing "It's All for You."

THURSDAY, JANUARY 23

I didn't have the energy or initiative to know what to do with myself between Evenings at Eleven. I sure as hell couldn't go sight-seeing with Judy, even if she'd been the type. I knew I'd be lousy company, I felt too unhappy to inflict myself on friends, even if I could find any, which I couldn't. The only person I knew was Dennis, and he was sick.

I wandered about Regent Street, window-shopping aimlessly in the stores and the arcades. I saw a black brocade jacket with a velvet collar that would make a great companion piece for my cape. Thirty pounds. In an art gallery I saw a wonderful serpent by Oliver Messel. One hundred and twenty pounds.

Why was I bothering to look? I couldn't afford these things.

As the sun began to set, I thought Maybe I'll go the theater. You're supposed to do that in London, you know, there are so many shows, and tickets are easy to get, and it's so cheap, not like New York.

I purchased a balcony seat for *Fiddler on the Roof*. I'd seen Zero Mostel in New York, but, somehow, the show had not impressed me. I decided to give it another chance here in London, with Alfie Bass.

I shouldn't have. The show was wonderful; timeless, universal, and profoundly moving. It made me feel awful. I left the theater with tears trickling down my face, feeling abjectly sorry for myself. Here were Jerry Robbins and Sheldon Harnick doing such magnificent work, such fine work, and here was I, striving for the same goals, and nowhere *near* anything like this. Someday, I told myself . . . someday.

Judy was an hour and fifty minutes late again tonight. *An hour and fifty minutes.* The Rolls didn't pull into the alley until ten minutes to one.

And by the time that happened, the crowd had become vocal in its annoyance. "We want Judy! We want Judy!" some of them were shouting, stomping their feet on the floor. And whistling. And shouting. It sounded like a Saturday matinee at Loew's Pitkin when the projector breaks down.

It was a Thursday night, not a weekend, and many people in this audience had to be up early the next morning for work. Now they wouldn't get home before two-thirty A.M. at the *earliest.* They had a right to be annoyed.

I'd arrived promptly at eleven, after leaving the theater, and had spent the past hour talking to Judy's dresser, Lorna Smith. Lorna was the head of Judy's London fan club and had offered her services to Judy for the duration of this engagement.

"They're married, you know," Lorna had told me.

I stared at her, wordlessly. Lorna was a pleasant, competent-looking woman who would doubtless have made a good nanny. She looked like she had never told a lie in her life. She's telling me the truth, I thought.

"No one's supposed to know," Lorna continued. "They had a secret ceremony last Thursday, in a chapel. She doesn't wear her ring in public."

I went out front in an emotional turmoil. So she'd actually done it, she'd married Mickey. The idea was hard to comprehend. I mean, she'd only *found* him on a scavenger hunt. Had Judy simply wanted to get married so badly it didn't matter to whom? Could she really love Mickey, that twerp? No, no, it couldn't be, no matter what she said onstage, or to the press. Judy would say anything, Judy could delude herself into believing anything.

I had wandered dazedly past the reservation desk. Michael, the captain, approached me with a solicitous air. "Your table is ready, Mr. Meyer."

Michael led me carefully down the stairs to a choice ringside table. After their gaffe last night, they were treating me royally now, seating me by myself at a table for four.

I sat down, still in a daze. Christ, so much was happening so fast. I'd forgotten how overwhelming the amount of fresh input could be when you were around Judy. She was right: with *her* life, she was about four hundred and twelve. And now she'd gone and married Mickey (it had to be on the rebound from me, it *had* to), and that meant that, sure as hell, she was gonna fink out on the recording session.

Goddamit! If I got nothing else from this whole fucking experience, I was damn well gonna get a recording of Judy singing my songs. At least singing "Hate Myself," at least that.

The crackle of the loudspeaker interrupted my ruminations: "Ladies and Gentlemen, Judy Garland has just called to say she *will* appear tonight."

There was a burst of applause, mixed with a groan of annoyance. Someone said "Why are we waiting?" and a man at the table next to mine said, "I don't care who she is; no artist in the world has the right to be so rude."

"Maybe something's wrong," said a woman at the same table.

"No," said her companion, "she does this every night, according to Philip."

I looked around. The mood of the room was not good. The people were restless and faintly hostile. Well, I thought, Judy has handled unruly audiences before, and then, in a surge of loyalty, I thought, These people are lucky to be in the same room with Judy, they should feel privileged. And then I thought, Should they? Should they really? Look what she's doing to you, do *you* feel privileged?

At five minutes past one Burt Rhodes started Judy's overture, and a few minutes later, the final, stirring octave of "Over the Rainbow" was resounding through the house and "Ladies and Gentlemen—Miss Judy Garland!" came over the speakers. But tonight, mixed with the tumultuous ovation this phrase always inspired, tonight Judy's entrance was greeted with a serious percentage of boos as well. Uh oh, I thought . . . they mean it.

Judy didn't bother saying I'm sorry I'm late or anything, she launched right into "I Belong to London," and as the audience realized she had no intention of apologizing, the feeling of hostility in the room became palpable. I could hear a murmur, an undercurrent of shock and disbelief all around me. She's kept us waiting over two hours, and she's not even going to apologize? these people were thinking.

After the number, I told myself. After the opening number she'll say hello and explain.

But I was wrong. After the opening, Judy plunged right into "Get Happy." Oh, Judy, I cursed her under my breath, you self-destructive jerk. You *know* better than that.

Because now the real trouble started.

The first thing that happened was someone threw a cigarette packet onto the stage. I remember the brand: Senior Service. The white and blue packet shot in a quick, clean trajectory from somewhere in midhouse and bounced twice at Judy's feet. The effect was simultaneously comic and horrifying.

Judy tried to kick the packet playfully off the floor as she sang, but now there were catcalls to deal with, too. "Who do you think you are?" someone shouted, and someone else yelled, "Tell us why you're always late!" and the nastiness in these voices was shocking to me.

"My, you're a noisy group—" Judy responded, between the lyrics of "Get Happy," and this provoked a shower of two or three more cigarette packets flung to the stage.

Judy bent down and tried to pick them up. "What will Mr. Delfont say?" she said into the microphone, referring to the owner of the club.

Now several people stood up at their tables and started giving Judy the raspberry, making rude noises with their mouths. The atmosphere was chaotic. A redheaded guy at ringside, stage left, stood up and began repeating the phrase, "Why can't you . . . why can't you . . . why can't you . . ." He said it over and over, he was obviously drunk, and after each repetition he looked down at the girl at his table, and smiled in a nasty, provocative way. Look what I'm doing, his smile was saying.

Hey, Red, hey, schmuck, I was thinking, is this how you want your girl to remember you? Sit down.

But "Why can't you—" this guy bellowed for the fifth time

and then threw himself up on the stage, where he sat with one leg hanging over the edge to the floor.

Seeing this, Judy decided the best way to handle Red was to try to embarrass him. She went over and held the microphone down to his mouth. "Go on," she said to him, like a school-teacher with an obstreperous pupil, "let's hear what you have to say."

It was a mistake. The guy grabbed Judy's hand, the hand that held the microphone. "Why can't you"—he said for the sixth time—"show a little respeck for the British public?"

There was a cheer from the crowd. Uh oh, I thought, let's not let this drunken shithead become a spokesman. I wondered fleet-ingly if I should hop up there and push him back to his seat. It would probably only incite him.

Red was struggling to his feet now and trying to take full pos-session of the mike. Judy didn't want to give it to him, but he was stronger and drunker than she was, and he wrenched it away from her. As he did, a glass, a water glass, was hurled from the back of the house. It shattered onstage, about three feet from where Judy was standing, throwing a dangerous spray of gleaming shards at her.

It was an incredible, shocking moment; though whether the glass had been thrown at Judy or at Red was hard to say.

"There, you see . . ." said Red, triumphantly, as though the glass's shattering had vindicated him. "Now just be courteous to the British public."

Considering the barrage of indignities being heaped upon her, Judy showed terrific guts. She put her hand on Red's arm and reached for the microphone. Red pulled away. He wasn't about to relinquish his moment in the spotlight. Judy stepped back and folded her arms across her chest. "All right look—" she said, to Red and the audience as well, "this has got to stop."

But Red, drunk with power now, decided he could do any-thing. Still holding the microphone, he brought his forearm up in the classic Fuck You gesture and then threw the microphone to the floor. It struck the stage with an amplified, metallic *thwonk*.

"That's it," Judy said decisively. She bent to the floor, re-trieved the microphone, and placed it on the seat of the stool midstage. She then walked calmly into the wings stage right, passing Burt Rhodes, who had come halfway downstage to help remove Red.

He was a little late. Red had returned to his table and was now accepting congratulations from his friends among the British public. Burt Rhodes turned back to his conductor's podium and said something like number twenty-eight, boys, and the next thing I knew, the band was playing for dancing.

Tonight's performance was apparently over.

I rose from the table and headed for the lobby. I didn't know what to do. Should I go backstage? Or go home?

Poor Michael, by the door, was fielding a storm of outrage as angry customers filed by on their way out. "Yes, sir . . . terribly sorry . . ." he was saying, over and over. "We've been having a great deal of trouble with her . . . yes, I know . . . yes, she's often late . . ."

And the people; they were so bewildered, so upset. I stood a few feet away, listening to the comments:

"Bernie Delfont isn't doing himself a bit of good. You're ruining your reputation here, you know."

"Appalling, just appalling . . ."

"We won't get home till three . . ."

"I don't care who she is, she has no right . . ."

And then there was one small lady in a wheelchair, one tiny, compassionate lady who broke my heart. She was being pushed to the door, and she overheard these remarks, and she said, straight out in front of her, to no one in particular, "Well, maybe she had a bad dinner . . ." and I had to turn away. In the midst of all this anger and invective there was one sweet, compassionate lady, whose infirmity had made her kind.

I was heading out. I'd decided to go home. What was I gonna tell her? Judy, all you had to do was say you were sorry? Judy knew that. I was certain that, subconsciously, Judy had provoked tonight's incident deliberately.

Michael saw me pass. "Mr. Meyer?" I turned to him. "Are you going back?"

"Oh, Michael, no . . . I think I'll just go on home . . ."

"You might go back, Mr. Meyer," Michael said to me. "I think she . . . I think she needs her friends around her now."

I hadn't thought of it that way, but Michael was right. Also, it would be Judy's style to claim her friends had deserted her in her hour of need, had left her to fend for herself at her low point. Oh, I could hear her: first the audience kicked me in the teeth, and then my friends left me there, bleeding.

Well, maybe there was something I could do, after all, even if it was just throwing a few lines. With trepidation, I walked round the corner to the alley that led to the backstage entrance.

There were several people in the Tad's Steaks dressing room, chatting and laughing, and I was glad to see the wake was going to be an Irish one, loud and tipsy, and not a Jewish one, tearful and keening.

Bernie Delfont was there, and Bumbles Dawson, a costume designer, and Traherne the doctor. Mmm, I thought, what a good idea, a doctor on retainer. Why hadn't *I* thought of that?

Judy came out, and I smiled off my lugubrious attitude. "Well," I said, "you've got enough cigarettes to last you awhile. If I were you I'd charge Bernie here for cleaning his stage."

Judy laughed. "Mmm . . . they were certainly an nn, *ac*tive group, weren't they?"

"Judy, here's what we'll do," said Delfont. He was a nice-looking chap with his hair parted in the middle, graying at the temples. "I'll release a statement, backed by Traherne here, that you're too sick to play the weekend. You'll return on Monday."

Traherne continued. "We'll explain you've been making a supreme effort appearing at all in your weakened condition, and that you've only been going on out of your deep sense of loyalty to the British public."

Don't use that phrase, baby, I thought, you'll set her off.

"In other words, hon," said Mickey, who was looking, if possible, even more fatigued than Judy, "the doctor is ordering you to bed for the next three days. You're suffering from nervous exhaustion."

Bumbles Dawson, Mickey, and I escorted Judy into her Rolls. The London paparazzi had been alerted and were waiting outside the stage door, and it was just like you always see—the pop of flashbulbs and the barked questions: "Will you be back to-morrow, Judy?" "Are you really ill?"

We pushed Judy into the car. Once ensconced in the plush backseat, Judy began to giggle. "That . . . nn, *red*headed fellow . . ." she chortled. "He was absolutely nn, *plotzed*."

Bumbles, Mickey, and I joined in her laughter. "I wish we had a . . . *film* of this evening . . ." Judy said.

"We can't even get a recording," Mickey murmured, sarcastically.

"What do you mean?" I asked him.

"We wanted to bring in equipment and get a sound recording of the show," Mickey elaborated, "but Glynn says it's against union rules." Glynn Jones was musical director of the club.

"Even if you pay them double scale, or whatever?" I inquired. This was a subject dear to my heart. A recording of the show would contain "Hate Myself."

"Glynn says no. It's got to be in a studio."

FRIDAY, JANUARY 24

All today it kept worrying me. Without a recording of the show, and without Judy's going into the studio to honor her commitment to Colby, how was I ever going to capture the priceless treasure of Judy's rendition of "Hate Myself"?

I was in the Burlington Arcade, buying some Spode for my mother, when the solution hit me. Marjorie had this elegant set of bone china that had been depleted by breakage through the years, and I think the reason she was eager to see me go to London was so I could replace the missing cups and saucers.

I was carrying a set of six cups out of the Arcade when I saw the sign; it was in the window of a travel agency, and it said: "Austin-Healy, MG, English Ford and other fine automobiles for rent."

The word "rent" leaped into my mind with a blinding reverberation. Of course! I could *rent* my own recorder, smuggle it into the club, and get "Hate Myself" down on tape. Right, I thought. If you want something done, do it yourself.

I was on my way home to drop off the cups. I stopped down-stairs in the foyer of the Tredenham Court, where the phone was. One pay phone for the entire house, and it was rarely free, but this afternoon I was lucky. I got out my pennies, my cop-pers, and opened the directory to "Sound Equipment—Rentals."

The most promising listing was a place called Location Sound, in St. Peter's Square, so I dialed it. On an English phone, you get your party on the line, and then, to clear the line for talk, you drop in your coins. Quaint, huh?

"Hallo," said a male voice, "Hughesden here."

"Yes, Mr. Hughesden," I said. "I'm interested in taping a live performance in a nightclub; what equipment would you recom-mend, and how much will it cost me?"

MONDAY, JANUARY 27

I was on the tube to St. Peter's Square. The tube and the bus, actually. Location Sound was in Hammersmith, something of a trip, but I was so obsessed with my idea that I would gladly have gone to Rangoon on roller skates.

Mr. Hughesden had been full of questions: first, was it possi-ble to jack into the club's sound system? I told him no, that wasn't possible. I didn't tell him that what I was attempting was illegal. It might have dampened his enthusiasm.

Well then, Hughesden had asked me, how big a room was I dealing with? And how close to the stage would I be able to get? Look, I'd said to him, I'll tell you all about it when I see you.

And so here I was, on a Monday morning, tooting off to Hammersmith. I hadn't seen Judy over the weekend, she'd been confined to her hotel. Colby and Hector had arrived Sunday night, from Cannes, where they'd been at a music convention. We had a lunch date coming up. I didn't say so on the phone, but they were in for a rude surprise.

Mr. Hughesden was one of those laconic, efficient people the English seem to do so well. Totally amiable and eager to be of help. I trusted him immediately.

"I've been thinking about your situation," he said to me, leading me into a large workroom with an overhead bank of bright fluorescent lights, "and I think the Nagra's going to be your best bet."

He stopped before a worktable on which sat a compact, reel-to-reel tape recorder. The machine was just a little smaller than the New York phone book.

"Your only problem here," Hughesden said, "is the five-inch reel. This box won't take a seven-inch. How long is your show?"

"About fifty-five minutes."

Mr. Hughesden looked doubtful. "Yes. Well, that'll mean flipping your reel about halfway through."

"That's not a problem," I said. "I can do it during applause." As long as no one sees me, I thought.

"The Nagra gets your best sound out in the field," Hughesden explained. "It's the machine all the film crews use. Swiss machine, it is. Quite expensive. Damn Swiss only make about six of them a year." He smiled, and I was happy to laugh with him.

"How much is the Nagra, by the day?" I asked him.

"Well now." Hughesden put his fists on his hips. "Are we going to use the Sennheiser microphone?"

I looked at him blankly. "I dunno. Are we?"

Hughesden's smile broadened. He obviously enjoyed teaching his neophyte customers the tricks of the trade. "I would, if I were you," he said, producing a thin pipe of gray steel about two and a half feet long. "The Sennheiser's multidirectional, you see," he went on. "Much the best mike for your purposes. German instrument, you know."

I glanced quickly into his eyes, but Mr. Hughesden betrayed no sign of emotion at the word "German." Cool guy, I thought. Hughesden had to be in his forties, he'd undoubtedly been through the Blitz. Oh, how do you know, I chastised myself. He's probably from New Zealand or somewhere.

I stared at the length of gray metal. It looks like a giraffe's dick, I thought, irrelevantly. Hughesden cleared his throat, quietly. "You told me on the phone you'd be sitting beneath one of the loudspeakers," he said.

"Yes, I can do that," I told him. The speakers in the Talk of the Town were set into the ceiling, and there was one directly above the table where Michael had seated me last Thursday. I was sure I could sit there again tonight.

"What you want to do, then," said my mentor, "is keep the Sennheiser facing upward, to catch the sound from the ceiling."

Yes, I thought, that'll be easy enough . . . as long as no one spots the strange, gray, snaky thing against the whiteness of the tablecloth.

"Good evening, Mr. Meyer," Michael greeted me and registered no more than mild surprise when I did not allow him to take my coat.

"I'm a little chilly, Michael, I think I'll keep it a few minutes," I said, following him awkwardly down the tiered aisle to the table that was apparently mine for the duration of my stay. If Michael noticed I'd put on some weight, he made no mention of it.

As Michael left, I furtively slipped the Nagra out of my coat and lowered it to the floor beneath my feet. I pulled the microphone from my sleeve and jacked it into the recorder, placing the phallic thing on the tablecloth, where it lay inert, blatantly obvious to anyone who might pass. Guiltily, I threw a napkin over its length and waited nervously, my foot tapping, for the first notes of Judy's overture.

When Judy got to "Hate Myself," I was afraid she might call me up onstage again, but she contented herself with introducing me from my seat. Inwardly, I breathed a sigh of relief. I didn't want to desert my recording equipment during the very moments I wanted most to capture—Judy's rendition of my song.

Sitting down again after Judy's introduction (the spotlight had hit me, and I prayed desperately the operator hadn't noticed the mike; I'd removed the napkin in the interests of clarity), I bent down as if to tie my shoelace and checked the recording level on the Nagra's indicator. It seemed to be okay, the needle wavering only occasionally into the red danger area that would mean overload.

During the applause that followed the "For Me and My Gal" medley, reel one ran out, and I flipped on a second reel. It took me less than forty seconds, and I didn't miss any of Judy's patter. I gave myself a mental pat on the back. If only the balance between the orchestra and Judy's voice was decent, the Nagra would produce a quality tape. The Sennheiser was directly below the speaker in the ceiling.

Please, God, I prayed, let this tape be born perfect.

As the audience filed out after the performance, I joined them casually, draping my coat over the recorder, which I carried by my side. In my other hand I held the Sennheiser like a walking stick, and I was affecting a slight limp. To the disinterested observer, I might have been a young man recovering from a ski injury.

I waited till the admirers and well-wishers had cleared out of Judy's dressing room, and then I went backstage. Mickey was making himself a Rusty Nail at the bar. He looked up as I entered. "Hi," he said.

Without a word I set the Nagra down on the floor and put it in the REWIND mode, letting it run the tape backward for perhaps a minute. Mickey stared at the machine with raised eyebrows. "What's up?" he said.

I set the volume dial at the fifty calibration and flipped the recorder to the PLAY mode.

"—Ow you're here . . ." Judy's voice sang from the machine.
"And now I know just where I'm going
 No more doubt or fear
 I've found my way . . ."

The quality was perfect. You could hear every nuance, you could hear the intakes of breath, you could hear the spit on the *T*s and the *P*s. I bit my lip. Somehow it felt like I wanted to cry. It was the frustration giving way to relief. But I wasn't about to cry in front of Mickey, nosiree.

"For love came just in time
 I found you just in time . . ."

Mickey's mouth was open; he was gazing enraptured at the two revolving spools. I heard a noise behind me, and I turned to see Judy standing in the door of her dressing room; she was holding a towel that was covered with makeup base.

"—To change my lonely life
That lucky day . . ."

The realization of what I'd done was illuminating Mickey's face. Judy still didn't understand. She was looking at the two of us, her eyebrows raised quizzically. "Where . . . where did this come from?" she inquired.

"I got the whole show," I told her proudly. "Including the talk, the overture, and the applause."

Mickey was shaking his head and grinning. "Where the hell did you get the machine?"

"I hadda go to Hammersmith, to this place called Location Sound—" I began, and related the story of how I'd found Mr. Hughesden, how he'd shown me the equipment, how he'd given me a fast course in Recording 101, and how it was costing me three guineas (ten dollars) a day.

Well, you should have seen Judy and Mickey light up. We threw ourselves into the Rolls, took the Nagra to the Ritz, and spent the next hour and a half going over the recording, checking the quality, listening to the balance between voice and orchestra, commenting now and then on the performing values.

It was close to dawn when I put on my coat. As I tucked the Nagra under my arm, Mickey eyed me speculatively. "Now wait a minute," he said, "when are you taking this thing back?"

"I told him I'd bring it back tomorrow," I said. "It's costing me ten bucks a day."

"Wait a minute, wait a minute—" Mickey put out a placating hand. "What's the hurry? Let's keep that thing a few days, let's get some more performances down on tape." He saw concern come into my face. "Don't worry, we'll pay for it," he said. "We want to study what Judy's doing up there."

"Oh, Johnny . . ." this was Judy now. "Do you have to go right away? I'd like to hear it again . . ."

"Judy," I said, "it's four in the morning."

"Well then . . . could I just keep it overnight?" Judy batted her lashes at me winningly.

"Oh, Judy," I said wearily, "you know what'll happen: if I lend you these tapes, I'll never see them again."

Judy turned to Mickey. "He thinks I'm Hedy Lamarr," she told him.

"And you are," I said. Judy was referring to Hedy Lamarr's being arrested for shoplifting. And I was kidding, but it was the truth. I knew Judy was completely amoral about returning anything.

She looked at me as if I'd wounded her dreadfully. "Don't give me those big cow eyes, Judy—" I said to her. "Remember, I'm the guy who was with you when you stole a wheelchair, when you stole that guy's wristwatch, when you stole the woman's eyeglasses—"

"What about my jewelry?!" Judy snapped at me suddenly.

"Oh, will you forget that?" I cried, a little more loudly than I'd meant to. "That jewelry was lost, not stolen."

"Larry Lowenstein stole it."

"Larry did *not* steal your fuckin' jewelry, Judy, and I don't wanna hear that anymore, awright?" I raised my voice menacingly at the end of this phrase, and suddenly it felt like we were right back in the thick of our intimacy. Judy must have realized how this sounded to Mickey, because she dropped her combative tone.

"Oh, go buy your mother some Spode," she finished, sarcastically. She'd heard me mention the cups and saucers.

My God, I was thinking, this is a woman you once loved . . . still love, will always love; and you're making a fuss about a coupla lousy tapes?

"Here," I said impulsively, handing Judy the reels. "But I want these back tomorrow, okay? Without fail."

"I promise," said Judy. And she took the tapes.

"Mickey, you're a witness to this."

"John, I promise you; these tapes won't leave the hotel," Mickey said.

And, as it turned out, they very nearly didn't.

TUESDAY, JANUARY 28

I was in Fortnum & Mason, on the phone to Mr. Hughesden. I told him we'd be keeping his Nagra and Sennheiser a few days more, and to transfer the billing to Mr. Mickey Deans, care of

the Ritz Hotel. I told him I was sending him his three guineas
for yesterday, but from now on Mr. Deans would be responsible
for the rental. I reiterated this, emphasizing Mickey's name.
Knowing Judy, I was not about to become liable to Hughesden
for two thousand dollars' worth of sound equipment.

I saw Colby and Hector enter the tearoom, looking prosper-
ous. Fine, I thought, they can buy me lunch. My cash had almost disappeared, spent on food, lodging, and the compulsive
acquisition of theater seats.

At lunch the discussion was solely about Judy and how we
could get her into the studio. I told the guys I was dubious
about our chances.

"They're going to New York to shoot a commercial with
Mickey Rooney," I said, despairingly.

"Really?" said Bob. "Last night she was talkin' about goin' to
the Virgin Islands for a rest; she says she's exhausted."

"It doesn't matter where she goes," I said glumly. "Once she
leaves the country it's all over; forget it."

"She owes us the session," Hector put in. "We paid her the
money."

"Oh, she'll do the session," Bob said, confidently. "It's just a
question of when."

"But what do we do with the studio?" Hector said, gesturing
excitedly. "And the musicians? The session is all booked!"

The three of us sat there silently, lost in our mutual dilemma,
munching our watercress sandwiches, drinking our Earl Grey
tea. Finally Hector looked at me.

"So are they married, or what?" he asked me.

"Yeah," I said, "they're married."

Hector rolled his big, Peter Lorre eyes. "I thought she was
supposed to marry *you*," he said.

"It's a long story, Hector," I said. I didn't want to go into it.

Colby wiped his mouth with his napkin. "Ah guess we
should get them a wedding gift," he said.

I was back in the Burlington Arcade, looking in windows. A
wedding gift, of *course*. It hadn't occurred to me, and I didn't
really understand why I felt compelled to make a gesture like
this, but it seemed somehow terrifically ironic, and very *big* of

me, you know? To get Judy and Mickey a gift. It was taking this very Noel Coward, civilized view of things; no, it didn't work out with me, the gift would say . . . but I hope things will be better with you.

But what to get them? You couldn't really get Judy something for the house, like a blender. Judy wasn't really what you'd call domestic, was she? And you had to get something they'd both enjoy, like a piano.

But what if they split up? Who'd get the piano? As I sniffed around the Arcade, I decided the best thing would be to get them separate gifts, so that when the split came (oh yes, they'd split eventually; it was merely a question of time) they wouldn't have to take a cleaver to the piano.

I settled on a handsome set of cuff links for Mickey, and a cameo brooch for Judy. I had them wrapped separately, in two velvet jewelry boxes.

Yes, I thought, heading home to my shabby lodgings, this will be a very effective gesture: I'll look noble, and they'll be ashamed.

And that'll be good, I thought.

And who should show up at the club tonight but Ron Anton, my benefactor from BMI, with his wife, Jane, and Thea Zavin, BMI's legal counsel.

"Ron—" I cried in surprise, releasing him from a bear crush hug, "what're *you* doing here?"

"We just ate our way through France," Ron informed me. "What's been happening?"

"Tell you later," I said, because Burt Rhodes had started the overture.

The band was sounding particularly good this evening, and across the table I watched Ron's face light up with anticipation. I could guess what he'd told Thea: "Hey, dig this," he'd have said to her, in Beaune or Lyon or somewhere, "one of our writers is having a thing with Judy Garland, and she's singing his song in London; let's hop over and take a look, it'll be a kick."

Judy did not disappoint him. When she got to My Spot in the program, she called me up onstage, and, as she sang "Hate Myself," I did a reprise of my dance, this time leaving the sequins on her sleeve intact. Again there was a terrific response from the crowd.

As I rejoined my friends, I could see Ron beaming. "This is a BMI writer," he said, proudly, clapping a paternal arm around my shoulder. "Now listen," he continued, "I understand Bob Colby's in town. Does this mean we'll be getting a record of some Johnny Meyer songs?"

"We're supposed to go into the studio on the fourth," I said, feeling like a liar. I knew damn well it wasn't gonna happen. But I didn't want to tell Ron. Not now, when he was so elated for me and so pleased. It would just be an awful downer. Maybe, somehow, we *could* do the session, switch the dates around or something.

There had to be a way.

THURSDAY, JANUARY 30

At five-thirty today a summit conference was held at the Ritz, to determine just how Judy was going to fulfill her contractual obligation to Colby's company, Blue Records.

After the initial pleasantries, Judy retired to her bedroom, characteristically leaving the business discussion to the gentlemen.

Bob opened the conversation by telling Mickey how excited they were about the session, and how they'd booked the best musicians in London.

"And a really fahn arranguh, Johnny Spence," Colby said in his Mississippi drawl. "He's been workin' with Tom Jones, Humperdinck, just the top names in the business."

"Oh, he's the best," Hector echoed. "Jahst the best." Hector's enthusiasm was endearing, but I could see Mickey pressing his lips together because he had to tell us no. Obviously, Judy didn't want to commit herself to February fourth.

"The thing is," Mickey said, "Judy feels she needs a rest. The Talk of the Town has been a tremendous strain, and she really wants to get away for a while."

"Well ah can understand that," said Bob, "but we may not be able to secure these same people at anothuh tahm."

"Look, fellahs," Mickey countered, "what's the sense of getting Judy down on record when she's not at her best? She's been through four solid weeks of singing, the voice isn't what it's gonna be in a few weeks, after she's had a chance to rest. Let's do it in a month or so, when she's really feeling in top shape."

Bob and Hector exchanged a look. I knew what they were thinking. They were thinking, What about our thousand bucks?

I hadn't said a word during any of this. I had been a fly on the wall. Now, I quietly left the living room and knocked softly at the bedroom door. I wanted to know how Judy felt about things.

I heard her voice come through the door. "Mickey?" she said.

"No, it's John," I replied, turning the knob and pushing inward. Judy was sitting cross-legged on her bed. When she looked up at me I saw a mixture of joy and trepidation in her face, and I knew exactly what she was feeling; she was really glad to see me, but she was afraid I was going to press her about the session.

I came to the edge of the bed, and something made me put out my hand. The same something must have made Judy take my hand and surround it in both of her own. I stood there, watching Judy look up at me, and then I sat on the bed beside her.

"Why don't you come out and settle this one way or the other?" I said. Judy averted her eyes. "I wish I had a nn, *tape* of what's going on in there . . . what happened to that . . . machine?" Her eyes were roving the room, seeking the Nagra.

"Judy, you don't need any tape recorder . . ." I told her. "All you have to do is say Yes I will, or No I won't."

Judy stared down at the bedspread. "No . . ." she said. "I can't talk about this . . . it's not *feminine* . . ."

"I never understood what you meant by that," I said.

"It's the difference between being a man . . . and a woman," Judy told me. Yes, I recalled, that had always been her feeling: women did not discuss business. I wondered fleetingly what Joan Crawford would say to this point of view.

"Judy—" I urged her, "all you have to do is decide what you *want*. Now you can do that, I know you can, I've seen you. What do you *want*, Judy?"

But Judy shook her head rapidly from side to side, trying to avoid this inquisition. "I want . . . whatever is *best* . . ." she said. "I want to rest."

Well, that was concrete, anyway. She wanted to rest.

"So, then, you want to go to New York and do the commercial, is that right?" I said. "And then go to the Virgin Islands for a rest?"

Again Judy shook her head. "I don't know," she said. "I want to do whatever's best. I can't think."

"No, Judy look—" I said. I put my hands on her shoulders. "This is John, asking Judy—what do you *want?*"

Judy turned her head from my gaze. "Well, that's what I have a husband for . . ." she said. "To make these decisions. To figure out what's best."

I was watching her intently, trying to see behind the protests, trying to decipher what was really going on in her unbelievably complex mind. "Is it that you don't want to say anything to offend me? Is that it?"

Judy nodded slowly. "You . . . or Mickey," she said.

"But if you had your choice . . ." I pressed her. The sentence trailed off into the atmosphere. Judy wasn't responding.

"Judy," I said, finally, "you're not gonna offend anyone by telling me what you really *want—*"

She looked at me then, and I could see the unyielding impenetrability pour back into her eyes. "Right now," she said, "I don't ever want to sing again."

FRIDAY, JANUARY 31

Okay. Obviously, there was no further reason to remain in London. I went down to the Japan Airlines office in Hanover Square and booked a flight home for ten P.M. I returned to the Tredenham Court, paid my bill, packed my clothes, and took a cab to the Ritz to get my two reels of tape. It was eight in the evening, and I was cutting it close: I had to check in at Heathrow by nine, an hour before boarding.

Mickey let me in and vanished immediately into the bedroom, where I could overhear him in muffled colloquy with Judy. I walked into the living room and went to the fireplace, where I set my two gift packages on the mantel: cuff links for Mickey, the brooch for Judy. After all my disappointment, I still had the impulse to make this gesture. The velvet boxes sat innocently above the andirons, twinkling in their shiny wrapping paper and gold elastic string.

Judy and Mickey came into the room together.

"So," said Mickey, "you're off."

"Yeah," I said.

Judy came to me. "Let me say g'bye now, Johnny . . ." she said. "I'm going to lie down awhile before the show." She gave me the briefest of hugs, and when I squeezed her hand I felt no answering pressure.

"Good-bye, Judy," I said, and for some reason the phrase *you'll never see her again* ran through my mind.

Judy walked out of the living room, and I heard her shut the bedroom door behind her. Mickey did not move. "What time's your flight?" he asked me.

I told him.

"Sorry it didn't work out about the session . . ." he said to me. "But we'll get to it, don't worry."

I told him I wouldn't worry. I knew Judy would never record my songs. All I wanted now were my tapes.

But Mickey was holding out his hand. "So have a good trip," he said.

"You have my tapes, Mickey," I said. Mickey looked at me. "Yeah," he said. It was not an acknowledgment. It was just a word. "John, would you mind if Judy kept those tapes for a week or so?" Mickey managed to make this, too, sound not like a question, but a statement.

"I'd rather not, Mickey; you know how she is."

Mickey looked down at the carpet. "The thing is, John, she specifically asked me to tell you it would mean a lot to her."

"Yeah?" I turned from Mickey angrily. "Well, it meant a lot to me to come to London for nothing, you tell her that. Now gimme the tapes, Mickey."

Without answering me, Mickey crossed to the living room door and closed it, quietly and deliberately. He didn't take his eyes from mine.

"John," he said, "I'm sorry. I can't let you have those tapes."

He leaned back against the door, almost indolently. The whole closing-the-door act had been very cool, very confident, very in control. All right, pal, Mickey was saying, this is the showdown. It's you or me, buddy, and if there's going to be violence we don't have to disturb anyone, do we?

He took a step forward and posed, his weight on his right foot, his right thumb hooked in the front inch of his pants pocket. The stance was pure Brando, out of *The Wild One.*

Well, fuck you, Charlie, I was thinking. I'll beat the *shit* outta you, CMA agent or no CMA agent. I hadn't had a fistfight in my adult life, but I was ready for whatever Mickey wanted to throw at me. Who the fuck did he think he *was,* this small-time putz, appropriating *my* tapes, tapes he'd never *have* if it weren't for me? Some fuckin' nerve!

I kept my voice steady. "So what do we do now, Mickey? Wrestle on the floor?"

I saw indecision flicker in Mickey's face. He hadn't counted on my getting this angry. He could sense I had the strength of fury in me, that I was on the point of becoming dangerous.

He took a split second to decide how to play it and then crossed past me with half a smile on his lips. "Think you're man enough?" he flipped at me as he went by. He had to say something to save face.

He stopped by a cabinet that stood by the windows and opened its door. From the shelves he withdrew my two five-inch reels of tape, packaged in their white and crimson boxes. He tossed them to me negligently. "You better check 'em," he said. "We were rehearsing some tunes with the recorder on, and we may have used your reels by mistake."

Tight-lipped, I crossed to the Nagra, which was sitting on the floor in the corner. Fuming, I threaded the first spool, the one containing "Hate Myself," onto the machine and began to spot-check it, running on FAST FORWARD, playing a section, then running ahead.

You sonofabitch, I thought. If you've erased anything on my tapes I'll damn well grab a couple of yours. Mickey had been taping the show every night, I knew. I had seen a stack of reels in the cabinet. Come to think of it, with other performances down on tape, why was Judy after mine?

There wasn't time to wrestle with this question now. My tapes seemed to be okay, and I began to rewind them. I was so infuriated by Mickey's teasing (that's all this had been, this We-erased-your-tapes crap, a tease) and Judy's instigation of it (this had been her idea, I was positive) that I was ready to repossess my wedding gifts. From where I was kneeling I looked up to the mantel.

The two little boxes were gone.

I rose and faced Mickey. With a great effort I retained my patience. "Okay, Mickey. Very funny," I said to him. "Whadja do with the boxes?"

Mickey looked at me in genuine puzzlement. "What boxes?"

"There were two packages on this mantelpiece," I said, my tone hardening with each word, "a blue one and a green one. Now let's have them."

"John, I swear to God, I haven't seen them. Ask Judy."

Disgustedly, I yanked open the living room door and turned left. I was now facing Judy's closed bedroom door. I knocked on it loudly. "Judy, it's me, John. Did you see two little boxes out here?"

The door opened too quickly. She must have been pressing her ear to it, trying to overhear what was going on. Of course, I realized, this whole tape thing was another of Judy's manipulations. She liked nothing better than the idea of two males warring over her.

"Oh, are these yours . . . ?" Judy said. She held out the two velvet cases, unwrapped, one in each hand.

My mind reeled. I found it hard to believe Judy had done this, and yet how in character it was that she had. I'd seen her pull similar stunts time and time again, but of course when it happens to you, you never believe it.

"Look, darling . . ." Judy crossed to Mickey, who had come into the foyer. "Look what Johnny gave us." And she held her brooch out for display and handed Mickey his cuff links.

It was worth the entire trip to see Mickey accept those cuff links. Later, I kicked myself for not grabbing them back, after the dirty way they'd treated me, but seeing the look on Mickey's face was a priceless experience. He glanced down at the links, didn't really register them, glanced at me, realized what I'd done, couldn't meet my eyes, returned instead to the case again, and finally really saw what he was looking at.

"Mmm. Gee," he murmured. "'S very nice. 'S marvelous. Thank you. Thanks."

"Well," I said, picking up my suitcase, "I'll see you." And on the crest of this effect, with my tape reels in my pocket, I left the Ritz Hotel, and, two hours later, I left England.

And truly, that night, I left Judy's life.

Epilogue

EARLY MARCH 1969

Mickey called me, totally unexpectedly. He was alone, in New York without Judy, and he had the rest of the Talk of the Town tapes. Did I want to make dubs of the other performances?

"Why Mickey," I said to him on the phone, "that's very generous of you."

"I've got about seven reels, I'll drop 'em up, okay? I'm right around the corner."

So Mickey came over and left me the reels, and I made copies of seven different renditions of "Hate Myself." All too fast.

How curious, I thought, that Mickey should make this gesture now, more than a month later. Is he feeling guilty about London, or what?

No, I decided, he's simply being a decent guy. It had been a while, but I remembered how crazy Judy could make you. She put you under her influence; she could make you do things you'd never dream of doing. Make you lie, make you cheat, make you steal, dissemble, be false, be nasty, fill you with guile.

Yes, I recalled, before the Arlen benefit I'd barked at some production assistant (I remember his name, Steve Schoeffler) and, when I got back from London, I made a point of calling him (and a few others) to apologize. Sorry, I told these people, you have to forgive me . . . I wasn't myself. I was with Judy.

So the same thing had happened to Mickey, now that he was spending a week away from Judy. He was calling me to make amends. And he knew the best thing he could do for me was give me more recordings of "Hate Myself."

Mmm, I thought. Maybe it's going to be possible to be friends with Judy and Mickey after all.

SUNDAY, JUNE 22

But then she died.

Maybe you're too young to remember, or maybe you weren't around for it, but it was world-shaking and terrible. There was extensive coverage, and the television newscasters all spoke in that mock-serious tone that sounds so phony, the tone they reserve for celebrity deaths, and they made a big deal of laying out the body at Frank Campbell's, with too many flower arrangements, and people filing past the casket for two days, and the whole thing was not on any human scale, and it was just horrible. Horrible not only because the attitudes preceding the funeral were exploitative and ghoulish, with the media wallowing in the iconography of Judy's career (a lot of Little Dorothy numbers and now she's finally over the rainbow and that bullshit), but horrible, too, because her death was needless. The woman was only forty-seven years old, who said she had to die?

It was like some annoying computer error, like the figures were wrong on your bank statement . . . no . . . no, I wanted to say, this isn't right, please, go back and fix this, this isn't right, take her out of that box and bring her back the way I know her: alive and vibrant and sexy and funny . . .

Jenny Wheeler came up from Atlanta. Herbert and Marjorie very generously allowed her to stay on Park Avenue the night before the funeral.

FRIDAY, JUNE 27

At a quarter to one this afternoon, Annie Bryant met us outside the chapel on Madison Avenue and Eighty-first Street. The three of us took our places in a row of seats at Campbell's, among a vivid cross section of New York personalities. Arlen was there, and Mayor Lindsay, and Lauren Bacall.

We all listened as James Mason delivered a short eulogy. He spoke of Judy's warmth, her stunning vulnerability, her fantastic sense of humor. Nobody took Judy's talent as a comic seriously, he told us. If *I'd* been in charge of Judy's career, he said, I'd have put her in a series of wacky comedies. And then he spoke of an actor's heritage, and of how, when the memories of those who saw her are gone, when the last of these "registrations" has disappeared (I remember his using that word "registrations" and thinking how peculiar it was, and how apt), then, and only then, is that actor finally dead.

No, I contradicted Mason mentally, she's not. And she won't be. We have the films, and the films will keep her alive forever. People will know her from the films.

I couldn't see Mickey Deans from where I was sitting, but my heart went out to him. There were people in this room, I had heard, who were blaming Mickey for not watching Judy closely enough, for allowing something like this to happen.

Yeah, I thought, just try living with her for a week or so, pal. Then come and tell me about supervising Judy. I suddenly remembered the morning Judy fell and cracked her skull in that Cambridge motel. Christ, it could easily have happened to me. Easily.

We were out on the sidewalk in the bright June sunlight, Annie, Jenny, and me. "We few, we happy few," I thought, "we band of brothers." We'd been through the war together, the three of us, hadn't we?

"Shall we go have a cuppa coffee?" I suggested. It would be better than standing around on the pavement, squinting and blinking.

"No," said Annie, "I gotta meet my mom in Bed-Stuy. She's a little under the weather."

"I have to pack," said Jenny. "My flight's at four."

"Okay," I said, "I'll see you back at the apartment." I started walking quickly downtown on the west side of Madison Avenue, past the art galleries. I didn't want the women to see me cry. Don't ask me why, it was just some dumb, macho feeling of pride that the man has to be the strong one in a situation like this. I don't know. I just didn't want it.

I strode rapidly away down Madison, thinking Yes, that's it, it was like having survived a war. Some men have a war, something that gives them a chance at heroism, a chance to test their capacity for courage, for strength, for resourcefulness. They go over the top, far from home, and they either meet the challenges or they don't, and they learn about themselves.

Well, I never had a war. Never had a cause to believe in; not Kennedy, not civil rights, not Vietnam. All those concerns of the sixties that my friends had been so exercised over, these things didn't mean shit to me, just didn't move me, and I never pretended they did. I had no cause and no religion—I had nothing to believe in, least of all myself and my talent. The talent was no more than a facility. Amusing, yes, but nothing to be taken seriously.

. . . Which is why I embraced Judy so fervently, I thought, as the gallery windows began to swim in my vision; that's it, of course. Judy took my talent, my wit, my heart . . . and validated them for me, made them important, by pressing them into service for herself.

And I could go to bat for *her*, yes, that was something to fight for, that was, that was something to believe in all right. And in fighting, in believing so fiercely, I found myself stretched way beyond my limits, uncovering resources, uncovering strength and intelligence and compassion; yes, working for Judy I found all this . . . and in greater abundance than I'd ever dreamed was there. I was fantastic, I was as powerful and effective as I'd ever been in my whole life.

But then, in the midst of this terrific blossoming, this marvelous unfolding . . . she let me down, goddamit, she blew it for me. She was crazy, she was a fuckin' lunatic.

And now she's gone. She's gone, an inner voice said to me, there's nothing you can do about it, kiddo, and suddenly—like Tom in a Tom & Jerry cartoon when he runs off a cliff and hangs there suspended—suddenly I'm left in midair with all this strength, intelligence, and compassion . . . and nowhere to put it. Where are you gonna put it, asked the voice, now that she's gone? Where are you gonna find someone else who deserves you, who deserves the kind of support you suddenly find you're so good at?

Well, how about me? I asked the voice. How about I transfer this crusading energy to me and my musical?

I dunno, said the voice, it doesn't feel the same, somehow, doesn't feel right. What did *you* ever do to deserve this kind of support, the kind of topflight, powerful support you gave Judy? No, the voice went on, you better go back to playing in piano bars and writing the occasional industrial show. That's good enough for you.

I found myself standing by the window of the Zitomer pharmacy. Through the glass I could see a display of Mason-Pearson hairbrushes. "No," I said out loud to the brushes, "it isn't."

I about-faced on the avenue and started back toward the apartment, ten blocks away. There were phone calls to make on *The Draft Dodger.*

INDEX